FINDING
MAGIC

FINDING MAGIC

A Love Story

SALLY QUINN

HarperOne

An Imprint of HarperCollinsPublishers

HarperOne

FIRST HARPERCOLLINS PAPERBACK EDITION PUBLISHED IN 2018

Designed by SBI Book Arts, LLC

All photographs courtesy of the author unless otherwise noted.

Library of Congress Cataloging-in-Publication Data is available upon request.

ISBN 978-0-06-231551-9

18 19 20 21 22   LSC(C)   10 9 8 7 6 5 4 3 2

For Jon Meacham, who showed me the way,
and as always for Quinn
and forever for Ben

Prologue

THE SUMMER DAY

Who made the world?
Who made the swan, and the black bear?
Who made the grasshopper?
This grasshopper, I mean—
the one who has flung herself out of the grass,
the one who is eating sugar out of my hand,
who is moving her jaws back and forth instead of up and down—
who is gazing around with her enormous and complicated eyes.
Now she lifts her pale forearms and thoroughly washes her face.
Now she snaps her wings open, and floats away.
I don't know exactly what a prayer is.
I do know how to pay attention, how to fall down
into the grass, how to kneel down in the grass,
how to be idle and blessed, how to stroll through the fields,
which is what I have been doing all day.
Tell me, what else should I have done?
Doesn't everything die at last, and too soon?
Tell me, what is it you plan to do
with your one wild and precious life?

—Mary Oliver

Recently I came upon this perfect Mary Oliver poem, which I felt spoke directly to me. Its questions were mine: "Who made the world?" Its admissions were mine: "I don't know exactly what a prayer is." Rereading the lines sparked hours of reflections—more moments of contemplation, more memories of people and places in my life that have stayed with me forever, memories of love and magic.

I believe in magic, as I do in love. I always have. In certain ways, magic was my first religion, the one I was exposed to as a child and that has infused my days and imbued my life with meaning ever since. My own concept of magic was filled with mystery, no doubt influenced by my upbringing in the Deep South where I was surrounded by active ghosts and the practitioners of voodoo, occultism, astrology, palmistry, tarot cards, and psychic phenomena. Through the years, from those early childhood days of wonder to this very day, I have been redefining and expanding on the meaning of magic, and examining what I sought and what I found.

Starting from a very early age, I thought of myself as someone who didn't believe in God: I labeled myself an atheist as soon as I heard the word and understood what it meant. Most of that time I was not just an atheist but an angry atheist. At that point I never even equated God with love.

Throughout these years of self-proclaimed atheism, I didn't pick up on certain obvious clues that kept presenting themselves. I recall that one of my favorite cartoons pictured a young child asking his atheist father, "How do you know there's no God?" The father replied definitively: "You'll just have to take it on faith." I knew enough to laugh at that, but somehow a possibly more important interpretation didn't sink in.

At that early stage, I was probably closer to being an agnostic (another word I didn't know), but later I rejected that descriptor. I thought that any follower of religion was by definition an agnostic because we have no proof of the existence of God. Agnostics are doubters and skeptics because they have no real evidence to fall back on. My favorite bumper sticker, which nearly caused me to wreck my car the first time I saw it, has always been "I don't know and you don't either."

For decades, my dogmatic thinking kept me from recognizing how full of faith and love I really was. Ultimately, I discovered that I was never an atheist at all. I was actually a person of deep faith.

Once I realized that neither label—atheist or agnostic—fit me, I had to figure out what faith really meant. I knew that my own version was sparked by a sense of mystery and inexplicable enchantment. There were episodes in my past that were extraordinarily vivid and mystical. The ability to recognize the sacred quality of these experiences helped define my own beliefs. New layers of life opened up to me when I stopped resisting.

In the process of exploring my own concepts of faith and love, I realized I wanted to know more about how others—close to me and far away—experienced and lived their lives.

In the beginning, I approached my subject strictly as a journalist. Or so I thought. I questioned the whole rationality of religion and faith and spirituality. How could all these people around the world believe things that made no sense to me? How could their beliefs inform their lives the way they did? What I didn't realize then was that my interest was far more personal. I just wasn't ready to acknowledge it.

I eventually became aware, through studying, reading, talking, writing, and contemplating ideas I had never been exposed to, that most people (including me) were using some version of faith for the major issues they confront on a daily basis—love and loss, life and death, joy and despair, hope and spiritual challenges. Of course, we are all handling these questions in an infinite variety of very personal ways, bringing to bear our own backgrounds and embedded beliefs. For me magic includes faith and love.

When I originally decided to write this book, my plan was to focus largely on the founding of On Faith and my reasons for developing it. I thought I would likely also write about a few stops along the way in my personal search. But when my husband, Ben Bradlee, the love of my life, died in 2014, and I began to internalize my grief and process his loss, that plan changed. Looking closely at and dealing with my pain gave me a new lens to survey some of the major events in my past and to see whether I could try to understand the meaning of my life—with Ben and without him. It was only then that I began writing this memoir. The spiritually overwhelming years just before Ben's death as well as those since made writing this book a richer experience. The process surprised me in ways I never expected.

This is not a how-to or a self-help book, although I hope that some of what I write about caregiving and loving may offer something useful to others. I would never presume to tell people how to live their lives. This is simply a book about what worked and didn't work for me.

Once I would have said that most of us are looking for answers. In my quest for meaning, understanding, wisdom, and a sense of the divine, I found that the questions were equally if not more important than the answers. Some believe that we have one life, and others believe that we have many. That's simply one of the questions that arise in any discussion of faith. I happen to believe that there is a life after death. I don't know what form it takes, but the thought of it gives me comfort. Certainly, I don't know any more than anyone else, yet I believe it's legitimate to explore all the possibilities.

The stories I've focused on here were events and stages in my life when answers were elusive and questions abounded. It was by continuing to ask questions that I moved along my path. Each story had a moment where meaning crept in, where there was some revelation, a flash of recognition of something consequential and illuminating. Often these epiphanies—fleeting as they may have been—were incredibly important to me, but I didn't understand why at the time. Only in retrospect has their significance become clearer.

I'm fascinated by memory, by what our minds store, by how and why we remember certain happenings and feelings but not others. How could my siblings and I remember things so differently? What was it about these stories that resonated with me, that made them somehow sacred? What did I learn from them? What questions drove me to ask about these episodes in my life? How did they contribute to my spirituality? What magic did I find there? What love did I feel there? What did Ben's life mean to me? Myriad questions again . . . In many ways, the answers had always eluded me and only became clear during my ongoing spiritual quest. I have faith that if I keep embracing the questions, I'll always be moving forward. As Rainer Maria Rilke suggested, "Live your questions now, and perhaps even without knowing it, you will live along some distant day into your answers."

Looking back, I am astounded that I didn't realize earlier how pervasive spiritual questions and issues are in our lives. They give structure, purpose, and meaning for how we love and live, doubt, mourn, and celebrate over time. I now know that love is at the heart of my spirituality.

Everyone needs something or someone to believe in. It is simply part of the human condition. I feel sad that I didn't see this sooner and didn't take advantage of the opportunities for living an even fuller life. Because I didn't identify myself as a person of a specific faith, I had the misguided notion that I was less open to any true spirituality. It never occurred to me that my childhood experience with magic was not disqualifying at all but would become the seed that grew into the faith I have today.

Nobody can get inside another person's mind or heart. Nobody can tell you what is going to make you feel better, what is going to assuage your grief, lessen your pain, add to your joy and exultations and your own sense of love and magic and meaning. For everyone faith and love are so personal. They're related but intrinsically different. The challenge is to be receptive to the hidden wonders and mysteries of our everyday lives. You are the only one who can open those doors for yourself.

I am writing this memoir in the hope that others will not make the same mistake I did, rejecting for all the wrong reasons an entire dimension——the unknowable and unseeable——that embraces important aspects of who we are. In my experience it is the invisible that can have the most powerful impact on who we become and how we live. There are such riches out there for each of us if only we can be brave enough to explore them. It's not always easy. We need all the help we can get. I can't imagine how empty and lost I would feel at this moment if I hadn't allowed myself to acknowledge the significance of what we cannot see, of the magic and love in our lives. It has been said—and seems appropriate—that "Faith is like a blind person looking for a black cat in a dark room and finding it."

Whether or not you consider yourself a spiritual person, I hope you won't miss out on Mary Oliver's core question that many people try to answer. "What is it you plan to do with your one wild and precious life?"

Part One

MAGIC

And above all, watch with glittering eyes the whole world around you because the greatest secrets are always hidden in the most unlikely places. Those who don't believe in magic will never find it.

—Roald Dahl, *The Minpins*

Chapter 1

Children see magic because they look for it.

—Christopher Moore,
Lamb: The Gospel According to Biff,
Christ's Childhood Pal

My belief in the occult started with my earliest memories in Savannah, Georgia, where my mother, Sara Bette Williams, was from and where I was born.

Savannah is a magical place. I think it's the moss. Moss hangs everywhere, pale gray and twisted, limp and slightly foreboding but mysterious and enticing at the same time. The romance of the moss cannot be exaggerated. There always seems to be a place to hide. It feels dangerous, and a sense of the occult permeates the atmosphere. One can believe anything when in Savannah. I'm not a graveyard lover, but there is nothing like the moss-draped Bonaventure Cemetery where some of my relatives are buried. It is the most deliciously spooky place I've ever been. I do believe in souls, and at times I actually felt them when I was visiting. They are just out there waiting to be admired.

My mother's family was from Statesboro, Georgia, about sixty miles inland. Mother had spent her summers there as a child, and we spent our summers there when my father, Bill Quinn, was off at war, first in Germany during World War II, then again before he returned from the Korean War.

It was in Statesboro that my beliefs were formed. My mother was part of the McDougald clan, Scots who had immigrated to America in the eighteenth century and settled first in North Carolina then followed their kinsmen—and the lucrative turpentine trade—down to Statesboro, a small town on the way to Atlanta. The first McDougalds established a plantation outside of town in a tiny village called Adabelle after one of my ancestors.

These Scots were mystics, believers in the magic of the stones, time travel, and psychic phenomena. My great-aunt Ruth was one of them. She embraced all those qualities and beliefs. Ruth was the grande dame of Statesboro, a pillar of the community despite her unfortunate marriage to a roving hustler named Roy Beaver. She was short with a round sweet face, apple cheeks, brown curly hair, and soft brown eyes, and she had a sympathetic smile with a slight overbite. She wore silk dresses with lace collars and pearls and sensible shoes. She looked exactly like what she was, the nice Presbyterian lady who played the organ in church every Sunday. She did not look like a woman steeped in occultism, which she also was. A wonderful storyteller, she knew all the family lore. Belief in magic and our Scottish heritage were woven into our lives in Statesboro.

The McDougalds had bought a much larger plantation in Statesboro and had built a big house with columns right out of *Gone with the Wind,* where we visited Aunt Ruth. When I was little, the town had begun to grow up around the house as the family sold off more and more land until it was in the center of Statesboro. All the land that was left was several acres in the back that still held the old slave quarters, a tobacco barn, the stables, the corncrib, and some other outbuildings. It was a fabulous place to play hide-and-seek, and the kids had the run of the place.

These were my happiest summers. Daddy was off at war, but I was so young that I hardly knew him. My mother was relaxed and happy with Ruth, and there was so much to do that we would fall into bed exhausted at night. My cousin Jane, her brother, Johnny, and my baby sister, Donna (two years younger), were all there too. We always had a gang of neighborhood kids looking for something to do. Our gang included Iwilla, the daughter of one of the household staff, whose name—I later learned—had been shortened from "IwillariseandmeetJesus."

The heat is what I remember most. It was oppressive, particularly the humidity, and of course there was no air-conditioning. I liked the particular torpor that it induced and a vague sense of the surreal that seemed to overcome all of us. Mornings we would get up and go to the icebox, get out a cold, green glass bottle of Coca-Cola and sit out on the back steps off the kitchen. I don't remember wearing shoes all summer.

Big ceiling fans whirred in all the rooms of the house and there were flyswatters everywhere, especially when we sat down at the dining room table for a country breakfast. Ham and grits and fried eggs and biscuits and redeye gravy were the staples. We'd rush to the table, laughing and giggling and talking. "Y'all want some moah grits," Ruth would say, in her thick Georgia drawl as she circled the table.

Suddenly, Roy Beaver would emerge from his bedroom dressed for the day in his three-piece white linen suit, his white shoes, carrying his white straw Panama hat. Silence would engulf the room as Roy took his place at the head of the table. We were all scared to death of Roy. He looked like Big Daddy in *Cat on a Hot Tin Roof.* He weighed at least three hundred pounds, if not closer to four hundred, and was never without a scowl on his red face, a handkerchief for wiping his forehead, and a thick smelly cigar in his mouth. Nobody spoke while he devoured his huge breakfast. We just waited until he finished and left for "work." Nobody quite knew what Great-Uncle Roy did for a living, but he always carried a huge wad of money in his pocket. One thing we did know is that he owned a bunch of shanties on the other side of town where the "colored" people lived and he was always going over there in his big white Cadillac convertible to "collect the rent."

Roy was a bad man, and Ruth knew it too. She never looked at us directly while he was around. As soon as he had departed, though, the chatter and stories began and Ruth would say something like, "Did y'all heah the rattlin' on the hall floah upstaiahs last night?" and then the stories began.

We had a number of ghosts at the McDougald House. Family lore had it that whenever any one of the McDougalds died, a ghost would pull chains across the floor of the long upstairs hallway, which ran the length of the house from porch to porch as did the downstairs hallway. The rattling of the chains would keep everyone awake all night. Sometimes it would go on for nights at a time. The night my great-uncle Outland McDougald died, the noise from the rattling chains "like to have scared us all to kingdom come."

That summer when Daddy was away, my great-uncle Horace died and everyone in the house heard the chains making crashing noises up and down the halls. I heard them too. At least I think I heard them. There was a huge thunderstorm, with lightning crashing around us, and I got in bed with my mother. I could hear people sobbing and wailing all night until I finally fell asleep at dawn. The next morning Ruth showed us scratch marks on the floor in the upstairs hallway.

As it was the Deep South in the early 1940s, all the domestic staff were black. Many of them were descendants of slaves who had worked the McDougald plantation. They were Baptists. They went to the church across town where they lived in the shanties that Uncle Roy owned. They were all Christians, just like Ruth, but they had another religion too. Just as Ruth was a devotee of Scottish mysticism, they were adherents of voodoo, which they practiced regularly.

One Sunday we woke up around six A.M. to the smell of frying bacon. Ruth put on her chenille bathrobe and slippers as did my mother and they went into the kitchen to see what was going on. Nobody was there. The bacon was cooking, the coffee was percolating, there were eggs in the pan, and the grits were bubbling. Orange juice was out and poured in the glasses.

Ruth turned off the burners, and she and my mother waited until the staff showed up an hour later. The house staff had no idea who could have done this. They were terrified. Ruth was completely sanguine. She calmed them down. It was just the ghosts, she told them, and they clearly meant no harm.

One summer when we were visiting, we came in for breakfast and found Ruth sitting on the divan in the parlor holding a shawl and weeping. She had dreamed that night of her mother, she told us, and her mother asked to speak to her. She wanted to let Ruth know that though she had heart problems, her mother was watching over her. Her mother told her that she would leave Ruth something in the parlor so that she would believe her. When Ruth went into the front room, she found her mother's shawl—the one she had been buried in—on the divan.

Ruth was uncanny in that she was able to predict people's deaths, including her own. My grandmother Sally, her sister Ruth, my mother, and her sister, Maggie, were all psychic. Actually, I believe everyone has this potential. When I say psychic, I'm not talking about the person who hangs out a shingle and, for a certain amount of money, can look at a stranger and predict what's going to happen. Rather, I mean people who are truly clairvoyant or who have extra senses, who see or feel phenomena beyond the reach of regular people. They are sensitive to the supernatural and often have extraordinary understanding or certain extraworldly influences and perceptions.

The stories in my family of psychic premonitions run thick. My aunt Maggie was living in Florida when she foresaw a terrible plane crash in the Okefenokee Swamp. Through a well-connected friend who understood her abilities, she contacted the authorities and told them where the crash site was.

All their psychic abilities were random. They never knew when they were going to see or feel something that was about to happen. Sometimes they would go through dry periods of foreknowledge, but other times, they were vibrating with psychic energy and could foresee all sorts of things. It could be very unsettling. Sometimes they were completely wrong, but most times they were eerily right. When they were in full psychic mode, it was as if their antennae just shot up and picked up signals that were meant just for them.

To me, there was nothing unusual or even surprising about the stories of psychic prowess of many in my family. My sister, Donna, and I felt we had psychic powers too from time to time. We just took it for granted.

I found myself looking at the stars and the sun and the moon. I wondered what they were doing up there, but never seemed to question that they belonged there and knew they had a purpose. I was especially mesmerized by the moon from a very early age. It became almost an obsession, but a happy one. I was always looking up. Only much later, once I began to study astrology, did I learn about the signs of the zodiac and my own sign, Cancer. Cancers are known to have psychic abilities, which fed right in to my family's propensity for the occult. We are also ruled by the moon.

· · ·

In the melting pot of Georgia, African, Creole, and European traditions all come together to inform spiritual practice. In this vein, voodoo is as much a part of my upbringing as Celtic mysticism. In many ways the voodoo part of my religious education is harder for people to deal with, mostly due to misunderstanding of its intent. There is good voodoo and bad voodoo. I was exposed to both. I also learned that good voodoo is the real voodoo: respecting nature, loving all creatures, feeling gratitude for all we have, respecting ourselves and others.

The practitioners of occultism in our household were careful not to allow me to see any actual ceremonies, but I picked up a lot from just being around the kitchen or on the porch as we sat together, my bare feet dangling from the steps. I watched and listened closely. I would hear the singsong chants, see the candle lighting. I heard the dialects spoken, but never heard anyone speaking in tongues. I remember vividly some of the women talking to me about how to ward off evil. There are many different rituals in voodoo, many potions, and, yes, dolls with pins in them. Rituals were generally done in the evening because the spirits were considered to be more available then. I somehow came to understand that it was beneficial to have something that belonged to a person you want to be affected by the ritual, even a lock of their hair. Candles are essential to any ritual, for the light, for illumination, for transcendence. Certain herbs and oils are important and, of course, water, the "gift of life" in all religions, especially as a form of baptism. You have to master incantations as well. The most crucial thing about initiating spells or hexes on people is you must absolutely believe in it. If you don't, nothing will happen. You can mix potions and stick pins in dolls, but it will be all for naught. I absolutely positively believed in it 100 percent. In those early years of my young life, I believed in it the way I believed in God. I believed in it the way I believed in Jesus.

When I said my prayers at night, I got down on my knees and folded my hands together. "Now I lay me down to sleep, I pray the Lord my soul to keep. If I should die before I wake, I pray the Lord my soul to take." Then I would recite the names of everyone I wanted God to bless: Mama and Daddy and my baby sister, Donna, and Aunt Ruth. The other names varied according to my mood. It never occurred to me that God was not listening and that he would not protect those I prayed for. Nevertheless, I had a backup. Voodoo. I always put positive spells on those I loved. As for the negative spells, I was too scared to do them then.

Although I listened wide-eyed to the voodoo stories in the kitchen, I remember thinking I would probably wait until I was older before I tried them. I was only about four when I first saw it work.

We had a dachshund named Blitzkrieg. We called her Blitzie, and I adored her. She was my first dog and we were inseparable. My mother adored her too. Shortly before the war ended, while Daddy was still fighting in Germany, Blitzie got terribly sick. She became listless and weak, eating and drinking almost nothing. My mother and I took her to the vet in our blue Chevy that had a rumble seat and wide running boards. I sat in the back stroking Blitzie all the way.

The vet said there was nothing wrong with her. All she needed was a little rest. Mama didn't believe it. She said the vet was a "dumb son of a bitch." She had a tendency to swear, which upset my father who only said "God Almighty" when he got really, really mad. We were up all night for the next two nights with the dog who just kept getting sicker and sicker. By the time we took her back to the vet, she was practically in a coma. He examined her again and said she would be fine, she just had to ride it out. We took her to the car and went back into his office for a prescription. When we got back to the car, Blitzie was dead. I had never seen my mother so upset. I was devastated. My mother grabbed my hand, pulled me back to the office, and started screaming at the SOB. "I hope you drop dead," she sobbed.

And he did. We heard about it a few days later. When we got the word, I was shocked that nobody in the household was surprised. "Uh-huh," the cook said, nodding. Ruth just raised an eyebrow. My older cousin, Jane, had an odd little smile on her face. That would not be the last time I saw the power of a hex.

· · ·

That gauzy, hot summer in Statesboro came to an end. Daddy came home. The war was over. He had been promoted to a full colonel, or a bird colonel as they were called in the army. He was a war hero. He had been in intelligence, or G2 in army lingo, and had distinguished himself in the war. He had been a part of Operation Dragoon and at the Allied landing in the South of France, had helped capture and interrogate Hermann Göring, and had arrived in Dachau the day after liberation. He had a staff photographer with him who had taken a huge number of pictures, some of which are in the Holocaust Memorial Museum today. He had had them made up into scrapbooks that he brought home with him, full of the infamous pictures:

ditches filled with naked skeletal creatures who once must have been humans, all dead. Hundreds of shriveled faces of emaciated people of indeterminate sex in striped uniforms staring blankly into space as though they had no idea what was happening. A few, but very few, slightly animated, if slightly dazed. The Americans, in uniform, looking almost equally shocked.

When Daddy came back from Germany, we moved to Washington and bought a house in Arlington, Virginia, near the Pentagon and Arlington Cemetery. He kept the scrapbooks in a small study off the living room. I was four years old when I found them. They were in black cloth covers with strings holding them together. I don't remember how many. No writing on them. No explanations. Just the pictures. That was enough. The pictures seared into my mind. I was mesmerized. I had no idea what I was seeing.

He and my mother had not discussed the war with me. All I knew was that the Nazis were very bad. I was too young to read the papers, the radio was just background noise to me, and we didn't have TV then. I kept looking at the bodies. Why were they all piled up in a ditch? How did they die? They must have starved to death. I saw the glazed-eyed people in their uniforms. What were they doing? What were the soldiers doing? Why were they all standing around? Why did Daddy have these awful pictures in the first place? For a while I didn't tell him I had seen them. But when he wasn't there and my mother wasn't looking, I would run into the study, slide the scrapbooks out of their semihidden space in the bookcase, and pore over them with curiosity, horror, and disbelief. I felt as if I were doing something wrong, that I shouldn't be looking at them, but I was so disturbed by them I couldn't stop. Finally I got up the courage to ask my mother about the photographs. She was upset that I had found them. She waited until my father came home and they went into another room to talk. When they came out, my father put me on his lap and we went through the scrapbooks together. He described what the pictures were and what had happened. He answered all my questions. There was only silence. After a bit, I asked him a last question. "Did God know about this?"

"Yes," he said. "God knows about everything."

"Then why didn't he do anything about it?"

"That's part of the mystery of God," my father answered.

I got up and ran to my room, threw myself on the bed, and began to cry. I was hysterical. I couldn't stop. My whole world had been shattered. God—kind, loving, all-knowing, all-powerful God—had let this happen. The God I prayed to every night on my knees had let this happen. Those people must have been praying too. Their children must have been praying. God didn't answer their prayers. He let these horrible things happen to them. He let these evil people do these things. If he couldn't or wouldn't protect them, why should I expect him to protect me? Why should I think he loves me, cares about me, wants me to be happy? In fact, if there really were a God, the God I believed in, he wouldn't have allowed this. No loving God would be responsible for this. Suddenly, it became clear to me. There was no God. There couldn't be. It was impossible. I stopped crying. It was hard to accept but I had to. I quit saying my prayers. There was no God.

Chapter 2

Hope can be a powerful force. Maybe there's no actual magic in it,
but when you know what you hope for most and hold it like a light
within you, you can make things happen, almost like magic.

—Laini Taylor, *Daughter of Smoke and Bone*

Moving around as much as we did, we became dependent on
family unity in our small circle. All we had, really, was one
another.

Daddy had a leprechaun named Geronimo living in his ear. When
he would come home from work—after he had fixed his bourbon
on the rocks—we would clamber up on his lap and he would reach
into his ear with his little finger and pull out Geronimo for us to have
a conversation with him. It was kind of a Q and A. We would ask
Geronimo questions about our lives—we always wanted to know
where we were going to be stationed next. It turned out that these
Geronimo sessions often led to talking about issues of morals and
values. God was never mentioned.

Geronimo was very wise. (Later, as a parent myself, I tried to
bring Geronimo back into our lives, but I couldn't match my father's
happy—and wise—blarney.) These conversations were where we
were taught to be decent human beings with integrity and honor.

Honor was my father's favorite word. He was a West Pointer and the motto "Duty, Honor, Country" was engraved in his heart and mind, and over time—under his tutelage—came to be engraved in the hearts and minds of our family.

Central casting couldn't have done a better job choosing my father for an Irishman or a general. He was tall, handsome, and athletic with a ruddy complexion and a head full of thick black hair. He remembered jokes and told them better than anyone I knew. *Raconteur* was a totally apt descriptor for him, a word with his name on it.

I loved my parents so much. And they loved me. I grew up believing I was lovable and knowing I was loved. What a gift. I've had struggles and defeats in my life and certainly have questioned my own actions or judgments at times, but I have never had a crisis of confidence. My parents gave me that.

I once said to a reporter during an interview that I never walk into a room full of people thinking, *Will they like me?* I always think, *Will I like them?* She almost dropped her jaw. I later thought it sounded conceited, but it was true. I think that annoys some people. I don't need flattery or praise or honors or awards. Those things have never mattered to me. I'd much rather celebrate other people than be celebrated myself.

My mother was like that. She was always happy for my father when he was promoted or given medals (many medals) or new commands or awards. She was always happy for my success and that of my sister and brother, but she never drew attention to herself. She was not, however, the little housewife. She was a pistol. She loved parties and always had a glass of champagne in her hand. She loved people, and they loved her. She was the one who would walk over to the person standing alone at a party and bring him or her into the conversation. She made everyone feel good about themselves. She had a mischievous sense of humor and could give as good as she got. She was smart, but not an intellectual. She was very strong, but not steely. She was the quintessential Southern belle.

The most important thing about my mother, though, was that she was the best mother in the world. If you asked her what she was most proud of and what her greatest accomplishment was, she would say raising her three children.

. . .

I was seven when my father got his orders for his new assignment and we moved to Japan in 1948, in the aftermath of World War II. By then my baby brother, Bill, had been born. Bill was extremely fat, weighing around forty-five pounds when he was six months old. His eyes were little slits in his enormous pudgy cheeks. He looked like the Zen monk Hotei, known in Japan as the "Fat Buddha."

Yokohama was like nothing I could have imagined. Standing on the deck of the ship as we docked, I looked down at the wharf and felt as if I had been plunked into the Land of Oz. Below were hundreds of men with funny hats and hairdos, strange three-quarter bloomers, and zoris or socks with toes in them. They were shouting in a language I had never heard as they pulled ropes and lifted gangplanks while other onlookers, women in kimonos wrapped in obis, stood shyly up against odd-looking buildings, giggling at the new arrivals. I was exhilarated. It was transformative. I knew then that what I wanted to do was to discover new things, new people, new ideas. I was overwhelmed with curiosity.

Daddy's first assignment was in Sasebo, on the island of Kyushu in the southern part of Japan. The officers lived on a bluff above the valley, in an area that was called Dragon Heights. The noncommissioned officers and enlisted men lived below in Dragon Gulch. I never thought much about that class distinction until I was an adult, when I realized what an appalling concept that was.

We settled into a charming traditional Japanese house with sliding doors and tatami (straw) mats. My parents were out at official functions every night, so Donna, Butchie (our nickname for Bill), and I would eat with the Japanese staff whom we came to adore. We all learned Japanese very quickly as only Emiko-san, the number one girl, spoke English. Her daughter, Mariko-chan, was between my age and Donna's so she became our number one playmate. The staff all kept little Shinto shrines next to their beds. Only once did I ever hear them talk about God or praying or religion. The shrines were simply there as an extension of themselves. They never talked about the war. It might as well have never happened. I didn't learn any of their stories. I never asked. Daddy said the Japanese had a lot of pride and that they would be ashamed to talk about it. I could understand that.

I loved Japan and I loved the Japanese—their language and their food, their customs and their culture. Mostly though, I was awed by their rituals. They seemed so elegant, so precise, so thoughtful, so spiritual. I felt as if I had been Japanese in another life. The tea ceremonies, the bowing, the dressing, the honoring of every gesture, every word, every person. The Japanese took honor to another level. Honor was everything—a way to connect to the divine. The Shinto chants were mystical and mesmerizing. So many things were sacred. I learned about the custom of hara-kiri, where a person stabs himself and cuts out his guts in a formal ceremony to expiate shame. It seemed totally terrible but somehow beautiful at the same time.

My first encounter with real shame was in Sasebo. It was the first time I questioned my own sense of honor. We lived next door to a very nice family who had a little girl my age. She was beautiful. Not only that, but she had a stunningly gorgeous mop of scarlet curls. She looked like Orphan Annie only prettier. Everyone commented on how beautiful she was and what spectacular hair she had. I liked her, but I couldn't stand being around her with other people. I wasn't exactly ugly, but nobody ever complimented me when we were together. It was always about her. I was jealous, really jealous.

One day in autumn we were playing outside in piles of vibrant red, yellow, and orange leaves. I suggested to her that we dig a hole, fill it up with leaves, and cover ourselves with them. She looked like an autumn leaf anyway. We dug and dug and filled up the hole and then I told her to get in and I covered her with leaves. I told her not to move, that I had a surprise for her. I ran back to the house and got a pack of matches. I came back to the hole where she was wriggling and giggling and telling me to hurry up. I looked at the pile and saw some of her gorgeous curls escaping from underneath the matching leaves. I saw myself lighting a match and tossing it into the pile. I imagined the flames leaping up around her, flames the same color as her hair. I visualized her screaming and writhing in pain. In my mind's eye, I saw her go up in a puff of smoke.

The next thing I knew I was breathing heavily, barely able to inhale, perspiration dripping down my forehead. I yelled at her to wait one more minute, raced back to the house, put the matches away, and rushed back with a bottle of water and poured it over her head. She squealed with laughter as she pushed the leaves away, then grabbed me and tossed me into the pile, pulling wet leaves over me, and together we laughed and laughed.

I suppose if I were Japanese, I might have cut my stomach open. As it was, I fought off the emotion of jealousy, as I have tried to do all my life. When I do feel it, my throat gets dry, my stomach clenches in knots, and I get nauseated. At the time of this awful incident I knew perfectly well that what I had done was wrong, very wrong. The knowledge came not from any religious teaching, but from a moral compass that was beginning to develop from what I was learning from my parents.

Getting caught playing doctor at a friend's house by her mother was nothing compared to that, but it was bad enough that I went home and hid in the armoire all night. My parents were frantic and had the MPs searching for me up and down Dragon Heights and Dragon Gulch. Finally I couldn't bear my mother's sobs and crept out, so ashamed I couldn't look at them. My mother, who had heard about our game from my friend's mother, consoled me, telling me that it was normal and that most kids experiment when they are little. She was so different from my friend's mother, who made me feel evil and dirty. I never played with that friend again.

. . .

My favorite doll was named Polly. She was very pretty with dark blond pigtails, a sweetheart mouth, blue eyes, and long black lashes. She wore a yellow cotton pinafore with blue-and-white trim and a ruffled white collar and skirt. I adored Polly. She was really my best friend. We were inseparable. One afternoon we were having a tea party in the playhouse, a small enclosed templelike structure in the backyard, when my mother called to me. She sounded urgent, so, thinking something was wrong, I dashed in to see what the matter was.

A typhoon was approaching, she said, and we had to batten down the hatches. The whole household was busy covering the sliding doors and propping up bags and pillows against them to prevent leaking. My mother and I were helping stock a safe room with food when the typhoon hit suddenly. We had very little warning. In my haste to get back to the house, I had forgotten Polly. I was frantic. I started to run out to get her when my mother stopped me. A fierce wind was already whipping branches against the house, and the rain was coming down in thick, dark sheets.

We all herded into the tiny safe room and sat together in terror as the storm lashed around us. Polly would die. I just knew it. Then Emiko began to chant and soon the others picked up her prayers. They were praying for us, said Emiko, but also praying for Polly.

After many hours, the howling and crashing and moaning subsided. I couldn't get to the playhouse fast enough. There was Polly lying on the floor looking disheveled, her dress half torn off, her hair a mess. The right side of her upper lip was missing as was one hand. It looked as if it had been gnawed off. But the little temple was intact. How could that have happened? Then I heard a crashing noise. Polly's tea set had fallen off the table. I looked closely in the gloom and saw a group of large black rats sitting on the table, and the floor, eating the last of the cookie crumbs and staring at me malevolently.

I shrieked and grabbed Polly, running as fast as I could toward the house, which had, happily, sustained very little damage. When I showed Polly to Emiko, she held her tightly and cried. Finally she said, "The gods saved her. If we had not prayed for her, she would have died." I wondered who these gods were and if they had really saved Polly. Still it didn't shake my "faith" that there was no God. I always loved Polly more because of her imperfections.

. . .

One day a wizened old Buddhist monk came riding up to our house in a donkey cart. Completely filthy, he was dressed in a tattered robe and disintegrating sandals. He had wisps of graying hair on his chin and his head. When he got out of the cart, it was clear he was starving. He came to the entrance in the back. He said he had been traveling a long way from Nagasaki and had not eaten for days. He asked if the staff would give him a bowl of rice. They did. He was so weak he could barely stand, and they offered to let him stay with them in their quarters and feed him. They told Mother and Daddy, who said he could stay as long as he liked. He stayed for three weeks.

Then one day he decided to leave. It was time for him to go, he said, although he did not know where he was headed. They tried to persuade him to stay, but he was insistent. He asked to speak to my parents as he was departing. He came into our living room carrying what looked like a giant clamshell with hinges on the side where the other half had been. Four feet wide and nearly three feet high, it had been painted white but much of it was worn. Obviously handmade, the inside had a raised design with a gold background and a painting of a blue lake with a large leafless tree covered in snow. A background of snowy hills completed the still, serene, peaceful winter scene.

The shell had been in his temple in Nagasaki, he told us. There was another half to the shell. When Nagasaki was bombed by the Americans during the war, he grabbed the shell and hid in the underground storage room of the temple. Because it was so heavy, he was only able to carry one half of the shell. The temple and everything else in it had been destroyed. Somehow he had found a donkey cart and had made his way to Sasebo. The shell was his only possession.

He bowed and presented it to my parents. He said he wanted to thank us for taking him in and saving his life. He would leave us the shell because he had no use for it now and it would be too difficult to carry with him. He was happy it had found the proper home. He said a prayer for us, bowed again, and left. My parents took the shell with them for their next twenty moves. When I got my first apartment in Washington, I persuaded them to give it to me. It is hanging in the living room of my house today. It is one of my most sacred possessions.

Again, only in retrospect do I see that my encounter with the Buddhist monk was a positive experience even though he was part of a formal religion. From the moment I met him I was drawn to the aura that surrounded him. Maybe his very foreignness and the light he seemed to give off drew me to him because in my mind he seemed more in the realm of magic than religion.

• • •

Shizuko was our nurse. She took care of Butchie and Donna and me. Emiko was number one, but we adored Shizuko-san. She was young, in her twenties but very wise for her age. She was kind and gentle and loving. She spoke Japanese to us. She also taught us all the customs. She taught Donna and me how to dress up like geishas. She got us little kimonos, pinks and reds with cherry blossoms, and obis and zoris (traditional Japanese sandals made of cloth and straw) and getas (flip-flops attached to an elevated wooden base). She made us up with white faces and little bow mouths. She showed us how to do tea ceremonies and flower arranging and how to bow. She taught us Japanese nursery rhymes and songs that I remember transliterally as: "Den den mushi mushi" and "Ame ame fude fude." The translation of the latter had to do with a rainy day and a little girl knowing her mother would come with an umbrella. I can still sing the "Rainy Day" song, but I'm not sure anyone would recognize it.

One day Emiko-san came to us with a very sad face. She was sorry to tell us but Shizuko had become very sick and had to go to the hospital. She didn't tell us what was wrong with her. Nothing was the same again. It was as if a light had gone out of our lives.

Donna and I begged our parents to let us visit her. One day they took us with Emiko to the hospital, where Shizuko was in the cancer ward, with only weeks to live. The place was horrible. It looked like a primitive barracks with one long dark room, concrete floors, and a bare lightbulb or two in the ceiling. There were rows of metal beds with patients in various stages of dying, many of them moaning or even crying out in pain.

Shizuko was at the end of the room, so we had to walk past everyone to get to her. She looked emaciated, and her eyes were sunken into the hollows of her cheeks. Her skin was ashen. However, the most horrifying thing was that she had small burn scars all over her body, including her face. When we tried to hug her, she flinched in pain. She could barely talk.

"Shizuko-san," I asked her, "what are those burns all over your body?" Emiko was translating.

"They are brands," she said.

"What do you mean?" She explained that because they had no anesthetics at the hospital, they would take a small branding iron and brand the patients with the red-hot metal to take their minds away from the unbearable pain of the cancer. Shizuko nodded to the branding iron sitting on her bedside table. I wasn't sure if she was welcoming it or dreading it. She was clearly in pain and exhausted.

Emiko said we should go. We had only visited for a few minutes, but I couldn't wait to leave. I knew there was nothing I could do for her. I couldn't even hug her good-bye. We all cried on the way home. Mercifully, Shizuko died a few weeks later. When I found out she had died, I thought again about Polly and wondered why Emiko's gods had saved my doll and not her.

. . .

Kyoto is one of the most sacred cities in Japan. It is a destination not just for Japanese, but for seekers from around the world. With its many temples and Shinto shrines dotting the landscape, the city's serenity beckons those in need. Kyoto looks like a storybook, particularly in the spring with clouds of cherry trees bursting with blooms, petals raining down in the breeze, shaved-head monks in dark robes with saffron shawls, and beautiful women in face paint and pastel kimonos strolling the temple grounds, their faces somewhat hidden by twirling parasols. The fall is breathtaking as well, the flaming maple leaves as ubiquitous as the pale-pink blossoms in spring. Arching temple bridges reach from one side of a pond to another, ducks calmly gliding underneath them. Every scene is a vision of a Japanese screen or scroll, inked out by the artists or gilded with a fine hand.

We lived in Kyoto for a year after Sasebo. Emiko-san, her daughter, Mariko-chan, and Teichi-san, our houseboy, came with us. We were very happy in Kyoto. I was totally culturally in sync in a way my friends were not. This was my place. I belonged. I felt Japanese. There's a phrase I learned much later—*genius loci,* or the spirit of a place—that comes to mind now as I think about my ease in Kyoto and my love for the city. I was overcome by its peacefulness, intoxicated by its fragrances, its colors, its essence.

On Sundays my parents took us to the Imperial Palace Hotel for lunch, our greatest treat of the week. The dining room was extremely elegant with crisp white tablecloths and other guests whispering to each other over champagne cocktails. After lunch we would take our dinner rolls, carefully hidden in our napkins, and go outside to the koi pond in the immaculate Japanese garden to feed the bright orange tubular fish, puckering their lips in and out, waiting for their turn as though they were about to kiss you. For some reason, our little ritual of tearing off tiny bits of bread and throwing them to our favorites seemed like making wishes. "Hi, precious fishie. I wish my front teeth would grow in." It wasn't just wishes that I was making. It was prayers I was praying, even if I didn't realize it. The fish were magic. They had special powers, I just knew it. We didn't go to church in Kyoto; we went to the Imperial Hotel pond. That was our religious experience on those special Sundays.

My front teeth did grow in soon afterward. Gorgeous new pearly white, if a little big for my face, front teeth. I no longer looked like a baby or a toothless old lady. It was a short time before we were to leave Kyoto that I was riding my bike down the steep hill in front of my house when Donna, not looking, ran out in front of me. I swerved to avoid hitting her and went headfirst over the handlebars and landed right on my face.

It wasn't until I had regained consciousness, with my mother holding my blood-soaked head, that I realized I had knocked out both of my beautiful new teeth plus a third one next to them. I was rushed to the dentist, cleaned off, and told I had to wait until the swelling went down and my gums had healed. It was then that the most rudimentary plastic caps were placed on what remained of three of my front teeth. They were so ill-fitting that I looked like a freak and lisped when I talked. Even worse, they were a hideous luminescent green and glowed in the dark. My humiliation was complete. I didn't smile at night for years.

The weekend before we left for Tokyo—where we were going to live for another year—we went back to the Imperial Palace Hotel for lunch. I was still having trouble eating properly, trying to adjust to this new atrocity in my mouth. After lunch we took our rolls and ran out to the pond to feed the fish. But as I stepped up to the edge and spied what I used to think of as lovely creatures swirling around in seaweed, all I could see were huge orange monsters. They weren't my friends at all. I had wished/prayed for new teeth and I got them, but then they were taken away. It was the first time I had known betrayal. I hated those fish, and I knew I would never believe in them again.

. . .

Daddy went to work for General MacArthur in Tokyo, and we had a big house in the Yoyogi district. Again we had our household staff, now family, with us. Donna and I were enrolled in the Yoyogi school for the fall when Daddy got his orders to go to Korea. He was to be the commanding officer of the Seventeenth Infantry Regiment, which was on the front lines between North and South Korea. It was 1950. I had just had my ninth birthday. The war had heated up, and Tokyo was a battle town. Soldiers in uniform and fatigues were everywhere. U.S. Army trucks rumbled down streets, and helicopters whirred overhead. There was a sense of urgency, anticipation, and, as always with war, a sense of excitement in the air.

General MacArthur had not wanted my father to go and had tried to persuade him that it would be better for his career to stay at command headquarters in Tokyo. But my father was a warrior through and through. There was nothing that could keep him away from the field or the front. He couldn't wait. I had never seen him so energized. My mother was nervous, but there was an air of resignation about her. She had been through the drill before.

I was a voracious reader by then. The first thing I grabbed each morning at the breakfast table was the *Stars and Stripes* newspaper. It was nothing but a litany of killing and wounding and overtaking towns, as well as artillery and troop movements; and it seemed that the Seventeenth Infantry Regiment was always in the news, pressing the enemy at every turn. I was traumatized. I worshipped my father. He had managed to survive one war. I was worried that he would never survive another. I knew there was no use praying for him.

I began to get terrible stomachaches, severe enough that I would double over with pain. I had a burning sensation in my gut that wouldn't go away. I fought back nausea constantly. I couldn't swallow. I didn't eat. I became weak. My mother was frantic.

The day my father was to leave I couldn't get out of bed. He came into my bedroom. The curtains were drawn; it was exceptionally hot at the end of August. I was sweating through my nightgown. He put on an encouraging face and urged me to try to eat something, just for him. He hugged me. I clung to him and started to cry.

"Please, Daddy, please don't go." He pulled away.

"It's my duty, Sal," he said.

He turned and walked to the door where my mother was waiting. They whispered something urgently. I could hear her muffled sobs. Then he was gone.

A week later I was in the pediatric ward at the U.S. Army's General Hospital in Tokyo. I hadn't eaten or drunk anything other than water in over two weeks. I was so weak I couldn't stand, and I was exhausted from the stomach pain. The nurses put me on an IV. My mother spoke with the officer in charge of the ward. He examined me. They did x-rays and blood tests and found nothing wrong. He said he thought it would only be a few days and then I'd be fine. Mother didn't want to leave me, but there was no place for her to stay. It was an open ward with beds, little cots and cribs, crying babies, and moaning children. I was scared but too sick to do anything but lie there. She stroked my forehead with her beautiful hands, looked lovingly at me, kissed my cheek, and gave me a huge hug. "I love you, darlin'," she said. "I'll see you tomorrow."

I didn't see her again for months. The major in charge of the pediatric ward had instituted a rule that no parents would be allowed to visit their children unless they were dying. The hospital was swamped with wounded soldiers coming in from Korea and they were very short-staffed. The reasoning was that when the parents came to see their children and then left after visiting hours, the place would erupt in chaos. Children screamed and cried, and it was too much for the few nurses to handle.

The major reasoned that if the parents never came, the children would remain calm and manageable. Naturally, the parents obeyed. This was, after all, the military.

The parents obeyed except for my mother. She joined the Gray Ladies, a volunteer auxiliary nursing group. They were there to help the overwhelmed staff. She put on her uniform and came to the hospital every day. The first day she made a beeline for the children's ward. I was lying in bed and I could hear her heels clicking on the linoleum floor as she approached the ward. I recognized her step. *Tap, tap, tap*. I thought I would expire with joy. I managed to sit up and stare at the door with anticipation. I thought I could smell her perfume, Sortilège, always my favorite. (Years later, I learned that the name also means "sorcery." Somehow that came as no surprise.) But the major was one step ahead. He saw her and barred the door. I could hear her pleading, begging to be let in. He was telling her it wouldn't be fair to the other children and that he couldn't break the rules. A rule was a rule.

Emerson's quote "A foolish consistency is the hobgoblin of little minds" was apropos of the major. His was a little mind. It was the first time, but certainly not the last, that my mother tried to penetrate the barriers, but the staff had been warned about her and she never managed to succeed.

My mother later told me she had gone to see General MacArthur's wife to plead with her to be allowed to visit me. Mrs. MacArthur was horrified to learn of the situation. Apparently, she had General MacArthur demand to know why this practice was allowed to continue. Unfortunately, he also became convinced that the hospital was so short-staffed that its employees couldn't manage the parents in addition to the sick children.

I had gotten stronger because of the IV, but every time the nurses and aides had tried to feed me anything, even Jell-O, I threw it up. The stomach pain continued. The doctors gave me something for it, but it didn't really work that well. They kept giving me tests but never found anything. According to one doctor, whatever I had was psychosomatic. To this day, I think he was right.

A library trolley would come around and I would go through books by the dozen. That was the only thing that kept me sane. What made me crazy, though, was reading about my father and his regiment in the *Stars and Stripes*, which I knew I shouldn't be doing. By this time, Daddy's regiment had become famous. He had acquired the nickname "Buffalo Bill," and the regiment he led quickly became "the Buffalos." Although they were on the front lines and taking more casualties than other units, soldiers all over Korea were trying to join them. I was at once proud and distraught. I was certainly riveted.

The major's daughter, a few years older than I was, had to have eye surgery. After her surgery, she was required to be in a darkened room. The major didn't want her to be alone so he put me in the room with her for company, where I was unable to read. What was most painful, though, was that her mother came to see her every day.

My mother was allowed to send me some spending money. Every once in a while a nurse would put me in a wheelchair with an IV hookup and wheel me downstairs to the hospital PX (Post Exchange). One day I went down there and a new batch of wounded soldiers had arrived from Korea. They were being brought in from vans on stretchers. Some of them had missing limbs, some had bandages over their eyes. Some were silent, some crying or moaning. The nurse wheeled me over to the side of the hallway to let them pass. After they had gone, we went into the PX.

Inside, my eyes spotted a cross. It was plastic, about eight inches tall and four inches wide and it was the most hideous shade of luminescent chartreuse green. The soldier behind the counter said it glowed in the dark. (It reminded me of my new teeth.) It had a little stand. There were other crosses too, but they were all gold or silver and much too expensive. This was really the only one I could afford. I thought about it for a moment. I knew Daddy was upset with me for not wanting to go to Sunday school and I knew he suspected that I didn't believe in God though I had never admitted it out loud. I did believe in Jesus, mostly because he was a real person and I didn't hold him accountable for the suffering in the world.

I decided to buy the cross. I couldn't think of anything else I could do for my father. I felt so helpless. I gave it to the nurse who mailed it to him. He got it. He wrote me back the most wonderful letter. He told me it was the best present he had ever received and that he would keep it with him always until the day he died. He did.

I had had enough. After several months of being on an IV, I had no veins left. My arms were black and blue, my wrists were shriveled and bloody. My hands and ankles and feet were so bruised that I could barely rest them on the sheets. Sometimes they would have to stick me over and over before they could find a vein. (To this day I can't have a blood test without lying down and almost passing out.)

At one point I actually began to think about Jesus, about the pain he suffered. I didn't think of him as the son of God, in large part because I didn't believe there was a God. And anyway, if there had been, how could he have allowed his own son to suffer so? I wondered if my father was scared or suffering. I wondered about all those soldiers, some only seven years older than I was. They were in Korea fighting and bleeding and dying without their mothers too.

I didn't want to go on living. I didn't see any way I was ever going to get out of the hospital. I was never going to get well. I still couldn't eat. I was never going to see my parents again. I just knew my father would get killed. My best friend in the hospital was a little boy my age named Mikey, who had leukemia. He was in the bed next to mine. When I first got to the hospital, he wasn't all that sick, but he suddenly got worse. Even then his parents weren't allowed to see him for the longest time. Mikey and I talked a lot at night after the lights had been turned out. We both decided that we wanted to die. Mikey didn't have to decide. He really was dying. One day they put up an oxygen tent over his bed. That's when his parents were allowed to come. His father came back from Korea. They didn't leave, even at night, but sat in chairs by his bed. It only took a day or two. You could see the plastic tent go up and down as he breathed. Then the breathing got slower and slower and finally it stopped. His mother screamed and started to cry. So did his father. Mikey was dead. I knew what I had to do.

I had to die. That was the only way I could get to see my parents. I willed myself to die. I already wasn't really eating, but I concentrated very hard on getting sicker.

One night shortly after Mikey died, I started feeling very hot and had excruciating pains in my stomach. My temperature spiked. I could see the nurses were really worried. The doctors still had no idea what was wrong, but a surgeon came in and said they were going to have to do an exploratory. They called my mother and told her they thought I was dying. They also called my father and told him to come back from Korea.

As Mother was getting ready to go to the hospital, Teichi, our houseboy, came into the living room. He was dressed in a white kimono with a sash and carrying a dagger. He knelt down before her and looked up, tears streaking down his face. He held the dagger in both his hands and pointed it to his chest. He was going to kill himself, he told her, by plunging the dagger into his heart so that he could exchange his soul for mine. The gods would be satisfied with this and would allow me to live. Already distraught, my mother was horrified and called the rest of the staff in. They managed to talk him out of it before she left, but she wasn't totally convinced that he wouldn't try.

My mother came and my father arrived from Korea. I had never been so happy in my life. It worked! It worked! Now I really could die. They did the surgery, and when I came to, my parents were standing over me, holding my hands. I recovered within a week and was allowed to go home. We were a family again. My father was safe.

As it turned out, my appendix had ruptured and I probably wouldn't have survived without the surgery. By the next week, I was so well that my father left to go back to Korea. That night I started getting a stomachache. The next morning I threw up. I tried to hide it from my mother, but she found out. I begged her not to take me back to the hospital, but she thought if she didn't, I really might die.

Again the doctors had no answers. It was decided that I needed better care, and we received orders that I was to be evacuated to Brooke Army Medical Center at Fort Sam Houston in San Antonio,

Texas. My mother, sister, and brother were to come as well. What they didn't tell us was that we would be traveling on a hospital plane with a group of the most severely wounded soldiers.

I can't decide which circle of hell in Dante's *Inferno* best describes that trip. The plane was filled with litters three rows across and five high. We were all assigned litters. There was no place to sit or even sit up. The plane was packed with young soldiers, most of them on IVs as was I, many of them minus one or several limbs. There were severely burned soldiers who were barely recognizable.

Blood was everywhere: dripping from the top litters down onto the lower ones, running along the floor in rivulets, soaked into towels and bandages, on people's hands and arms, and all over the nurses' clothes. I remember the blood well—particularly its smell—but mostly I remember the sobbing, shrieking, wailing, gasping, moaning, begging. It never stopped. "Please, God, help me," they cried. "Please, make the pain go away, please don't let me die." Or almost as frequently, "Please let me die."

Most heartbreaking of all were the soldiers' anguished cries for their mothers. My mother spent most of the trip walking (or rather sliding through the blood) up and down the aisles trying to comfort them. She stroked their foreheads if they weren't burned, she kissed them gently, she held their hands, she listened to their pleas, she told them they were loved. She wrote down the names of family and friends in case they died, promising to write. She lit their cigarettes and brought them chocolates, if they could smoke or eat. Most of them smoked. They asked her to pray for them. She did. I wanted to. I tried to. All I felt was anger. Again I was thinking, How could God let this happen? What good would praying do? I knew a lot of them would die anyway. And they did.

They were dying right and left. The orderlies would come, zip them up in body bags, and take them who knows where on the plane. Quite a few litters were empty when we arrived in San Antonio. I was frustrated because I was too sick and too weak to walk up and down the aisle and help them out. But my sister, Donna (only seven years old then), did what she could, talking to the ones on the bottom litters and even lighting their cigarettes too. She was like a little mascot. Ten years or so ago she attended a reunion of my father's regiment, the Buffalos, and a much older man came up to her and said he remembered her. He had been in one of those litters and she had lit his cigarette.

I don't recall much about arriving in San Antonio and being taken by ambulance to the hospital. It was May. I was getting better. I began to eat a little at a time. Moving to San Antonio had been a good thing. I could see my mother every day, I wasn't reading the *Stars and Stripes,* my father would be coming home that summer, and I wasn't totally surrounded by wounded soldiers. Soon I was allowed to go home for visits. My first real meal was Mexican food. Nothing has ever tasted so good.

We lived in a tiny apartment off the post with very little money. My sister was in school. Butchie was having a hard time because he only really spoke Japanese. I was determined to get well. The sooner I did, the sooner we could go to Savannah and Statesboro. I didn't want Daddy to come home from war and find me sick. By the end of June, after Donna got out of school, they told me I was well enough to leave. I never did get a concrete diagnosis but clearly there was a cause and effect, with my illness connected to my father being away at war.

Shortly before I got out of the hospital, my mother had come to visit me. She told me of all people in the world, she had run into the dreaded major from the pediatric ward in Tokyo. She said she was so filled with rage that she turned on him and spat out the words, "I hope you drop dead!" According to my mother, he died shortly thereafter.

. . .

We moved back to Savannah and stayed much of the summer at the DeSoto Hotel beach club on Tybee Island, spending our days getting sunburned beside the sea and eating french fries on the boardwalk and our nights sleeping under a whirring fan, listening to the waves lapping at the shore.

As we settled into Savannah, my mother decided she wanted us to have our portraits painted. I had had my portrait painted in Kyoto, but it had been after I knocked my teeth out and my face was still terribly swollen. This one would be better, she promised. There was a young artist, Sally Kravitch, who lived in her parents' big house on Victory Drive. Apparently she was all the rage in Savannah, with a list of names of people who wanted their portraits done by her. Mother made an appointment for my first sitting. Just before we were to leave, my step-grandmother, who was German and would have fit right in with a group of Nazis, pulled me aside. "Don't touch anything when you go in the house," she whispered. She pulled out a white lace handkerchief and pressed it into my hand. "If you accidentally touch something, use this to wipe your hands right away." I took the handkerchief and shoved it into my pocket. "Why do I need to do this?" I asked. "Because," she hissed, "they're Jewish."

I was totally confused. I knew the Nazis had killed the Jewish people—who hadn't done anything wrong—for no reason. What was so bad about them that I couldn't touch anything? Were they dirty? Did they have germs? For some reason I didn't tell my mother what Granny had said. They didn't get along very well and I didn't want to cause any more friction. However, I couldn't understand why my mother would take me to a house that might be infected and cause a health problem.

When we got there, the door was opened by one of the most beautiful girls I had ever seen. She was blond and blue-eyed and looked a little bit like my aunt Maggie. She couldn't have been more gracious and welcoming as she led us into the living room, which I remember as painted in all pale creams and blues and much grander than Granny's house. Beyond the living room was a small studio, full of light, where she asked me to sit. I was very nervous. I kept looking around for signs of contamination but everything seemed pristine, sunny, and airy. Sally charmed my mother and put me totally at ease. I was disappointed when the afternoon was over. We were stunned at how much of a likeness she had created of me, even in that one sitting.

We made arrangements for another sitting. I don't remember ever going back because Daddy came home unexpectedly and we had to leave Savannah for the next assignment. I never saw the portrait she was working on and never told my parents about Granny, but having met Sally only reinforced my disbelief in a God who would allow anyone who was a Jew to be killed.

. . .

Daddy came back midsummer. He walked up the driveway at my grandmother's yellow brick house on Habersham Street. He was wearing fatigues, he was sunburned, and his black hair had turned pure white. He looked like a god. My heart nearly burst with love.

Chapter 3

When your life is filled with the desire to see
the holiness in everyday life, something magical happens:
ordinary life becomes extraordinary, and the very
process of life begins to nourish your soul.

—Rabbi Harold Kushner, "God's Fingerprints on the Soul"

General Wild Bill Donovan, who had been the wartime head of the Office of Strategic Services (OSS) during World War II, appointed my father to head the transition from the OSS to the Central Intelligence Agency. Daddy had been with the G2 in the Seventh Army in Germany during World War II and had a background in intelligence. We moved back to Washington toward the end of summer. One day my mother was gossiping on the phone to a friend when Daddy came into the room and spotted something in the ceiling light fixture, moved slowly and carefully toward it, and dismantled it. Then he took my mother and me outside. He told us the house was bugged. We had to be very careful about what we said. The house was swept by the OSS the next day. This was our new life.

Before school started, we moved to a house we had lived in earlier, on North Nottingham Street in Arlington. My best friend was a Catholic. I had never knowingly met a Catholic before and was very curious about what this label even meant. How was she different from me? What did she believe? I understood that she and her family ate only fish on Friday and that some people called them "mackerel snappers." That was about the extent of what I knew about Catholicism. One Saturday she invited me to spend the night and go to church—she called it Mass—with her the next morning. My parents didn't object, and my curiosity overcame my anti-religion feelings. I was a little nervous but kind of excited as well. What I experienced was far from what I had expected. The Mass was beautiful, mysterious, and moving. I loved the theater of it all—the priests in their fancy garb, the incense burning, the music, and most important, the language, the Latin. The best part of it was that they weren't saying anything I couldn't believe, mostly because I couldn't understand it. I could just sit and feel something transcendent, something I hadn't experienced before. The Mass didn't make me think I was turning to religion, but it did give me a sense, for the first time, of what worship was truly about.

· · ·

That summer the polio epidemic hit, terrifying everyone, especially mothers. The swimming pools were closed, and we were not allowed to go to the movies or any big events. My parents would hardly let us out of the house to see our friends or play with others. Every day the paper had stories about people dying or being paralyzed, and most horrifying, spending the rest of their lives in iron lungs. Polio really was viewed as a plague. With all the quarantines in effect, by the end of the summer the number of new cases decreased a bit and the hysteria seemed to die down. We were finally allowed to go to school that fall.

One day I was walking home from school, wearing my favorite black-and-white pinafore dress and my black patent leather Mary

Janes. It was a lovely fall afternoon and the sun was shining through the dappled dark-green leaves, on the verge of turning brown. For some reason I felt so happy I thought I would burst. I knew my mother would be waiting for me at home with my favorite treat, vanilla custard. She would hug and kiss me and tell me how much she loved me. My mother loved me to pieces, I used to tell my friends. Suddenly I was overcome with a horrible feeling of dread. Something terrible was going to happen to my mother. I started running as fast as I could. When I got to the door there she was, her beautiful soft hands outstretched toward me, and of course, there was the Proustian smell of the vanilla custard wafting from the kitchen. I raced inside and sat down to eat but knew immediately that something was wrong. My mother sat down and put her head in her hands. She had a terrible headache, she said. Her back hurt. She had no energy. I was scared. My mother never got sick. When Daddy got home, she said she wanted to lie down. I could see that her out-of-the-ordinary behavior worried him. Sometime that night he took her to the emergency room, while my grandmother, Nana, watched us.

Mother had it. She had polio—lumbar polio, she was told, the worst kind. Incurable. They took her to the army hospital at Fort Belvoir. Children under twelve weren't allowed to visit their parents. The irony and the pain of this after having been in the hospital in Tokyo without my mother being allowed to see me was almost more than I could bear. Happily, because the old wooden pre–World War II hospital was only one story, my father would wheel my mother's bed to the window and we would stand outside and talk to her. At night Daddy would come home and try to be upbeat. Nana usually did the cooking, but sometimes he would take everything in the icebox, put it in a pot, and call it the "Mystery Dish," usually something unrecognizable and awful. We were always sad at dinner, but Daddy tried to make things seem lighter, at least joking about that night's dish. The problem was he never had any good news.

Mother was still very sick. I thought I would never see her well again. I believed she might die or be paralyzed for the rest of her life. I knew I couldn't live without her. I cried all the time but stubbornly refused to pray. What was the point? There was no God. How could that good and loving God that others talked about do this to my mother, the most wonderful person on Earth? I wanted to shriek and stomp on the floor and show my rage. I found that the most helpless feeling in the world was to be angry and not have anyone or anything to be angry at, no object for my anger. It would not be the first time I would know that kind of frustration and anguish. Finally I decided to take the situation upon myself, as I had in the hospital in Tokyo. I willed her to get better.

Mother recovered and, contrary to the doctors' predictions, walked out of the hospital. It was a miracle, they said. They had never seen this kind of recovery in a case this bad. Some people said that God had answered our prayers. I didn't say anything. Mother told us she had to get better because she loved us so much and she had to be there to take care of us. I believed then that she willed herself to get better. God had nothing to do with it. When we got home from picking her up at the hospital, at our insistence Daddy made her the Mystery Dish for dinner. She said it was a good thing she got better because if she hadn't, we would all have died from eating Daddy's cooking.

. . .

In these early preadolescent years I was obsessed with *Alice in Wonderland*. I wanted to be Alice in part because I often felt I was in my own version of Wonderland. I had practically memorized the books. My time in the hospital in Tokyo had been a through-the-looking-glass experience. It was surreal. Life was surreal. Somehow *Alice in Wonderland* didn't seem all that far-fetched to me. Everything was jabberwocky. I learned someone was making a movie of *Alice in Wonderland* and was feverish with excitement. So were all my friends, though no one was as ecstatic as I was. It was coming soon to a theater near me, on a Sunday afternoon. My friends and I were all going to go together. I was beside myself. I could barely sleep, the level of anticipation was so high. It was certain to be the highlight of my life. Finally the big day arrived.

Daddy woke me up, saying it was time to go to Sunday school. Daydreaming as I was, I certainly didn't want to go to Sunday school. I hated Sunday school and fell back on my usual thinking that it was all a big lie, anyway. It just seemed so stupid, the teachers sitting there telling us these treacly stories about Jesus and having to sing songs with lyrics I didn't believe—"Jesus loves me, this I know, for the Bible tells me so. Little ones to him belong, they are weak but he is strong. Yes, Jesus loves me, Yes, Jesus loves me. . . ." Who were they kidding? Had Jesus loved all the little Jewish children? All those young men on the hospital plane coming back from war? Did Jesus love them, too?

I quickly lied to Daddy, telling him I had a terrible stomachache and couldn't possibly go to church. He absolutely hated lying and knew right away that I wasn't telling the truth. I curled up, rubbed my stomach, and moaned, not looking him in the eye. He stood there in silence for a bit. "Are you really sick?" he asked. "Yes," I groaned. "I'm sorry about that," he said, "but you ought to think about it because if you're really too sick to go to Sunday school, then you're too sick to go to *Alice in Wonderland* this afternoon."

What did he just say? I didn't believe I had heard correctly. Not go to see *Alice in Wonderland*?! He knew how I felt about it being the most important day of my life. How could he even suggest such a thing? "I mean it," he boomed, "either you get out of bed and get dressed now or you're not going to see the movie this afternoon."

What could I do? I couldn't suddenly have a miraculous recovery on the spot—the proof that I had been lying would be evident and he might punish me by not letting me go anyway. Besides, he wasn't a cruel person. He couldn't possibly not let me go. It was unthinkable. I decided to call his bluff. I rolled over and moaned again, curled up even more, and whispered that I felt horrible. He turned and left.

What riled me even more was knowing that Daddy was not himself a churchgoer. He would drop us kids off at Sunday school and then come home for another couple of hours' sleep and return to pick us up. He and Mother never went to church. What kind of a lesson was that? I was so mad that I almost did get sick. I had to figure out a clever way to get unsick. I stayed in bed for a few hours, then went to my mother and asked for some Pepto-Bismol, which she gave me. I suddenly had a miraculous recovery. I asked her if she would tell Daddy that I was better and feeling well enough to go to the movie. She said she would. She knew I had lied, but she didn't feel that strongly about it. I could hear them having a heated discussion in the kitchen. After a while, she came back upstairs. She shook her head sadly. He would not relent. She had done her best, but he would not tolerate dishonesty.

It was the first and last tantrum I ever threw. It was a pretty good one too. I may even have threatened suicide. I certainly threatened to run away from home. Of course my mother knew that that would never happen since I was a double Cancer and Cancerians were such homebodies that they would never run away. It was all to no avail. I missed the movie and spent the afternoon in my room sobbing in dismay and rage, even hating my father for the moment. I literally made myself sick. I now realize that what I never got over was the moral issue at stake. Yes, I lied. That was wrong. I never should have. On the other hand, he was trying to force me to believe something that was so personally offensive to me that I couldn't do it in good conscience. My lie was a little lie compared to the big lie he was insisting I live. I never forgot it.

. . .

Enterprise, Alabama, is the peanut capital of the world. In the center of the town square is a kind of modified Statue of Liberty, holding a pedestal with a boll weevil on top. When the boll weevil hit Alabama and destroyed the cotton crops, the farmers planted peanuts instead and made fortunes by diversifying.

My father got his first star when we were in Enterprise. We didn't live at Fort Rucker where Daddy was stationed after his Washington assignment, because there were no quarters for dependents. Enterprise was a tiny town then. We lived in a new housing development, surrounded by red dirt. Across the street, the less affluent white neighbors lived in shacks or trailers. My friend's house had no separated rooms unto themselves, just ropes or clotheslines with sheets hung over them to define spaces for privacy. I had never seen that kind of poverty. It was shocking to me.

I was in sixth grade. The first day of school was in September and it was still swelteringly hot. I was the only child wearing shoes. Everyone else was barefoot. Lunch was a bag of salted peanuts poured inside the green neck of a glass Coke bottle. It was almost as dramatic a culture shock as the move to Japan.

Children were regularly beaten by the teachers for the mildest infractions. They would be marched up to the front of the room, made to lie across the teacher's desk on their stomachs, and hit with paddles. Nobody seemed to have a problem with this. I was horrified and so were my parents. They'd never heard of anything like it. The humiliation was more than I could imagine. I lived in terror that I would do something wrong and be hauled to the front of the class. I felt sure that I would not let that happen. I would run out of the school and never return again. Happily, that never came to pass. My teacher, who was probably in her early twenties and didn't really have her heart in the paddlings, was married to a lieutenant at Fort Rucker. I didn't think I was going to have a problem. Nevertheless, what really got to me was that the kids were all Southern Christians. We had to pray in school in the morning. What kind of Christians would publicly humiliate and beat their children in front of others for such little things? Just another reminder that there was no God.

My parents always found good friends and managed to have fun anywhere, but Enterprise was no garden spot, and the surroundings and culture began to wear on all of us, especially Mother and Daddy. There was a lot of tension between them. Daddy was away a lot on maneuvers and Mother was left alone with us, with nothing much but her bridge club to keep her occupied. One night, after he had been away for a while, he came home to dinner. Unfortunately there was no dinner. My mother still was not home from bridge. Fuming, he went into the kitchen, made something for dinner, and called us to the table. Just as he did, my mother drove up and flounced into the house, not really greeting my father or apologizing for being late.

"Where have you been?" he demanded in a controlled but stern voice. He looked especially commanding in his uniform. "I came home to an empty kitchen and I had to cook dinner myself." I had never once in my life heard my parents argue, and I had certainly never heard my father use this tone of voice to my mother. Before she could answer, I piped up in a singsong, teasing voice, and exclaimed, "Poor little housewife!" I'll never know what possessed me to say that.

With that, my father threw his napkin on the table, his face drawn with rage, stood up from the table and said, "Goddamnit, Bette, that's it. I'm leaving." He charged out the door and drove off. I'd never heard him swear either, except his occasional "God Almightys." I was thunderstruck. What had I done? What had I said? My father had left us because of me. How could I ever forgive myself? I ran upstairs to my room and flung myself on the bed, quickly becoming completely hysterical. My mother came up to console me. She kept rubbing my back and kissing me and telling me it would be okay, but I knew it wasn't okay. Eventually I got the dry heaves. Mother became frantic. Sometime around dawn I heard my father's voice. He came up to my bedroom and put his arms around me. He held me for a long time until my tears subsided. He said he was sorry. He didn't mean he was actually leaving but he had to go back out on maneuvers for a few months. He loved me and he would be back. He knew—and my mother did too—how sensitive I was. It had only been a little over a year since I had gotten out of the hospital in San Antonio. I could tell they were worried I might have a relapse. He managed to convince me that everything would be okay and then he left.

He didn't come back for months, a time period that seemed even longer than it actually was. I overheard my mother talking to my grandmother about how Daddy was living at the BOQ (Bachelor Officer Quarters) at Fort Rucker. He wasn't really on maneuvers at all. I just knew they were splitting up. It took everything I had not to get sick again, but the combination of knowing I had to stay strong for my mother and that I couldn't go back to a hospital again kept me resolute about not getting some unknown malady once more. We were all miserable, stuck in Enterprise, with Daddy gone and no idea what to do.

I took up praying again. I actually knelt by my bed. Maybe I was praying to Daddy to come back. Maybe it wasn't to God. I don't know who was the recipient of my prayers and hopes and best wishes, but I knew I had to do something and this was one of the few things I knew how to do, although I certainly had been out of practice.

In May, Daddy got his new orders. He was going to be stationed in Athens, Greece. We were going to go with him. Paradise. I'd rarely been so ecstatic. He came home, finally, to tell us the news. He would leave almost immediately and we would follow on a ship from New York. My mother—alone—would have to pack up everything, and all of us as well, and get us there. She was so thrilled, she didn't care. We were going to be a family again. Did my prayers help? I'll never know.

· · ·

As a family we were the happiest we had ever been in Athens. We loved everything about it—the weather, the blue skies, the whole Mediterranean ambience. We loved the sea, the mountains, the beaches, the whitewashed islands, the olive trees. We loved the culture, the music, the language and history, much of which was redolent in the ruins and monuments. We loved the Greek food—the salads, feta cheese, calamari, moussaka. We loved the Greek people, their personalities and temperaments. We loved the *den peirazei*—the insouciance, the lightheartedness—of it all, essentially an attitude of "whatever, don't worry." The whole place lent itself to some calm and peace that came over our family. We were unstressed and delighted by each day. Yet again I was in sync with the *genius loci* of the place. I *was* Greek and felt completely at home there. This would be a repeated experience throughout my life.

It was 1953 and Daddy was a major general by now. He was the number two in the JUSMAG (Joint United States Military Aid Group). My parents made huge numbers of friends in the military and the diplomatic corps, the CIA as well as the Greek shipowners, the Greek government, and even became friends with King Paul and Queen Frederika. It was a tight social community and they saw each other all the time. (At the time I began to suspect that Daddy was working for intelligence.)

The Hotel Grande Bretagne, across the plaza from the palace, was headquarters for all the action, and my parents often took us to lunch there on Sundays. The hotel restaurant had the most extraordinary homemade potato chips I had ever eaten. We also drove on weekends into the mountains near Athens, where we had lunches in small tavernas, always including dessert with freshly grown almonds and honey from wild beehives.

In the summer we would drive to Vouliagmeni Beach, south of Athens, where there was one tiny taverna on a cove. We watched the fishermen catch the octopuses in the cove, beat them on the rocks to tenderize them, and deliver them to the restaurant. When we finished swimming, we would take a table and order freshly grilled octopus as we sat in the shade and sipped our Fanta limonadas.

Some weekends in the summer our parents' friends would take us on their yachts to the islands. Often we would stay with their friends who had houses on Hydra or Spetses. We went to the Anglo American School in Kifissia, a suburb of Athens. It was tiny, international, and laid-back. Our friends were from every country imaginable.

In Greece, children were folded into the grown-ups' activities. We stayed up half the night and slept half the day. Greece was heaven.

I turned thirteen in Greece. It was there that I began to become a fully formed person. It was in Greece where I began to be a woman. It was in Greece where I learned the word *atheist*.

Here was a word for what I was—or at least felt myself to be. I wasn't alone. I wasn't weird. I wasn't sick. I wasn't evil. I just didn't believe in God. It's not that the existence of God had not been questioned before. I felt an enormous sense of freedom, emotional and intellectual (confirmation that my thinking was not wrong). In some odd way, that sense of freedom allowed me to be more spiritual, a feeling I hadn't recognized before.

I was so proud of my newfound word, my newfound identity, that I announced to my father that I was an atheist. Naturally, he went ballistic. (A decade later, the atheist community in the United States was led by a shrill woman with a mustache named Madalyn Murray O'Hair, not the compelling sympathetic leader one would want for a new movement.)

As they had my entire childhood, my father and mother continued to try to send my younger siblings to Sunday school and me to church while they slept in on Sunday mornings after their late-night "bacchanals." From this point on—and after the personal catastrophe of missing the *Alice in Wonderland* movie—I simply refused to go.

Right around this time my father went to Paris for a meeting. When he returned, he brought me a present. He had little trinkets for Donna and Butchie. He saved mine for last. It was a shoebox, inside of which was a gorgeous pair of sophisticated, sexy black suede pointed-toe French heels with a sweetheart cut. I could hardly contain myself, they were so beautiful. My first pair of heels. I slipped them on. A perfect fit. I threw my arms around my father, practically weeping with gratitude.

"You can have them on one condition," he said. I suddenly had a wrenching feeling in my stomach.

"What?" I asked.

"You can have them if you go to church."

I was faced with an enormous moral crisis. What should I do? Take the coveted shoes and go against everything I then believed by going to church services or refuse the shoes, not go to church, and live with a clear conscience.

"Okay," I said.

The next Sunday, our chauffeur Yiorgos drove my brother, sister, and me to Sunday school and church, respectively. I deliberately ran late so the church would be filled when we got there. I sashayed up the middle aisle all the way to the front where I proudly took my seat before the altar. I wanted to make absolutely sure that everyone saw me in my new high-heeled French suede shoes.

They knew what was on my body. It was none of their business what was in my soul. After that there was no way my father could keep me out of church. That was the only place I had to wear the shoes. I often wondered how he felt about bribing me like that. He must have realized a pair of French heels couldn't change someone's mind about believing in God. Although I have to admit, they came close.

· · ·

Greece was a place where I became more open to certain moments of transcendence. I had experienced moments like these before, but hadn't been able to give a name to them. In Greece, however, I began to recognize them for what they were—magical happenings beyond any explanation rooted in the physical world.

Greek Easter is a red-letter day in the Orthodox Church. King Paul and Queen Frederika celebrated with a great party at the palace where whole lambs were roasted on spits and the king cracked eggs with all the guests, a traditional ritual. Each person has a hard-boiled egg and cracks it against one held by another guest. The one whose egg does not crack will have a year of good luck. I cracked eggs with the king. My egg did not break.

We also went—as a family this time—to the Easter services at the Orthodox church. I couldn't help but remember my first experience at the Catholic church with my friend. From the moment we walked into the church, this felt similar in many ways. The service was held at night, with the church completely lit up by flickering candles. All the priests were in extremely ornate robes with what appeared to be crowns on their heads. The chanting and singing were mystical. Rose petals were strewn everywhere. There seemed to be awe on the faces of the congregants. I was envious, wanting to feel that awe. I wanted to believe what they believed. I wanted to celebrate with them. It struck me that this was religion as community. Something about everyone praying and believing together was especially powerful, even overwhelming in a good way. It was different from being alone in a room trying to conjure up an elusive God. Church that evening included an inexplicable presence in addition to all those people and me. I felt something I had never experienced before, something I didn't have a name for but knew it to be real and true.

. . .

Christmas that same year in Athens was another moment when I experienced some similar otherworldly feelings. I was always im-

bued with a sense of extreme anticipation on Christmas Eve—of ex-
pectation, joy, and magic. Even though I was thirteen now and had
stopped believing in Santa Claus long ago, I had that sense again
on this particular night. I don't know what I thought was going to
happen; I just felt as if I were about to jump out of my skin. Though
I didn't realize it, I might have been anticipating something spiritual.
The birth of Christ is obviously a powerful story. For some reason I
didn't connect the story of Christ with my disbelief in God. I remember trembling with excitement all evening.

Our family ritual was that we opened one present on Christmas
Eve and saved the rest until the morning. We also had to perform for
my parents. Every year, we did the same little playlet from *The Little
Match Girl*, for which I wrote the script and produced and starred in
the show. Donna played the rock against which the Little Match Girl
leaned when she was bone-weary and weeping. Butchie played the
tree in the background. I always gave a bravura performance, after
which we opened our one present, had dinner, left out cookies, milk,
and a note for Santa (Butchie still believed), and went to bed, knowing we would probably not sleep a wink.

Of course I was looking forward to opening presents the next
morning. I really loved surprising my parents and siblings with
things I knew they wanted. What I didn't look forward to was the
letdown I knew would follow after it was all over. I never analyzed
that familiar letdown until recently when it became clear that it also
was a spiritual letdown. Whatever I was anticipating around the
birth of Christ had not been fulfilled.

I went to bed Christmas Eve and went to sleep right away. I woke
about four A.M., not listening for the sounds of Santa's reindeer on the
roof but for something else. Our house was on a hill in Psychiko outside
of Athens, and my room looked across the valley to the mountains

on the other side. The light was beginning to dawn around the top of the mountain, the moon was beaming, and the stars were out by the millions. The outline of the terrain in front of me looked so like that of Bethlehem, or at least what I had seen in paintings and imagined.

My mind went into paroxysms of fantasy and I saw the wise men on camels following the star, I saw the manger, I saw Joseph and Mary, and I saw the baby Jesus being born. If you had put me in front of a lie detector and asked if I had really seen it and I said yes, it would have registered that I was telling the truth. To this day it still seems absolutely true. I believe I saw it. I still have an ache in my heart when I remember this scene.

I had been sitting up and I collapsed on the bed and fell into a deep sleep. Everyone had a hard time waking me the next morning. I could barely concentrate on the presents. The whole idea of exchanging gifts now seemed silly and meaningless to me. I think I was in a state of transcendence. It wore off finally, and sadly. From then on I have been trying to recapture that feeling every Christmas but have never fully succeeded.

. . .

Shortly before we left Athens, after nearly two glorious years, to move to Germany, we were invited on the yacht of one of my parents' friends. It was a day trip. We stopped at several ports, swam off the boat in the Aegean Sea, and had a sumptuous lunch. As we were heading back to Piraeus I slipped up to the bow of the boat and stood there for most of the return trip. The setting sun was on my face and the wind was blowing my hair. I felt truly happy. I wanted to stay right there for the rest of my life.

Then I had the oddest sensation. As if I were watching flashbacks of my life, except I was seeing flash-forwards. My whole emotional future passed before me. I felt everything, good and bad, that after-noon that I have since felt. Exhilaration, devastation, fear, strength, pride, envy, despair, peace, love many times over, hate, fear, appre-hension, need, lust, anticipation, guilt, excitement, shame, greed, uncertainty, ambition, insecurity, compassion, giving, nurturing . . . I could go on. The kaleidoscope in my brain just kept twisting and turning, showing me the various rearrangements of my emotions and experiences that were yet to come. I was at once terrified and thrilled. It was a true psychic experience. From then on, everything that has happened to me has been something that, no matter how joyful or painful, I have somehow anticipated. Since then, I haven't had an emotional experience that did not seem already familiar to me. I realized that day that I would survive and thrive. That moment gave me enormous strength.

Chapter 4

I would not want to live in a world without magic, for that is
a world without mystery, and that is a world without faith.

—R. A. Salvatore, *Streams of Silver*
(The Legend of Drizzt series, Book V)

While we were stationed in Göppingen, a tiny town outside of Stuttgart, Germany, my parents—after a short stint for me at Stuttgart American High School in Ludwigsburg for the children of diplomats and the military—decided to send Donna and me to a girls' boarding school in Switzerland. Donna was in the lower school and I rarely saw her. I was the youngest in the upper school, which was essentially my freshman year in high school. The other girls were all British and had completed their equivalent of high school in England. They were attending for one year to be "finished."

The school was in a tiny town, Château-d'Oex, in the French-speaking part of Switzerland. A Disneyland chalet right out of the movies, it was called "Le Torrent" for the torrent of water that flowed down the snow-covered hills above into a stream on the grounds of the school.

Our headmistress was a crazy woman, middle-aged, with masses of wild dyed bright-red hair; she had a huge bosom and wore very high-heeled shoes. She was hysterical, literally, and shrieked a lot.

The rumor was that her husband had hung himself in the basement years earlier.

We were only allowed to speak French, and for each word of English we were overheard speaking we would lose one of the five francs of our precious weekly allowance. We learned very quickly to speak French. We had classes in the morning—typing, French, and French literature. After lunch we skied all afternoon, returned for late tea, had more classes, and then went to bed. Weekends we went to the tearoom for tea dances with the local boys and students from the exclusive boys' school Le Rosey, in nearby Gstaad.

It was one of the most wonderful years of my life.

The British girls were fun, rowdy, iconoclastic, and mischievous. I bonded with them immediately, and we were constantly looking for ways to get into trouble. Sundays were great because we had no classes and skied all day. I became an excellent skier. We returned to school, had tea, and then went to mandatory church or vespers. This time I looked forward to church. The minister, who spoke in whispers, was a weather-beaten cipher of a man, with stooped shoulders and a defeated mien. Every Sunday he gave a number of sermons, starting in Lausanne, then up the train route to Montreux, Vevey, and finally Château-d'Oex. We were his last stop at 6:00 P.M., and by then he had lost any juice he might have started out with that morning.

We, the bad girls, sat in the back row and behaved appallingly throughout the entire hour while he intoned about sin and hellfire and damnation. There wasn't a believer among us. Everything he said sent us off into gales of laughter, which we would try to stifle to no avail.

One of our classmates, a slightly porcine girl with an unfortunate priggish personality, was not exactly Miss Popular. She always sat in the row in front of us. Much to our delight, she broke wind noisily all the way through the service. This undid us. The minute she began, we would be falling off our pews, biting our hands to keep from screaming with laughter, and inevitably wetting our pants—not exactly a spiritual reaction. We would stumble out of the church at the end of the service, exhausted from trying to contain ourselves and always in the most charitable mood. We loved those Sundays with the flatulence of our friend in front of us and the good father. If church had always been that much fun, I might have become a regular for life. As it was, after that, whenever I thought about religion, all I could think about was wetting my pants from laughing. That wouldn't change for a very long time.

. . .

In those days there were very few ski lifts. We used the lift every day for regular skiing; however, several times we had the most fabulous excursions. One weekend we attached sealskins (*peau de phoques*) to the bottom of our skis and spent an entire day climbing. It was exhausting and exhilarating at the same time. We would climb for an hour or so and then stop to eat an orange. Nothing could have been more beautiful than being in that pristine snow in the silence on a gorgeous, cloudless day overlooking the Swiss Alps. Our guide yodeled. It was too much.

We slept that night in a public cabin at the top of the mountain. There was a wood-burning stove and mats on the floor. We made cheese fondue. Because you positively cannot drink water with melted cheese, we drank Kirschwasser, which was also in the fondue. There was no drinking age in Switzerland. I got totally smashed. We were all exhausted and sunburned and crashed as soon as we had finished eating.

We woke the following morning to the sun blinding us as it poured through the windows, had a breakfast of meat and cheese, bread and oranges, put our sealskins in our backpacks, fastened on our skis, and prepared to ski down the mountain on perfect white sparkling untouched deep powder. We were all good skiers and we seemed to fly down the slopes. Sometimes when writers write, they say they don't know where the words come from. It's as if their thoughts are being channeled from some unknown source. That's how I felt that day. My skis hardly touched the snow. I was completely fearless. I sailed over moguls, jumped ridges, and slalomed around logs and trees with a sense of freedom and abandon. I had never had such a thrilling sensation. I may as well have had a line from the sky that kept me aloft, safe from danger as I careered down the slopes. If I had been religious, I would have said that God was holding that line, allowing me to go beyond my own limits. But I was not religious.

. . .

One day a beautiful Scottish couple arrived at Le Torrent. They looked as if they had just stepped out of Balmoral Castle. She was sophisticated with a pile of burnished curls pulled up on her head, an elegant fitted suede coat trimmed with sable, patterned stockings, and smart pumps. He was dashing in a fitted bespoke suit and cravat, his shoes perfectly polished. They were charming and gracious to everyone, her ringing laughter carrying throughout the chalet, his deep voice commanding and reassuring. Both of them oozed self-confidence and an easiness in their own skins. They were the most social of animals. I thought they were incredibly glamorous.

They were there to enter their daughter in the school. Just looking at the two of them, you could easily imagine the aspirations and expectations they must have had for their divinely beautiful daughter. In fact, the daughter was a different story. She was the saddest girl I had ever seen.

Her face was mildly out of balance. Her nose was not aligned, and her eyes were too close together and slightly off-kilter. She didn't look directly at people when she spoke, and her speech was so nasal it was hard to understand. She was gangly, not quite walking in a straight line. Today, we would identify her as a special needs child. The only problem was that there weren't places for this kind of student then.

Her parents were clearly loving and concerned, but seemed at a loss for how to handle the situation. No doubt they had high hopes that this school would work for their daughter. Unfortunately, the administration of Le Torrent wasn't inclined toward any integration of outliers, and we—her classmates—were just as bad.

The next few weeks must have been a horror for her. Nobody paid attention to her except to tease her. She didn't speak French, and, besides, she had no one to talk to. She couldn't keep up in class, couldn't ski, sat alone at meals, and spent most of her time by herself in her room, crying, so I was told. I was not one of the perpetrators, but that doesn't absolve me. I have to admit that I was uncomfortable being around her, so I avoided her. I didn't know how to talk to her and she had a hard time carrying on a conversation, even in English. The teachers were frustrated and short with her. It was painful to observe.

One day a couple of the girls raided her bedroom when she wasn't there. They came back triumphant; they had found bloodied underpants and wads of bloody toilet paper. It seems that she had gotten her period for the first time while she was there and had told no one. Some of the girls thought it was funny; others, including me, were mortified for her. This was too much. Something had to be done. Finally a group of us went to see the frightening headmistress, a terrifying and unsympathetic woman, and told her what had happened. She didn't say a word, just listened.

Shortly after that, this poor girl disappeared from school. We never saw or heard about her again. She may have been gone, but the memory of her was forever seared in my brain. I couldn't get over my shame and guilt. I may not have been directly responsible for her pain, but I didn't do anything to stop it either. My behavior was despicable. It was unchristian in the largest sense of the word. I clearly had not had the Golden Rule uppermost in my mind. Years later, when my son was born with special needs, the memories of our mistreatment of that young girl came flooding back. So did the pain. I will never forget her.

Chapter 5

The universe is full of magical things
patiently waiting for our wits to grow sharper.

—Eden Phillpotts, *A Shadow Passes*

Growing up in the military is a singular experience. We never lived in one place for much longer than a year and a half. I practically had to be pried out of Switzerland. I've rarely cried so hard as when we had to leave Le Torrent. Donna and I returned to Germany with our parents to pack up for our next assignment.

On the move again, our family came back to the United States, first to Fort Carson in Colorado Springs, then, six months later, to Fort Lewis, near Tacoma in Washington State, where my father was taking over as the commanding general. In Tacoma, my closest friend was Jeannie Schwartz. She was a year older than I and the smartest friend I'd ever had. She lived right next door on Generals Row. Her father, a doctor, was the commanding general of Madigan Army Hospital. We spent hours at her house talking about books and ideas. She had a great library and was always lending me books.

I was intent on enlarging my vocabulary, partly to impress her because she seemed to know every word in the dictionary. One day when we were hanging out, I was looking through the books on her shelves and came across a book with the word *anti-Semitism* in the title. I had encountered that word recently but hadn't absorbed its meaning. Wanting to show off my newfound word, I turned to Jeannie and asked brightly, "Oh, are you anti-Semitic?" Of course, I didn't know what it really meant and may not even have pronounced it properly, but she knew what I was asking. She looked at me, shocked. "Sally, of course not," she said. "I'm Jewish."

I looked at her, shocked myself. I had no idea she was Jewish. How was I supposed to know? How could you tell? I always wondered that about the Nazis. How could they tell people were Jewish? I was shocked because I didn't know. My parents had never said a word about the Schwartzes being Jewish. I was appalled and ashamed that I had offended her. I was also deeply embarrassed to have shown my ignorance. I wanted to sink through the floor. All I could think of was Granny in Savannah telling me not to touch anything in Sally Kravitch's house, and all I could do was bow my head and say meekly, "I didn't know."

Jeannie smiled and then actually laughed. She sat me down and gently explained what the word meant. I told her about my father and Dachau and the Holocaust albums and Granny. I certainly didn't understand where anti-Semitism came from even when I knew what it meant.

We hugged at the end of our talk. I went home and asked my parents if they knew the Schwartzes were Jewish. "Of course," they said. "Why didn't you tell me?" I demanded. "Why would it matter?" my father asked. And of course, he was right. It didn't matter. Not to us, anyway—or so I thought.

As I found out later, it did matter to him.

· · ·

Whenever we moved, there was always a new school to adjust to, new friends, a new house, a new culture. What that meant was that we established our own family rituals that remain meaningful to me today. They weren't really religious rituals, but they might as well have been. When we moved into a new house, we would greet the house. When we left, we would say good-bye. I used to go around and kiss the walls of each room. The fact that my parents would always have a party the night they moved into a new house, I now see as a way of blessing the house for the short time we would be there.

So in two years I had added two more schools to my list that, by the time I finished my elementary and high school education, tallied twenty-two schools. After four other high schools—Ludwigsburg in Stuttgart, Germany, Le Torrent in Switzerland, Cheyenne Mountain in Colorado Springs, and Clover Park in Tacoma—we had returned for a third time to Washington, D.C. I was now ensconced at Mount Vernon Seminary, an all-girls school (where we wore uniforms) on fancy Foxhall Road where a lot of Southern girls boarded. Donna was there too, and we both loved it. My senior year went by very quickly since I spent most of my time studying—I had my sights set on getting into Smith—but I did find time to start smoking that year, learn to drive, have my first kiss (I was a late bloomer), and play Alice in the school play, *Alice in Wonderland*.

We moved from a fairly temporary place in Chevy Chase to generals' quarters at Fort Myer just across the river in Virginia. This time our house was on the parade ground across from the chapel, overlooking Arlington Cemetery. Living there, which we did from 1959 until sometime in 1964 (although I was away at college for most of those years and only there on visits and during the summers), had an enormous effect on my life. By the time we got to Fort Myer, my parents had long since given up on sending us to Sunday school or church. They never went, and we were old enough to point out the hypocrisy of the whole thing. We were living across the street from the chapel, and I don't think they ever set foot in there except possibly for weddings, christenings, or funerals.

Funerals . . . there were a lot of them at Fort Myer, sometimes as many as four a day, right outside our front door. All you had to do was look out a window to see throngs of black-clad and uniformed mourners surrounding a casket, some weeping softly or loudly, others silent, looking stricken. The casket would be lifted by soldiers onto the caisson drawn by horses and the procession would turn in to the cemetery followed by a line of black cars. There would be a graveside service and then "Taps," which we could always hear. Sometimes my brother and sister and I would follow the caisson and stand behind the trees at the cemetery, watching the ceremony. Military funerals are always moving, especially for those killed in battle.

These years coincided with the beginning of the U.S. involvement in the Vietnam War. We saw the toll that was being taken long before the general public did. We saw the grieving families of the boys and men who were dying. None of this made any sense to me. Early on, I had come to believe that the Vietnam War was a really pointless war, so very different from World War II or even the Korean War, though I had questions about that as well.

Mostly I had questions about God. Once again God was at the forefront of much of what I was observing in my life. The funeral-goers would come streaming out of the chapel, having just prayed to God. They would stand in front of their loved ones' graves with a military chaplain praying to God. What in God's name were they praying for? The dead? That they would go to heaven and not hell? That God should rest their eternal souls?

Sometimes I would turn away from these funerals in outrage. It all seemed such an exercise in futility and absurdity. I would go back to our house and lie on my bed, which faced the chapel, and I would listen for the next horse-drawn caisson, the clop, clop, clop of the horses' hooves on the pavement, day in and day out, serving as a reminder of my lack of faith in God.

. . .

The summer before I went off to Smith, I worked at the Pentagon in the intelligence unit called G2, of which my father was head. (These were the days of rampant nepotism.) I was in the office of protocol, where I had a top secret clearance. I'm not sure that meant much because even the menus at the office were top secret. We certainly didn't want the Russians finding out about our dining habits and flower arrangements.

I fell madly in love that summer. It was the first love of my life. He had just gotten out of the Marine Corps, after graduating a year early from prep school, and was entering his freshman year at Princeton. He was so much more sophisticated and manly than any of the other boys I had dated. He was born in July as well, another Cancer; I was a double Cancer—clearly, this was a match made in heaven, or at least in the stars. I began to read more about astrology, which would become more and more important to me as I grew older. I had our charts done. We were soul mates. I read his palm. He had a long life line, which showed he'd make lots of money and would travel. He also had a solid love line. We spent the entire summer together in a swoon. It gave me an enormous amount of confidence to be entering college with a fabulous guy to call mine. Maybe there was a God. . . .

. . .

Smith was everything I had hoped it would be. At that time, there were no dorms; instead, each student was assigned a house to live in. I was assigned to Talbot House. I loved all of it—the girls in my house, my courses, my teachers, the campus, and particularly the theater. I immediately decided on becoming a theater major and plunged into the first play as soon as I got there. Everyone was so smart. In those days, the Ivy League schools—Harvard, Yale, Princeton, et cetera—were all men. Many of the women at Smith, Wellesley, Radcliffe, and a few others might have been at these men's schools had it been a few years later.

We stayed up late most nights discussing the meaning of life. Nobody ever spoke of religion. I read everyone's palms, because I had taken up palm reading again the summer before my first year of college. I had been doing palm reading on and off since all those years ago in Statesboro but began doing it again seriously at Smith.

That fall, my inamorato invited me to Princeton for the weekend of the football game with Penn. It was a nightmare. I was sick. My girdle was so tight I couldn't breathe. My heels were so high I couldn't walk. He was enthralled with a very sophisticated beautiful blond model from New York. It rained all weekend. He hardly spoke to me. I cried all the way back to school. A week later I got a letter from him breaking up with me. "It ain't no mo'," he wrote.

I continued to feel unwell and got terribly sick at Thanksgiving. The illness turned out to be mononucleosis. I've often wondered if he came down with it too. When you're in love, even if you're a nonbeliever, God's in his heaven, all's right with the world. But this God of mine was elusive.

· · ·

I dated a lot the summer after freshman year, but none of them was The One. I was still mourning the loss of my first love. The one person I did go out with, whom I found more interesting than the others, was several years older than I was. He was very smart and had a great sense of humor. He invited me to spend the day with him at the family farm in Virginia and I accepted. The day before we were to go he called me. He sort of beat around the bush for a bit. I knew he was trying to say something. Finally he came out with it. "I'd like to bring a friend with me," he said. "Fine," I said. I was a bit relieved because I was nervous about being alone with him. I hardly knew him though we had met through friends. "Well," he said, clearing his throat, "I wanted to tell you that he is a gentleman of color. I hope that won't be a problem for you." I was completely at a loss for words. I simply didn't know what to say. A gentleman of color? That meant he was a colored person. I had never socialized with a colored person. That's what we called them at home. The "N" word was never acceptable in my family; only white trash used the "N" word. We had a few "colored" girls at Smith but I didn't know them.

I could feel the blood rushing to my face. I was embarrassed, but also terribly uncomfortable. I didn't know how I would handle it. The silence continued. "Well," he said, "I'll see you tomorrow." I worried all afternoon. I worried about my feelings and how I would deal with this, but also I worried about his possible discomfort. Later that afternoon he called back to say his friend wasn't able to come. I was both relieved and humbled, feeling guilty. I knew his friend wasn't coming because of me.

When he picked me up, I could tell he was a bit cool. We drove out to the country house, had a picnic, and went to the pond to swim. Sitting on the pier, we were just talking and getting to know each other. He had gone to Amherst, the men's college only seven miles from Smith. I had dated a few guys from Amherst. I asked him if he belonged to a fraternity. He said he did and told me the name of it. "Oh," I said enthusiastically, "isn't that the kike house?" I had no idea what *kike* meant nor that it had any negative connotations. He looked stunned. "Sally," he said, "I'm part Hebe." I had no idea what that meant either, but I somehow assumed it meant he was part Jewish. Much later I figured out it was short for *Hebrew*. "Oh," I said, "one of my best friends is Jewish." With that, we gathered up our things and drove home in silence. I never heard from him again.

I had never associated racism and anti-Semitism with religion. It was only as I grew older that I understood how closely related they were.

. . .

One summer I met Senator John Tower at my parents' house at Fort Myer, Virginia, shortly after he had won his seat in a special election. I was twenty. My parents were hosting a party for Senator Barry Goldwater. Senator Tower seemed to take an interest in me from the start. There were all these other famous and successful people at the party, but he spent most of his time talking to me. I was good at these parties. I had grown up with my parents entertaining and was very comfortable in the role of junior hostess. In fact, often my parents would take me to embassy parties with them, and on occasion I would go alone with my father if my mother wasn't feeling well. I wasn't shy at all and wasn't surprised that Senator Tower enjoyed my company.

He was singularly unattractive—tiny and plump with little eyes, a puffy face, and very small swollen hands and fingers. Still, he was interesting, talking about politics, and he lit up when he learned that I was a theater major at Smith with a minor in political science. He had taught theater at Midwestern University in Texas before going into politics. We agreed that the two, politics and theater, weren't so different in the end. I didn't mention that I had become what some considered to be a flaming liberal at college. He said he'd love to show me around the Senate and asked me if I'd like to have lunch in the Senate dining room one day and a tour.

Even though I had worked on Capitol Hill for Senator Goldwater, a friend of my parents, my first summer in Washington, it had been a few years and I thought it might be fun to see it again from Senator Tower's perspective. Tower was a friend of Barry's. It never occurred to me that he might have ulterior motives. Call me naive.

Tower's secretary called to make a lunch date for the following week. I wore a pink-coral-and-white linen print dress with a bolero jacket to work. It was in the middle of a sweltering summer. I wanted to look nice but not too dressy, summer professional. Shortly before lunch his secretary called. Unfortunately the senator had a very important emergency meeting and couldn't make lunch. Could I possibly come by his office on the Hill around six P.M.? He would give me a tour and take me to dinner instead. I knew what a senator's schedule was like, but dinner?! That was not in the plan. I stuttered and stammered. I really didn't want to have dinner with him (he was married, of course), but I didn't know how to say no without implying that his intentions were not honorable. So, feeling very uneasy, I said yes.

I showed up at his office right on time. He offered me a drink, which I declined. I didn't drink anything but wine or champagne then, and nobody ever drank either or served them except at formal Washington dinner parties. He apologized for the late hour. He had been tied up in very important meetings, and of course there would be no tour of the Senate since everything was closed. He had made reservations at the most posh French restaurant in Georgetown,

Chez Francois. To my disappointment, he asked for a discreet ban-
quette indoors. It was incredibly hot outside, and in those days there
was no air-conditioning. Everyone was sitting outside trying to
catch a breeze. He motioned to the waiter, snapping his fingers, and
calling out "garçon, garçon" ("boy" or "waiter" in French) in his
Texas accent, only instead of pronouncing it correctly, as in *gar son*,
he said *gar con* as in con man. I was horrified, as was the waiter.

Still, he was a senator and commanded a certain amount of defer-
ence even though he was acting as if he were the president. He had
no idea what he was ordering and refused to ask the waiter for help,
so I suggested a few things on the menu and ordered the wine. He
began to tell me how beautiful I was and how sexy and how smart.

When he pulled out his wallet at the end, it was a cheap wine-
colored gold-embossed one, which sold on the Ponte Vecchio in
Florence for about $4.00. I remarked that he had an Italian wallet,
anything to deflect his attention. He narrowed his squinty eyes and
drawled, "You don't miss a trick, do you?"

I was beginning to squirm and was so desperate to get out of there
I nearly knocked over the table as we left. However, I was not to
escape so quickly. Once we were on the street, I tried to hail a cab,
but he grasped my arm rather tightly and insisted that we go across
the street to a rather sinister-looking nightclub called L'Espionage,
which had a masked and cloaked man painted on the entrance.

We were led upstairs to a cozy, dimly lit little parlor with love
seats. I thought I was going to die. He plunked us both down, still
holding tightly to me, and confidently ordered two brandies. He was
definitely on home territory here. Without loosening his grip, he
took my hand in his pudgy little one.

Going into survival mode, I quickly offered to read his palm. Being
the egomaniac that he was, he succumbed. His palm was sweaty and

showed little character; it was a palm of such pure debauchery that I shuddered. But I rambled on for dear life to keep him distracted. By the time I had exhausted my repertoire he had knocked back his brandy and was preparing to order another.

With that I leaped up from my seat and announced that I had to get up at dawn the next day to get to work. While he was paying the bill I dashed down the stairs and out to the street and was hailing a cab when he appeared. "I'll come with you," he said, pushing me into the cab.

"No, no, you don't need to," I practically screamed. "You live on the Hill and I'm at Fort Myer. It's the opposite direction." My protest was to no avail. Before I could say another word I was in the backseat of the cab, gasping out my address, and he was on top of me. I was in shock. He threw his weight over me, putting his hands up my skirt and grasping at my underpants. I was desperately trying to fend him off, pleading with him, "Senator, Senator, please stop," and begging the cabdriver to hurry.

The poor driver, an elderly man, was clearly distraught. He could see what was happening, but hearing my assailant's Southern accent as he grunted amorously and aware I had called him senator, the taxi driver was afraid to do anything except speed. I think we were probably going about ninety miles an hour as we pulled through the gates of the army post just across the Potomac River from Georgetown. Tower had managed to partially pull down my underpants as I was beating at him and trying to wriggle free. He was surprisingly strong. I also noticed he had unzipped his trousers. Finally I shouted at him, as haughtily as I could, under the circumstances, "Senator, kindly remember your status, both marital and senatorial!" I actually said that.

Just at that moment, thank God, the cab screeched to a halt, and the driver got out to open the door for me in front of our quarters.

"We're here, ma'am," he mumbled, and I think Tower suddenly realized I could start screaming and the general and several MPs would appear on the scene. He reluctantly let go of me.

I tumbled out of the car and sprinted to my front door, locking it behind me once I had gotten inside. I went upstairs to my room and began to sob. That would not be the last time I cried about this. In fact, I was upset for years afterward every time I thought of it.

I was overwhelmed with guilt and shame. How could I have been so stupid? Why did I agree to have dinner? Why did I let him take me to the nightclub? Why didn't I just insist on taking the cab home? What did I do to make him think it was okay to behave that way? I must have been leading him on in some way for him to think he could get away with it. I was devastated and traumatized.

I didn't tell my parents or Barry Goldwater about it for years. When I finally did, it had been so long in the past that I don't think they realized how much it had affected me. Besides, Tower was still a senator, a friend and colleague of Barry's, and a social friend of all of theirs. I think Daddy and Barry just wanted to sweep it under the rug. My mother was much more upset. She wouldn't have anything to do with him after I told her. Still, there was not the kind of outrage I had hoped for or expected. It was, after all, the days of the old boys' club. That's what powerful men did. And they got away with it. Only he didn't—at least that time.

In 1989, five years after Tower had chosen not to run for reelection, President George H. W. Bush nominated him to be secretary of defense, a post the retired senator and former chairman of the Senate Armed Services committee badly wanted. From the moment his nomination was made public the damaging stories started appearing. Tower had a drinking problem; he had questionable relationships with defense contractors; and most of all he was a terrible womanizer and probably guilty of sexual assault. I had heard rumors about his sexual exploits over the years and there were always endless jokes about his office being constantly filled with "babes," but then that wasn't exactly a unique situation in the Senate. I had only told a few close friends of mine about what had happened between Tower and me. I was still so mortified. (Actually I still am. Now, though, I'm angry as well.)

I was married to Ben at the time of the nomination. I had obviously told him the story. He was properly outraged and disgusted but not surprised. He had always thought Tower was a repugnant little "pissant."

One day during the hearings I was at home when the doorbell rang. I answered it and two FBI agents were standing there holding out their identification, asking if they could come in. I ushered them into the front hall but did not invite them into the living room. We stood there staring at each other. They were clearly uncomfortable and wouldn't look me in the eye; instead, they were shifting from foot to foot.

They had come, they said, because they were vetting Senator Tower for the job of secretary of defense and had heard the story about his sexually assaulting me. They would like to ask me a few questions. I refused to confirm it. "But you don't understand," one of them said to me, "this will be totally confidential."

I burst out laughing. "Are you kidding?" I said. "Where do you think the *Washington Post* gets its stories? From guys like you who leak."

They left empty-handed.

Shortly after that visit, John Tower's confirmation was defeated. As was reported in the *Washington Post*, it was the first time in history that a new president had been denied his first choice for a new cabinet position, the ninth time that any cabinet-level nominee had been rejected by the Senate, and the first time since Eisenhower's choice for secretary of commerce that a cabinet nominee had been turned down. One of those voting against Tower was Kansas senator Nancy Landon Kassebaum, the only Republican to vote no. I later learned from a friend who was working for Teddy Kennedy that Nancy had voted against Tower after she heard my story.

"It couldn't have happened to a nicer guy," said Ben. Barry and Daddy were not displeased either.

Later, Anita Hill made a decision I did not. She agreed to testify "confidentially" about Supreme Court nominee Clarence Thomas. I could have been Anita Hill, or something close.

The common belief is that forgiving always makes you feel better. If you hold a grudge, you're only hurting yourself more than the person you are angry with. As the saying goes, you take the poison hoping someone else will die. People say that letting go is the best revenge, that holding a grudge is like a cancer, that forgiving is the healthy thing to do, the right thing, the Christian thing. "Forgive us our trespasses as we forgive those who trespass against us." I don't buy it.

Of course there are some things you can and should forgive. However, I don't believe in forgiveness without an apology, a sincere apology. There are too many nonapology apologies. They happen in love, in business, in politics, in foreign policy, in every area of life. "I'm sorry if I offended you" or "I'm sorry if you were hurt" are not apologies.

In this case, even an "I'm sorry I tried to rape you in the back of a cab when you had just turned twenty and were innocent and I was a U.S. senator" wouldn't be good enough. Some things can't be forgiven unless there is true remorse. Tower never apologized for anything.

Aaron Lazare, in his book *On Apology*, wrote about a time when two friends betrayed his trust, which led him to "question both my trusting approach to relationships and my overall ability to judge people." It occurred to him that if they "would sincerely apologize, our relationships could be restored." He elaborated:

> *This idea, which may seem simple and obvious . . . was an epiphany to me, a sudden, spontaneous realization of something I felt was important and perhaps even profound. I was intrigued that an apology, which appears to be such a simple event, could change so much.*

Bishop T. D. Jakes once said to me when I was interviewing him about his book on forgiveness, "I may forgive. But I never forget." That's true for me as well.

The important thing about this incident in my life is that it was so searing and so traumatic that I never got over it. I can't help thinking now that if he had raped me, it would have affected my views on sex, love, trust, and maybe even marriage, all things that have given me great joy throughout my life. No, this experience didn't ruin my life. It really didn't change my life, but it made a huge impression on me in many ways. I wasn't the same person after that incident. I became more cynical and less trusting. If I had been a nonbeliever before that happened, this experience certainly wouldn't have changed my view. It wasn't that I had suffered the worst trauma anyone could suffer. But I felt that I had seen the face of evil, up close and personal. I was aware for the first time what it truly felt like to be dehumanized. There was too much of that in the world.

. . .

My sophomore year I returned to Smith no less confused than I had been at the end of my freshman year, by which time I still didn't have a clue what I was supposed to be doing. Consequently, this next term I dove immediately into the theater and stayed there. I found I had a particular talent and proclivity for the theater of the absurd, especially Ionesco. It would serve me well in life and help prepare me to eventually work in Washington.

That fall we had an assembly at John M. Greene Hall and attendance was required for the whole student body. The speaker was a young woman named Marian Wright, the first black woman to enter Yale Law School. There was considerable snickering among the students. *Why did we have to listen to this colored girl talk?* they said. I was curious.

I ended up being stunned by the effect that her speech had on me. What happened next changed my thinking entirely. Marian talked about her life. She spoke eloquently about growing up black in the South, with no hint of anger or bitterness or self-pity. Her tone and manner were so contained that her story was all the more powerful. I had goose bumps and was deeply moved. I couldn't believe what I was hearing.

She—this "colored" girl—was not my equal; she was undeniably my superior. She was brilliant, funny, persuasive, authentic, and certainly engaged in work that mattered.

I had never seen anyone like her.

On the way back to Talbot House with my Southern friends I was silent. They were laughing and tittering and making jokes about Marian. Had they not just seen what I saw, heard what I heard? Then they broke into song:

Alabama niggers should be free,

hail to the N double ACP;

Throw Jim Folsom [former governor of Alabama] out the
    door:

Roy Campanella [black baseball player] for gov-e-nor.

Hail Autherine Lucy [first black student admitted to the
    University of Alabama],

Hail Autherine Lucy.

Yo so big and black and juicy,

how we loves you, Autherine Lucy.

Hey, hey, what's all the fuss?

We wants to ride in the front of the bus.

I was incredulous. The words were immediately burned into my memory. I felt shocked and outraged and yet I said nothing. Another shameful moment. I just ran into the house and up to my room to get away. Who was I? I thought of myself as someone who was looking for meaning, yet I had just seen myself behave by being silent when I should have spoken. Right then I felt devoid of morals, ethics, and values. I felt I had no sense of myself. Was I not a person of courage? Not only did I need to find myself, but I needed to find friends who were enlightened and knowing and learn from them.

Chapter 6

What you can do, or dream you can do, begin it.
Boldness has genius, power and magic in it.

—translation by Irish poet, John Anster, inspired by lines
from Johann Wolfgang von Goethe's *Faust,* Part I

During my college years I had occasional psychic moments. By this time I really didn't think much about it; it was simply part of my life. The phone would ring and I knew who it was before answering. I would know what someone was going to say before he or she said it. I would sense when something bad was going to happen. I knew what the end of some difficulty or disagreement would be well before there was any resolution. These are not uncommon phenomena. Many people have similar experiences. My mother understood what was going on. She would often ask me what I thought of something when I knew what she wanted to know was what the future would bring.

I used to laugh at the lyrics of that Doris Day song: "Que sera, sera, whatever will be will be, the future's not ours to see, que sera, sera." I most definitely sensed that the future was ours to see.

One afternoon I was in my room at Talbot House when I was overcome with dread. Something terrible was happening to my mother. I had to get to a phone. I rushed down the hall to the one phone on my floor and called home. My family was still living at Fort Myer at the time. The phone rang and rang. No answer, but I let it ring. It was not possible that there was nobody home. We had several military orderlies at the house and one of them was always there. I held on. The phone must have rung fifty times. I wouldn't put it down. I was frantic. I just kept hanging on listening to that distant—and unanswered—ring, determined not to hang up.

At last an orderly answered the phone and put Mother on. She was hysterical, crying so hard she couldn't talk. "Mother, what happened?" I asked. She was gasping and couldn't catch her breath. She was trying to talk to me, but I couldn't understand a word she was saying. I held on, just listening to her cry. I didn't know what to do. I didn't want to hang up and leave her alone. Just then I heard a man's voice calling for her.

"Mrs. Quinn?" It was another one of the orderlies. I heard him say, "Jesus," then yell to someone else, "Get General Quinn. Tell him to come home right away."

"Mother!" I was screaming at her. "What has happened? What's wrong? Put him on the phone." She was composed enough to hand the phone to the orderly.

"She's okay," he managed to sputter. "The bathroom is completely flooded. Your mother looks like she's been drowned. Let me call the dispensary and I'll call you back." He hung up. I tried to call Daddy. I called back and the line was busy. The orderly had called the army dispensary that was right next door to our quarters. They sent over medics, and Daddy had come home, while I sat on the floor in the hall next to the phone waiting. Finally he called.

Mother had been taking a bath that afternoon. She had the water running when suddenly someone threw a jacket over her head and pushed her under the water. He held her head down until she thought she was drowning. She inhaled some water. While this was happening the phone started to ring—it rang and rang and didn't stop. The tub was overflowing. As she was about to drown, the man took his hands off her and ran out of the bathroom, but not before the room was flooded. She managed to get out of the tub, soaked, naked, and distraught. That's how the orderly found her.

The intruder turned out to be a GI who lived in the barracks on the other side of the parade ground. They found a number of my father's missing items in his bunk, three watches, some cuff links, and other things that he had previously stolen from our house. The soldier had not expected anyone to be at home. He said he didn't know what to do about my mother so he tried to drown her. When he heard the phone ringing, he got scared and fled. He was sentenced to seven years. My mother, then in her early forties, was so traumatized she never got her period again.

• • •

Weekends at Smith in the winter were especially lackluster and dull. But there was always the possibility of dates. If one of us had a date, we'd fix up our other friends with their friends. Since I hadn't met anyone I really cared about, I would choose to hang out in the theater, although not much was going on there during weekends. We didn't have TVs. The idea of actually studying wasn't considered, at least not by me.

One Friday morning in February I got a call from the older brother of a friend of mine who wanted to know if I would like to go skiing in Vermont that weekend. I had never dated him because he was known as a wild man. The idea of going with him alone to Vermont was terrifying. However, he wanted me to bring a friend for his Harvard roommate.

I had heard of his roommate because he was notorious. Apparently once, under the influence, he had stolen a police car in Cambridge, among other things. I said I'd look around and get back to him. I found a friend who was a bit apprehensive, but we were both bored and decided to go. The boys said they would pick us up Friday afternoon and we would drive up. We would be staying at "Fat City," a cabin in Vermont that several Harvard guys rented and that had a terrible reputation—worse even than one of the fraternities at Dartmouth that had the nickname "Animal House" and later served as the model for the movie of the same name.

"Fat City!" exclaimed one of my friends. "Are you both out of your minds?" We figured if we clung to each other the whole weekend we would be fine. Besides, we really wanted to ski.

The drive up was a nightmare. Our "dates" were drinking and speeding along winding, snowy country roads in the pitch-black of night. We were scared to death, but it was too late to do anything about it except keep begging them to slow down. Mercifully we arrived at Fat City in one piece, to find several other guys who were already crashing there. One of them showed us to our room, which was on the first floor opposite the living room. Immediately we both made sure there was a lock on the door. Everyone was tired and went to bed, thankfully without incident.

The next morning we got up, grabbed our skis, and hitched a ride to the slopes with one of the other "houseguests" staying there. The weather was perfect and we had a wonderful day of skiing. All we wanted to do was come home, have a bowl of soup, and go to bed. The boys, however, were ready to play. They seemed to have been imbibing most of the day, and things got bawdier and raunchier as the night went on. The tipping point came when our dates broke out in a lewd song: "Let's all git drunk and git nekkid, let's all git drunk and git nekkid, let's all git drunk and git nek-kiiiiiiiiid, and git in a great big piiiiiiile." The situation called for some serious action. It was time for some palmistry.

"Okay, guys," I said. "I'm now going to read your palms and tell your futures." They perked up. Nothing like talking to a man about himself. I wasn't as worried about our escorts. They were so far along they didn't pose much threat. There was a brooding, poetic-looking guy in the corner who had been eyeing us and who hadn't had that much to drink. He was exuding sexual tension. I chose him as my first victim. He was eager.

I settled in, looked deeply into his eyes, took his hand, smoothed his palm, and began to read. "You are a poet," I said. He looked startled. "You are deeply sensitive but nobody understands you. You have a brilliant mind, but you are wasting it on childish things. You choose the wrong companionship. You need to trust your own instincts and do what is right for you, or you will ruin your life."

I went on to predict certain fabulous things that would happen to him in the future unless he blew it. He was overcome with emotion and disbelief. Nobody had ever told him these things, he said. Nobody had ever seen so deeply into his soul. By the time I had finished, he settled back into his corner and spent the rest of the evening brooding over his palm.

The interesting thing was that even though I was trying to divert his attention away from my girlfriend and me, I really did see those things in his palm. I think that's why he reacted so strongly to what I said. I was unnerved by it. Once I had read his palm, the others were hounding me to read theirs, which I did. I felt sad reading my friend's palm. I didn't tell him exactly how sad. I left him staring pensively at his palm, and, the animals finally subdued, we went to bed.

Around three A.M. my roommate woke me up. "It's raining," she said. "It can't be," I told her. It was twenty degrees outside. Then I heard the sound of water splashing against our window. "How is that possible?" Next came the raucous laughter and the singing. "We are wee weeing on the window . . . We are wee weeing on the window." We peeked through the curtains and there they were, all of them except the poet, doubled over with laughter as they sprayed our window until they couldn't anymore. Depleted, they went to bed and we went back to sleep.

The next morning we insisted they take us back to school and there were no objections. They were too hungover to do anything else. We had a long silent drive home. They never asked us out again, nor would we have gone. I'm told the poet went on to become a successful writer. The others did not fare so well. For as long as I followed them, everything I read in their palms turned out to be true. Who said I had no religion?

I began to see the power of the mystical, the mysterious, and the magical. I had a glimpse of the spiritual as a possible substitute for religion—unorthodox as what I was seeing and feeling may have been.

. . .

Although I majored in theater, I took a lot of French courses because I had planned to spend my junior year abroad in France. (As it turned out that didn't happen because I was so swept up in the theater that I really couldn't go.) By the second semester of my sophomore year, I had decided I wanted to be an actress and spent the entire time at the theater, involved in every production. I sporadically dated a couple of guys, but my heart wasn't in it. I hardly studied at all and barely squeaked through.

I took a course in Molière, the French playwright, for theater, but also studied him in my French courses. Reading his play *Tartuffe* had a profound and long-lasting impact on me. I began to think more about religion. Up until that point, my views on religion had been about my not believing in God; certainly not believing in an omniscient, omnipotent, all-loving God, a personal God to pray to. *Tartuffe* was about hypocrisy and religion, something I vaguely had been aware of but had never really articulated. Now it seems so obvious I can't imagine it hadn't struck me before. The leaders of the Inquisition were "Christian," the South was "Christian" during the Civil War, the Nazis were "Christian," and the segregationists were "Christian."

After reading *Tartuffe*, everywhere I turned it seemed that people were proclaiming their faith at the same time as eschewing many of the basic tenets. Nowhere did it seem more egregious to me than during the civil rights era in the 1960s. Schools were being desegregated using National Guard troops, blacks and their white supporters were being murdered, black churches being blown up, and Martin Luther King was changing America. In fact, change was coming so quickly that it was hard to keep up, hard to formulate one's views before being confronted with other views even more powerful.

I was scared and excited when King led the March on Washington on the Mall. I half wanted to go but was afraid there would be riots, and my parents, also afraid, forbade me to. My German "Nazi" step-grandmother, a devout churchgoing Lutheran, had called from Savannah the day before the march to warn my family to leave town. "You have to get away from those African bullies," she commanded. That was almost enough to persuade me to go to the march. I watched every minute of the "I Have a Dream" speech on television and had chills throughout.

Fundamentalist Christians were denouncing King and the speech, left and right. How could they call themselves Christian? Again, they were proclaiming their Christianity without living it. "We're all brothers and sisters in Christ." "God made man in his own image." "Love thy neighbor as thyself." And not least, "Do unto others as you would have them do unto you." It seemed that those most bigoted were those who proudly proclaimed their piety. None of it made any sense to me.

The words in *Tartuffe* stuck in my mind and are still there today. Tartuffe himself is a pious imposter who convinces the gullible and wealthy Orgon that he is holy and should take him in, then swindles everything Orgon has away from him. Orgon is the only one who doesn't see through Tartuffe. In one brilliant scene, which stands up today as well as it did in the seventeenth century, Tartuffe's brother-in-law, Cléante, tries to convince him of Tartuffe's evil.

> There's true and false in piety, as in bravery,
> And just as those whose courage shines the most
> In battle, are the least inclined to boast,
> So those whose hearts are truly pure and lowly
> Don't make a flashy show of being holy.
> There's a vast difference, so it seems to me,
> Between true piety and hypocrisy.

How many times since I first read those words have I turned to the play, especially that passage, to remind myself that so little has changed? Hypocrisy is one of the repulsive aspects that lend themselves to religion and vice versa.

No place lends itself to hypocrisy more than Washington, D.C. One cannot get elected president without proclaiming one's faith, the more pious on the hustings, the better. Ironically, people don't talk much about their religion in Washington. Long ago, my friend the astrologer Caroline Casey called the place a "spiritual hardship post." We know what politicians have to do to get elected, we understand how distasteful it is, so better just pretend religion doesn't exist while we're here. The idea of living a double life is too embarrassing. The only problem is that in the pre-television and pre-Internet days, candidates could get away with extolling their religious beliefs out on the trail with nobody really paying attention. Now, though, hypocrisy sells.

It was after reading the play that religion, politics, human nature, and my own sense of morality were brought into clearer focus. *Tartuffe* has served me well as a beacon of authenticity throughout my life.

. . .

My senior year at Smith I was dating a guy at Harvard Law School and was spending quite a bit of time in Cambridge, Massachusetts. One weekend we went to a party with some friends of his. It was quite late, we had been to dinner first, and initially I could barely see through the haze of smoke in the room. I don't think it was all cigarettes, either. It was redolent of a funny smell, but at that point I had never been around marijuana so I wouldn't have known what it was. This was definitely a different crowd from the one that I usually spent time with. It was a very bohemian scene. I didn't drink liquor in those days. Nobody had wine so I must have had a Coke or water. I did smoke so I pulled out a cigarette. The next thing I knew this very good-looking, rugged older man with shaggy hair reached over and lit my cigarette, looking deeply into my eyes, a half smile on his face.

He introduced himself as Timothy Leary. I had heard of him, certainly; almost every college student in the Northeast had. He was a famous psychologist who had introduced psychedelic drugs, especially LSD, to the university and ran the Harvard Psilocybin Project. His motto was famous. "Turn on, tune in, drop out." Later Richard Nixon would describe Leary as being "the most dangerous man in America."

I was immediately taken with Leary, who really put a burn on me, as we said at the time. He began telling me about his project and how exciting the experience of taking LSD was. I was mesmerized. I found him extremely sexy, and he was doing everything he could to encourage that. I had no idea where my date went, and I didn't care, either. Leary asked me if I had ever had an ecstatic experience or an intense religious experience. I said I hadn't. "It will change your life," he whispered. We ended up sitting on the sofa. His face was very close to mine. His eyelids were half closed.

He talked about how many primitive tribes used psychedelics in their religious rituals and that taking them could be truly mystical, could bring you closer to God and nature. He invited me to come back to Cambridge and spend the following weekend with him. He offered to introduce me to psychedelics. I said yes. "We will have a spiritual experience," he promised. He took out a small cream-colored piece of paper from his pocket and a pen and wrote down his name and telephone number. He told me to call him at the beginning of the week and we would make plans. I said yes.

I don't remember leaving the party or discussing the conversation with my date. When I got back to Smith, I excitedly told a few of my closest friends. One of them was outraged. "Are you crazy?" she yelled at me. "All he wants to do is get you high so he can have sex with you. He's notorious for that."

She put the fear of God in me. I was a virgin after all. I didn't call him that week and I never heard from him. I'm not sure I ever told him my name. I didn't throw away his card, though. I put it in my wallet. I kept thinking I might get in touch with him at some point. There was something so compelling about him, and it wasn't just a sexual attraction. The appeal was the notion of having a true religious experience, of having a close-up encounter with the divine. That, more than anything, was what intrigued me and really turned me on.

I carried his card for years, transferring it with my other cards whenever I would change wallets. About twenty years ago my wallet was stolen out of my purse in a crush when I was boarding a train at Union Station in Washington. I didn't discover it right away. When I finally realized it was gone, it wasn't that I was so upset about losing the money or my driver's license. I was upset because I had lost my shot at taking LSD with Timothy Leary. I had missed my chance to have that particular transcendent moment, the idea of which I had held on to for so long. Until I lost his card, I had not realized it meant so much to me. Timothy Leary died that year.

. . .

Shortly after I met Leary I had had a reading of my astrological chart that was endlessly promising. I had worked the summer before as assistant technical librarian at the Institute for Defense Analyses, a conservative think tank. I had a great boss who was a lot of fun, but I knew nothing and cared less about being a military librarian. In fact, a librarian of any kind I am not. I was terrible at it and I hated the job. However, it paid well and I had to have a job every summer to earn my spending money.

What I couldn't understand was what had happened to the thoughts from that stellar reading. The only thing that had gotten me through that past year was the theater, but I knew even that wasn't enough. I also knew I was wasting my college years by not studying, but acting was the only activity I was motivated to engage in. It is clear now that I was looking for meaning in my life. I was too young (or too preoccupied with other things) to understand what the emptiness I felt was all about. There seemed to be a black hole in the pit of my stomach that was spreading to my head and heart.

Chapter 7

I have always been delighted at the prospect of a new day,
a fresh try, one more start, with perhaps a bit of magic
waiting somewhere behind the morning.

—J. B. Priestley

My tenure at Smith did not have a particularly illustrious ending. Having spent so much time in the theater and none at all in the library, according to the dean I graduated at the bottom of my class, the very bottom. I figured this was better than graduating second from the bottom. My parents were thrilled that I had actually made it through.

What I cared about was that I had been accepted at the Monomoy Theatre in Chatham, Massachusetts, on Cape Cod to do summer stock. Next stop, Broadway! I had been "discovered" by an MGM talent scout when I played Sabina in Thornton Wilder's *The Skin of Our Teeth* my senior year. He was going to make me a star. His name was Dudley Wilkinson. I carried his card around for years the way I carried Timothy Leary's.

The work schedule at the Monomoy was exhausting. We probably averaged four hours of sleep a night. Aside from acting, we did everything, including help with the building of sets, selling tickets, printing programs, and even sweeping out the theater. We took all our meals together and collapsed at the end of the day, only to try and memorize our lines. I was playing Lydia Languish in Richard Sheridan's *The Rivals*, so I had my work cut out for me. It had become clear, though I had my heart set on becoming a great tragedienne, that I was really cut out for comedy. I had actually played Lady Anne in Shakespeare's gruesome *Richard III*, and I made the scene so screamingly funny that people were rolling in the aisles. (Or at least that's how I remember it.) My penchant for comedy has served me well—especially as a journalist in Washington and even more so as a religion reporter. When you're looking for meaning in life, one of the things that stands out is humor. The expression "from the sublime to the ridiculous" becomes profound. In the end, one good way to get through life intact is to laugh.

While working at the Monomoy I wasn't dating at all. The men in the troupe were so involved with themselves that I don't think they knew the women existed. There was very little chance of meeting anyone. However, I did get a call from a guy who was a friend of a friend, asking me out. He sounded nice on the phone so I agreed to see him on the one night we had off.

He was tall, dark, and heart-stoppingly handsome. He was also brilliant, funny, witty, a talented musician, successful, wise, a great athlete, and kind. He had graduated from one Ivy League college and was already teaching, at the age of twenty-three, at another. I fell instantly in love. So did he. He was working on a book, staying at his parents' summer house nearby.

We were inseparable from the moment we saw each other, at least during the times I was free. I, however, began to get less than four hours of sleep so I could meet him at odd hours. I drank so much coffee trying to stay awake that summer that I still can hardly bear the smell of it.

We often would sneak out to the beach or to his car to make out but never did more than that. I was still a virgin and he knew it. I was so impressed with his restraint, but I have to admit I was a bit frustrated as well. Some nights when I was free I would go to his parents' house to stay over. He never once came into my room. It was all very chaste.

At one point that summer my parents decided to come up from Washington for a weekend. I couldn't have been more excited. I was anxious for them to meet my new love. I had told them I'd met the man I was going to marry. He hadn't actually proposed but I knew he would. It was just a matter of time.

My parents took us out to dinner and really seemed to like him. What wasn't to like? He was charming, polite, smart, engaging, everything you could wish for in a son-in-law. I was so proud of him. I was especially excited because he had asked me to go for a walk on the beach with him after dinner. He had something he wanted to talk to me about. There was no doubt in my mind that this was going to be the big moment.

It was a beautiful night, not too chilly as was often the case on the Cape. The stars were out by the millions and, of course, there was a full moon, which made the sand twinkle as we walked barefoot down the beach holding hands. I was in a swoon. I was wearing a blue-and-beige printed full-skirted dress that swirled in the breeze and made me feel like a fairy princess. I was laughing and chatting away, so full of joy I could barely contain myself. He seemed unusually quiet, but I just assumed he was gearing up for the big question.

Suddenly he stopped. He pulled me to him and kissed me, a long loving, lingering kiss. I thought I would faint. Then he held me away from him. "I have something to tell you," he said. I held my breath.

"I'm impotent."

At first I didn't think I had heard him correctly. I wasn't actually sure I understood what he was saying.

"Sally, I'm impotent," he said more forcefully. His voice was cracking with emotion. "I've always been. All my life. I've never had an erection."

He waited. I said nothing. I was in shock. I didn't know how to respond. I knew this was terrible news, but, as a virgin, I didn't actually realize how terrible.

"I love you," he said. "I've never been in love like this before. But I can't marry you. In fact, I can't be with you anymore. It's not fair to you. I have nothing to give you." The tears were pouring down his face now.

I tried to persuade him it was okay. That I loved him so much that we could overcome this. I insisted that sex wasn't the most important thing in the world, anyway. I just wanted to be with him. That was all that mattered. In my heart I'm not sure I believed that, but the idea of losing him was not acceptable.

He put his arms around me and we held each other for the longest time, overcome with emotion. Finally he said it was time to go and we walked silently back to the car and he dropped me off at the theater. I didn't kiss him. I just got out of the car and walked away, not looking back. He didn't say anything.

The following night I had to perform. I walked through my part in a daze. I still couldn't quite process what had happened and what it meant. I was so confused. I didn't hear from him. After the performance, my parents took me out for fried clams. I couldn't eat. They knew something was wrong, but I kept insisting it was just that I didn't feel well. They drove me back to the theater. They were leaving the following morning so I wouldn't see them again until the end of the summer. I was feeling desperately alone and bereft. When they stopped the car and told me good night, I started to cry deep racking sobs. My mother put her arm around me and stroked my hair. They were both begging me to tell them what was wrong. Embarrassed as I was, mortified really, I couldn't hold back any longer.

I related what I had learned the night before. I said, "He told me last night. He says we can't see each other again."

There was a long silence. My mother held me tighter and continued stroking me. "Oh, darlin'," she kept saying. Daddy said nothing.

We sat there in the car, not speaking for a while. Then my father spoke up.

"The guy's a Jew," he said.

I was stunned. This from the man who helped liberate Dachau?! But what did it have to do with anything anyway? What made my father think that my boyfriend was Jewish? What prompted him to say it? What made him react the way he did? In retrospect, I think he was trying to make me feel better. In Daddy's mind, the fact that my friend was Jewish precluded any marriage between us. He was opposed to my marrying outside what was his faith, not mine. His thinking must have been that since I couldn't marry the man I loved because of his religion, then it was just as well he had this problem that would make a marriage impossible in any case.

I never felt quite the same way about my father again. The pedestal I had put him on crumbled before my eyes. He had been like a god to me. Now, yet another deity had turned out not to be real.

. . .

I finally called my friend a few days later and insisted that he make a doctor's appointment to have a physical. He had never told anyone about his problem, not even a doctor. I offered to go with him, which I did, and waited in the car. After the appointment, he came out smiling. There was nothing physically wrong with him, he was told. It was psychological. He needed to start therapy immediately, which could take years. He drove me back and we sat in the car. He strongly suggested and I agreed that we shouldn't see each other anymore. Years (in the plural, clearly) was too long to wait and I had a life to lead. Interestingly enough, my ardor for him had cooled. Even though I didn't really know what I was missing, I understood it was too important to give up. My sexuality was budding, and there was something mysterious and magical there that I felt I couldn't reach without consummating our love. I had a spiritual feeling for him, but I seemed to know I needed more.

We hugged good-bye, I got out of the car, and watched him drive away. The sadness I felt was all-encompassing.

Years later I read that he married somebody famous. I was happy for him. I also was so grateful to him that he had had the strength and courage to let me go.

Chapter 8

That's the thing with magic. You've got to know it's still here,
all around us, or it just stays invisible for you.

—Charles de Lint, "Ghosts of Wind and Shadow," in
Dreams Underfoot: The Newford Collection

The day John F. Kennedy was shot in November 1963 I was at
our home in Arlington glued to my television, as was everyone
in the country and many around the world. The only time I took a
break was to walk over to Arlington Cemetery to try and see where
they were going to put the grave.

Until then, I had never officially been to a funeral. In fact, I was
against any kind of ceremony or ritual, even though, and perhaps
because, I lived at Fort Myer, a U.S. Army post next to Arlington
Cemetery and watched the daily funerals, the sounds of the horses
clopping along carrying the caissons, the bugles playing "Taps."

When I think of it, I imagine that my time in the hospital in Tokyo
and on the plane ride back had so scarred me that I couldn't bear the
idea of death or the thought of any kind of ritual surrounding it. Let
people die and be buried quietly alone was my view. Why did we all
have to be dragged into this prolonged suffering? I didn't yet understand the importance of ceremony for those left behind.

I watched every second of Kennedy's funeral on television at least a hundred times. Every perfect detail, every meaningful gesture, every heartbreaking moment has stayed with me until this very day and always will. Surprisingly, it gave me great comfort and enormous pride. I am so grateful I was able to see it all. For the first time I understood how important ritual was—in the case of JFK, how important it was for those who were immediate family as well as for those of us who felt we knew him, and for our country. It was another example of how binding and transcendent ritual can be, how visceral and fundamental it is to us as humans but also to us as a community. The religious part of it was as crucial to the funeral as anything else. In fact, without that, it would not have been as meaningful.

Jack Kennedy's funeral changed my views about ritual and religion in more ways than I will ever know.

What I couldn't know at the time was that my future husband, my beloved Ben, was involved with the Kennedys the whole time, meeting Jackie at Bethesda Naval Hospital on the night of the assassination, being part of the funeral planning, and participating as an usher.

. . .

Shortly before the funeral, my father had received orders for Germany again. He was to be the Seventh Army commander, stationed in Stuttgart. I didn't want to miss the opportunity of living in Europe once more. We left in January of 1964 and found ourselves for the second time in the same part of Germany. This time, however, we lived in a huge house up on a hill overlooking the city—high on the hog, as my father noted. Next door was the residence of the chancellor of Germany. My father had his own private train, plane, helicopter, and limousine, and we had a huge household staff. It was a far cry from the good ole days when, as my mother liked to say, "in the army, we always travel on our stomachs."

My sister and I hadn't spent much time in Germany the first posting we lived there because we were away at school in Switzerland for most of the year that my parents were there. We did, however—soon after we had arrived at that first posting in Germany—visit Dachau.

Just walking through those arched gates with ARBEIT MACHT FREI ("Work makes you free") inscribed on them was horrifying enough, but touring Dachau with my father describing what he had seen that day so many years earlier—the trenches full of bodies, the skeletal living humans with glazed eyes—brought back so many memories of those photographs I had seen as a child. I was filled with rage—rage at what and who, I didn't know at first. It couldn't be at God because I didn't believe in the existence of God. How could anyone come to Dachau and ever believe in a loving, personal God again? Reading the plaque that was displayed on a large stone that stood where the crematorium had operated—DENKET DARAN WIE WIR HIER STARBEN ("Remember how we died here")—I was sure that I was an angry, confirmed atheist.

Coming back to Germany for the second time, I went back to see Dachau, and again, I was filled with rage. This time, though, I was angry at myself. I felt as though I had somehow been brainwashed in the ensuing years. How could I possibly have mellowed so that I thought the religious rituals of the Kennedy funeral were meaningful? What a sham it all seemed, worshipping a God who would let this obscenity happen. I was convinced that I would always feel the same way and never have a breakthrough to an understanding of any alternative meaning.

It wouldn't be until much later, when I read Viktor Frankl's brilliant book *Man's Search for Meaning*, that I realized that even within these houses of horror one could find meaning and one could find the good in others. Finding meaning in one's life didn't necessarily require religious faith, but that comprehension would be a long time coming.

. . .

I began dating a handsome lieutenant in the German army, the son of social friends of my parents. He was so good-looking that the army used his picture on its official recruitment poster all over the country. He was not a career officer but had graduated from the University at Tübingen and was now serving only for two years.

Joachim (the "J" is pronounced like a "Y"; everyone called him Yo) and I spent many weekends in Baden-Baden, about an hour and a half from Stuttgart on the French border. It had been a resort spa for the kings of Europe in the old days, who went there for the salt spring baths to take the cure, or Kur. The place became known as "the playground of kings."

Yo's father was *Direktor der Kur* overseeing the casino and spa, but the town was filled with nightclubs and fabulous restaurants as well. Yo had access to all the facilities for free so it was great fun. We stayed with his parents at their spacious apartment where we had separate rooms.

Joachim's father and mother, whom I liked very much, were both German Protestants. His father was bald and portly with a red face and a big smile. He had impeccable Old World manners. His mother was pretty and petite, a very graceful figure. Both of them were intelligent and had good senses of humor, but there was an air of sadness about them and a certain posture of defeat. I couldn't understand why. They had a wonderful glamorous life and seemed to have a great marriage.

One Sunday night when the maid was off, Yo's mother invited us to stay home with them and she would cook. We would eat in the kitchen. She made a delicious roast chicken with vegetables and we had plenty of good wine. It was after several glasses that the conversation took an ominous turn.

One interesting thing I had noticed was that since I had been in Germany that year, nobody had talked about the Holocaust. It was as if it had never happened, so eerily similar to the Japanese and their seeming denial that the war had happened. My parents' official German friends, their social German friends, my German friends, the men I dated, my coworkers—not a soul mentioned the war or its aftereffects. Several of the men I dated were older and had fought in the war. I did ask them about their experiences and to a man they were reluctant to discuss the war at all and would only say vaguely that they had fought on the Russian front. In fact, I never met a German who hadn't fought on the Russian front. Nobody had fought the Americans and nobody had ever been near a concentration camp, and interestingly, I don't recall anybody ever saying the word *Jew* or *Jewish*.

So it was in this kind of silent environment that night at Joachim's parents' apartment that the conversation about the Holocaust finally arose. Yo brought it up. "Why don't we ever talk about the war?" he asked. There was an anguished silence.

"We don't ever talk about it," he said a bit more forcefully. His voice was accusatory. His father asked if anyone wanted more wine and poured another round. We all drank. His mother began to clear the dishes.

"I want to talk about it," he said.

Both of his parents started talking at once. Flustered and nervous, they explained that the reason they had left for London in the late

1930s was because they realized what was happening. They had witnessed the rise of Hitler and realized that he couldn't be stopped. Besides, what was there to say? It was all so horrible. Best to forget.

Yo pounded his fist on the table. "No, it is not best to forget," he yelled. "We must never forget. If we forget, it will happen all over again."

I wanted to get up and disappear, but there was something so compelling about the conversation that I was riveted. Clearly distraught, they were wriggling like bugs pinned to a mat.

"Why did you run away?" Yo finally demanded, his face flushed with anger. "Why didn't you stay and try to do something or stop Hitler? If people had stood up to Hitler, if people had not run away like cowards, this may never have happened."

His mother started to cry. "You don't understand what it was like," she quietly replied.

His father began to weep as well. He talked about how powerful Hitler was, how a tidal wave of hate and power took over the country, how people, even some of their closest friends, had gone mad. He said how terrifying it was for those who opposed Hitler even if they weren't Jewish. He said they knew they were not strong enough to deter him and if they tried, they would be punished as well. They had a choice of either leaving or going along with Hitler's crazy schemes. He begged his son to understand.

At that point, Yo started to cry, and so did I. His parents were crying out of shame and guilt and remorse and possibly from recognizing their own helplessness at the time. Yo was crying because he was seeing his parents as human, weak and flawed. I was crying because I was a witness to such a painful exchange. Their suffering was palpable.

All of us sat weeping at the kitchen table, the dirty dishes still in front of us, and the half-drunk wineglasses still glistening in the candlelight.

Finally Yo's father spoke. "You have no idea," he said, as much to himself as to us, "what it is to look into the face of evil."

The only thing I could think about was all the unanswered prayers—the same thought I'd had as a child when I first saw the photos from Dachau.

. . .

I was twenty-three at this time and still a virgin. Yo and I had indulged in many passionate make-out sessions, but I simply wasn't ready. An older friend of mine had once told me that I should not just fall into bed with anyone. I must elect my first lover. It would be better not to be in love with him. That way I wouldn't be hurt. Yo was my age but had had a lot of experience with women. He had just broken off an affair with a Frenchwoman in her early thirties. I absolutely adored him and was wildly attracted to him, but I was not in love. He was perfect.

It was summer and we decided to go to Spain for a vacation. My father, the general, was not too happy about my going off with this good-looking German lieutenant. He suspected Yo might have ulterior motives, but my mother convinced him it would be totally innocent. Ha! Yo, who had the most beautiful manners of anyone I had ever met (the *Verbindungen*, university fraternities, taught manners as did the army), was so polite and correct with my father when he came to fetch me in his Volkswagen that Daddy was too charmed to object. Yo assured him he would take very good care of me. And off we went.

We made it to Switzerland the first night. We found a cozy bed-and-breakfast run by a nice German-speaking woman who served us Wiener schnitzel and showed us to our room, very utilitarian, sparsely furnished with a double bed, a lamp, a chair, and a dresser. The bed was made up, as were most European beds, with a duvet and no top sheet. We were both tired and crawled in as soon as we finished dinner, only to find that when one of us moved, the duvet would be pulled over to the side or fall off the bed. For some reason we were not in the mood for love and though we did attempt to be a bit amorous, the atmosphere simply wasn't conducive to seduction. Not only that, we couldn't stop laughing every time the duvet slid off the bed. Neither one of us slept well that night and we got up early, anxious to be on our way to a more romantic climate. Barcelona was our next stop. Perfect.

We drove straight through and arrived late afternoon, found a charming pension in the heart of old Barcelona, and settled in. We were tired from the long drive and immediately fell asleep. We woke at dusk. The temperature was hot and sultry, through the open windows. The city was just coming alive. Sounds of people laughing outside, smells of restaurants grilling meats wafted in the air, the churning of mopeds peeling down the streets—all portended excitement and anticipation. We began kissing, and soon it became clear to me that something important was about to happen. This time I didn't protest, didn't remove a wayward hand, didn't back away when he came to me. I wanted him to make love to me. No, I wanted to make love to him. He did. I did. We did. It was everything I could have imagined and more. He was skillful, adept, practiced, and loving. His every move was meant to please me and he succeeded. He showed me things about my body that I could not have known. I was enthralled, overwhelmed with disbelief.

So this is what it was about. How could I have ever known? Why had I ever waited? How could anyone possibly think that what we were doing was wrong, sinful, unacceptable? I never wanted to stop. And we didn't for days.

He was in love with me, and though I was not in love with him, I did love him. I finally understood the meaning of ecstasy. It's not exactly that I thought then of God. Yo was not religious and neither was I. But I had seen the painting of St. Teresa of Avila, the rapturous expression on her face when she thought of Christ. That expression had always seemed slightly unrealistic to me, a bit over the top. Now I could see what she was feeling. There was something sacred, holy to me about what we were doing, the merging of two bodies in an intimacy I could never have thought possible. Somehow it had to be the work, the creation of the divine. It was only when I first made love to Ben that I understood what the divine truly was. It began to dawn on me that as delightful and satisfying as sex can be, there was another dimension to it that I hadn't expected. It was a powerful spiritual experience.

. . .

Daddy was resigning from the army. He had had a disagreement with President Lyndon Johnson, and Johnson reneged on his promise to make my father chief of staff of the army and give him his fourth star. He was devastated. However, Daddy was never one to look back. He got a job at Martin Marietta and marched home to the lucrative work of a member of the military industrial complex. We had been in Germany a little over a year and a half, and my parents were ready to leave, as was I.

Yo and I had ended our relationship by this time. He realized I wasn't in love with him, and he had too much pride to stick around.

It was painful but we remained friends and I adored him and understood why he had to make this move.

It was soon after that, but before we returned to the States, that I met someone new. He was a young lieutenant, having been in ROTC at Harvard, now stationed at Seventh Army headquarters in Stuttgart. We invited him for dinner, and he and I immediately hit it off. He was smart, charming, and handsome. We had many of the same friends, and we were interested in the same things. His parents were divorced. His father lived in New York, and his mother was married to a French business owner and lived in an *hôtel particulier* on the Left Bank in Paris. We began seeing each other exclusively and spent a lot of time in Paris. His mother's dining room had a mural painted by Fragonard. We dressed for dinner every night, and the house was so big his mother would bring her evening bag downstairs in case she needed to freshen up.

He had a Ferrari, and we spent weekends trying out three-star restaurants around Europe. The problem was that my father was leaving Germany soon, and my friend had nearly a year before he got out of the army. He asked me to marry him and I said yes. I cared about him a great deal, but I wasn't in love with him. I was twenty-five by then—in those days dangerously close to being an old maid; I was in love with being in love and in love with the idea of being married. Being engaged gave me a sense of security. This was not particularly noble, but I felt it was the best thing for me, and my parents liked him a great deal. They were also thrilled that I be taken care of. It was all very old-fashioned. If it were today, I would have stayed with him in Germany when they left, but it seemed inappropriate if not impossible at the time. Actually, if it were today, I would not have gotten engaged.

I didn't get an engagement ring right away. We decided to wait until he got out of the army and pick one out together. He did give me his Porcellian pig, an emblem of the club he belonged to at Harvard. He was a fifth-generation Porcellian member and had a tiny solid gold pig with emerald eyes that had been passed down through the years. I had a thin gold bracelet and wore the pig on that as a single charm. I was happy with that.

. . .

I had had a fabulous time in Germany, working as a translator and tour guide at Daimler Benz, traveling constantly, meeting fascinating people, acting in the Kleines Theater in Stuttgart and on the army post, studying languages. However, as our time to head back to Washington drew near, I began to feel lost. I had no idea what I was going to do or where I was going to live until my fiancé arrived back in the States.

After a very emotional retirement ceremony for my father, I moved back to Washington with my parents and continued living with them, trying to plan my upcoming wedding. I was looking for a job, but was agitated much of the time, bored and depressed. Marriage seemed to be the only thing I had to look forward to. I viewed it as my escape.

Then I met Warren Hoge and immediately fell in love. Good-looking, sexy, and smart, he had a great personality and was a brilliant journalist. He had graduated from Yale the same year I had graduated from Smith, but we had never met. I was head over heels. It was mutual.

Unfortunately, my fiancé was on his way back for home leave and was coming down to Washington to stay with me. What was I going to do?

It had been a while since I had relied on occultism, but it had always been my fallback. With that in mind, I devised a plan. I knew that I would have to break my engagement. I couldn't marry him when I was so passionately in love with someone else. Also, I really cared about him and didn't want to hurt him.

He arrived, and it was clear that things were uncomfortable. I put him in the guest room and he took me to dinner that night at the famed Sans Souci restaurant, across from the White House. The conversation was strained, fraught, actually, and tense. I couldn't think of a thing to say. We ate quickly and went back to the house. All I really wanted to do was go to bed, alone, but I had to tell him. I fixed him a nightcap. Then I exclaimed, excitedly, "Why don't I get out the Ouija board." My mother and sister and my aunts in Georgia had always relied heavily on the Ouija board for advice.

He looked at me as if I were crazy. "What are you talking about?" he asked. He had no idea about this side of me. I knew he would never understand it so I had simply not bothered to tell him that I led a "life of the spirits." Besides, that area of my life had been relatively dormant since I left college.

By that time we had both had enough to drink so that he was a bit more willing to indulge me. I got out the board and placed it on the coffee table in the living room. I began to ask the board innocent questions, and the two of us placed our hands on the plastic heart with its needle and watched it move around. He began to relax. It was fun. Finally I got up my courage. I was concentrating with all my might. "Are we going to get married?" I asked. He looked at me quizzically.

With the fingers of both of our hands on the heart we waited for several minutes. The heart began slowly to move. I held my breath. We felt it under our hands as it headed toward the letter *N* and rested there for a while. He suddenly seemed alarmed. It began to move again. This time, and I swear I was not pushing it—he would have felt it—the heart went straight for the letter *O* and settled firmly there. He looked at me in disbelief. I was trembling. I could feel the energy flowing through my body and into my hands, and I could feel his energy too. There was an endless silence. His eyes welled up. Finally, he spoke. "May I have my Porcellian pig back?"

After that Ouija board moment, I knew that the occult part of my life from childhood had returned and that I would probably be involved with it for a while. I was right. There was always a part of me that could not deny the psychic energy I had been brought up with and the magic I believed in.

Part Two

MYSTERY

The most beautiful thing we can experience is the mysterious. It is the source of all true art and science. He to whom this emotion is a stranger, who can no longer pause to wonder and stand rapt in awe, is as good as dead: his eyes are closed. This insight into the mystery of life, coupled though it be with fear, has also given rise to religion. To know that what is impenetrable to us really exists, manifesting itself as the highest wisdom and the most radiant beauty, which our dull faculties can comprehend only in their most primitive forms—this knowledge, this feeling is at the center of true religiousness.

—Albert Einstein, *Living Philosophies*

Chapter 9

Science cannot solve the ultimate mystery of nature. And that
is because, in the last analysis, we ourselves are part of nature
and therefore part of the mystery that we are trying to solve.

—Max Planck, *Where Is Science Going?*

When I first read Einstein's words (see the Part Two epigraph), I had a shock of recognition. Beginning with the very idea that mystery is a "beautiful thing," I knew that my thinking and feelings were completely in sync with his observations. I'd always been drawn to mystery. Of course, by its very definition mystery is something that is difficult or impossible to understand or explain, very like many aspects of religion—from the Trinity to the origins of scripture to good and evil to who we are and where we came from. But one of the realities of the mysterious is that we often keep trying to reach beyond what we know to what might yet be known. We have hope for understanding. We have faith that we can move toward answers, that there's always more to discover, within ourselves and outside of ourselves in the larger and largely unknown world. Yes, we can bring new worlds to light both within and without (or beyond). At this point in my life I was coming to appreciate the beauty of mystery.

Sadly, mystery is not a valued commodity in Washington, except for the kind that's behind closed doors.

Washington is all about power, and seeking power often makes people, even good people, do bad things. I have spent most of my adult life in Washington, watching those seeking power, getting and losing it, using and abusing it.

It can be soul-searing, even for an observer. A power center cannot, by its very nature, be a spiritual place. That doesn't mean that the people who live here aren't moral, don't have values, don't have ethics. It does mean that the quest for power, in many cases, trumps those virtues. It's too bad more of those in power in Washington don't understand the value of mystery.

• • •

It was a different environment in which I arrived back in the United States in 1966 after living in Germany. The sixties were in full flower, and the atmosphere only reinforced my feelings about why astrology, voodoo, psychic phenomena, witchcraft, palmistry, ghosts, and other forms of magic would seem, on some level, to be a more fitting way to overcome the stresses of a power-obsessed city than any traditional religion or form of faith. Certainly at that time they were for me. This is what I believed. I still considered myself an atheist, but I was a true nontraditionalist.

Warren, though my age, was already ensconced as a journalist when we met, already part of the Washington scene. We began dating steadily from the first moment, and I spent most of my time living in his group house on the edge of the George Washington University campus downtown, five minutes from the White House. He had just left the *Evening Star,* and was the new bureau chief of the *New York Post.* Through Warren I met his journalist friends. To me they were the most interesting, exciting people I had ever known, so different from the people I had met in the theater world, which was very insular. These people seemed to be always in the know, well aware of everything that was going on. They followed each breaking story, they were constantly on the move. Nothing was routine. Nothing was ever boring. I was hooked. Like those in the theater world, they were almost all liberals, but as objective as possible in their reporting and if any of them was religious, I certainly never knew about it. Protestant, Catholic, Jewish—they all seemed the same to me. There was one thing that mattered. The story. Get the story; get it first and get it right. That was their religion. The First Amendment was their religion. That worked for me.

Warren and I had similar backgrounds. His father was of Scottish descent; his mother, Scottish and English. Both his parents' families and my mother's had emigrated from Scotland to North Carolina. My mother's name was Sara Bette. Warren's mother was Sarah Virginia. Warren's family had a special closet in their apartment where they hung and cured their country hams. My mother kept a jar of bacon grease next to the stove and cooked nothing without it. We all ate a lot of grits. My father was a functioning alcoholic. He only drank when he wasn't working, but when he started, he couldn't stop. Warren's father was periodically a raging alcoholic. It was often so bad that he would have to be taken to a swell drying-out clinic on the Upper East Side, and Warren was often the family member delegated to deal with his father.

Both families had had religious upbringings. My mother was a Scottish Presbyterian as was Warren's. My father was an Episcopalian, his family having converted somewhere along the line from Catholicism. By the time they were settled in New York, both of Warren's parents were members of the Riverside Church in the

Morningside Heights section of Upper Manhattan. It was founded
in 1930 by the Rockefeller family as a Baptist church but had long
before this time become interdenominational.

It was and is a famous church—the tallest church in the United
States. Its awe-inspiring nave is modeled on Chartres Cathedral in
France. By the 1960s it was already known as what the *New York
Times* later called a "stronghold of activism and political debate . . .
influential on the nation's religious and political landscapes." To be
a deacon there, as Warren's father was, was enormously prestigious.

Sunday was a big day at the Hoges'. The ritual would begin in
the morning when Mrs. Hoge would set the table for Sunday dinner
(lunch in the Southern vernacular) with her best crystal and china,
her best lace tablecloth. The ham would have been taken out of the
"smoke closet" the night before and put in the oven. We would all
dress in our best Sunday-go-to-meetin' clothes, white gloves and all.

What nobody knew until Sunday morning was what kind of state
Mr. Hoge would be in. We were all apprehensive and agitated until
he appeared. Had he had too much to drink the night before? Had he
been roaring drunk? Had he taken a knife to his wife's beautiful living
room damask curtains? It didn't matter. His mood might not be the
most cordial if he'd been on a binge, but his demeanor was perfect.

He could have drunk his way to China and back and yet he would
appear immaculately groomed, his hair combed to perfection, his
face perfectly shaved, and in some cases I often suspected he had put
a bit of white powder on his face. He would be dressed in full deacon's attire, silver-gray tie, tails, striped pants, the works. We would
all pile into his huge Chrysler Imperial sedan and drive slowly and
ceremoniously to church. Mr. Hoge was a particularly big deal at
church. He was a tall, imposing, distinguished man with a majestic
carriage, a mane of wavy gray hair, dark brooding eyebrows, and

a strong determined chin. People kowtowed to him, revered him, followed him. He was on an equal par with the famous minister Dr. Robert McCracken, another Scot with a rolling burr, whose sermons lasted forty-five minutes but held most everyone rapt. At least while in church Mr. Hoge was the most pious of men.

Back at the apartment, Warren would carefully mix the Bloody Marys with no alcohol but lots of seasoning, which Mr. Hoge drank with little relish. Mrs. Hoge would place the ham before him at the table with a perfectly sharpened carving knife and he would slice the ham so finely one could almost see through it. We would pass the food, family style, and there would be polite chitchat about the service and the sermon. After Sunday dinner, Mr. Hoge would disappear to his study for a "nap." We would not see him again for the rest of the day.

The Sunday rituals were reminiscent of my time in Statesboro as a child. I was emotional about them. They had the feel of having an outsized importance that was mysterious and that I didn't altogether understand. They were close to religion for me, and also for Warren, who was as terribly conflicted by what he saw at home as I was. I later learned that although we both felt something wholly spiritual on these Sundays, his reverential feelings about going to church were connected to his love of the choral music, which still draws him to services.

Although my father didn't drink as much as Mr. Hoge, he certainly could tie one on. He almost never went to church, though he was unabashedly religious. The contrast of the sinner and the saint brought up all the old feelings I had about organized religion and what it meant. Mr. Hoge was a decent and honorable man who loved his family and worked hard to give them a good life. There was no question that church had great meaning for him. But he was clearly so conventional in his views that he couldn't distinguish between actual faith and belief and the posturing that accompanied the churchgoing life. For me it made no sense. Atheist though I thought I was, I always loved the services at Riverside, and I always wanted them to mean something to me as they did to Warren. I was, even then, yearning for something that I couldn't articulate.

. . .

In Washington Warren and I fell in with a group of antiwar types immediately, though they were journalists. Every night, it seemed, we were out at gatherings where people sat around on living room floors, standing outside in gardens, drinking wine and occasionally smoking pot, and always, always discussing the war. Norman Mailer came to town to lead a march against the war and we went as observers, of course. As journalists Warren and his friends couldn't participate. But our sentiments were with the marchers, the demonstrators, those speaking out against Vietnam. Warren and some of his friends were once reprimanded by an older journalist covering the White House for wearing JOURNALISTS AGAINST THE WAR buttons. As the war continued we became more and more adamant against it. The wrongness of it, the intrinsic evil of what we were doing seemed to mobilize all of us.

It divided so many families, including mine. I never discussed it with my father but he knew. My mother was against the war. She never discussed it either. My father didn't like Warren. He was suspicious of any young man who wasn't fighting in the war. Warren was in the Reserves. That wasn't good enough. When my father went to see *Dr. Strangelove*—though controversial, it was still one of the most popular antimilitary films of the decade—he wanted to know what Warren thought of it. Warren was reluctant to admit he liked it, knowing that my father would hate it because of the way it made fun of the military. Later, to Warren's shock, my father clapped Warren on the back, smiling and telling him how much he had loved the movie. "Boy," he said, "they really socked it to the air force."

One night in the heat of summer, Warren and I went to a party at a group house on Macomb Street in very staid Cleveland Park, an odd place for a bunch of hippie radicals to live. There was the usual Chianti, slices of pizza, and dips and chips. Seymour Hersh, a fervent antiwar activist, journalist, and radio commentator, was one of the occupants of the house, which had little or no furniture.

Sy was a well-known figure, a leader in the movement. Everyone looked up to him. He was a radical. He was also exceptionally smart, funny, and mischievous. He asked me if I'd ever smoked pot. I told him I hadn't. "Okay," he said. "Now's the time." I was really excited and nervous, but I decided I was ready to take the plunge.

Sy, Warren, and I went out on the front porch, looking out over the manicured lawns and beautifully kept houses in one of the most expensive neighborhoods in Washington. Of course there were no chairs so we sat on the porch floor, leaning up against the wall of the house in our jeans. Sy pulled out a package and paper and rolled a joint, lit it, took a huge drag, and passed it to me. I smoked at the time so that part didn't bother me. I tentatively held it between my thumb and forefinger the way he did. I breathed in deeply, expecting to float away into space. Nothing happened. The joint was passed around among the three of us until we finished it, me waiting for the effect. Still nothing. I began to feel a bit fuzzy, a little mellow. I giggled. However, in touch with the divine I wasn't. Others in the house were smoking too. Some were lying on the floor in a daze; some were laughing hysterically; some, I suspect, had disappeared into other rooms to have sex. After a while, Warren and I left and went home. I slept well. I woke up the next morning feeling cheated and deeply disappointed. I had wanted a sublime experience. I hadn't had one. It hadn't occurred to me how much I had been hoping to get a glimpse of something up there, something unreachable, something that would make me into, or rather help me to believe in, something larger than I was. Maybe I was hoping to find what Timothy Leary had promised. I resigned myself to the fact that that something was not there. Or if it was, I hadn't found the right path to it. I shrugged it off. My astrology, tarot, and other practices would certainly do me for the time being. In fact, I took a lot of solace from them. I would continue to for the rest of my life.

. . .

Warren and I broke up a lot. Whenever he felt we were getting too close, he would run away. It became a pattern. I would then date other people; he would get jealous and come back, then I would stop seeing the other people, and we would live happily ever after until the next episode. I had a number of jobs during this time, nothing I really loved and certainly nothing meaningful. I was rudderless and drifting. I wanted to get married. He didn't, but he didn't want me to be with anyone else, either.

So I started going out with one of his greatest rivals—someone who had been a year ahead of him at Yale, a brilliant musician, someone he really admired. He was good-looking, sexy, and talented. I suspected he was working for the CIA, which gave him an air of mystery. I liked him a lot, but I was not in love with him. It worked. Warren called me one night at my tiny studio apartment in Georgetown. He had driven his car up to the mountains of Virginia near the Shenandoah River and had almost driven off the edge. He wanted me back. He wanted to marry me. We got engaged in February of 1969.

The engagement announcement ran first in the Charlotte, North Carolina, newspapers, where Warren's family was from, and then in the *Washington Evening Star*. We were to be married on March 29. I bought a wedding dress. I ordered a blue velvet sofa to be made for our first apartment. His parents were thrilled. My parents were thrilled—sort of. Actually, Daddy didn't approve of my marrying a journalist, but I was getting long in the tooth so he was a little desperate to marry me off.

Warren clearly was not thrilled. Neither was I. I thought this was what I wanted, but the fact was that I didn't want to marry someone who basically had to be roped into it. More than that, though, I wasn't ready to be tied down. I wasn't the person I wanted to be. I hadn't accomplished anything on my own. I had little meaning in my life. I thought that by getting engaged, by getting married, I would find meaning, but it all seemed so shallow and empty.

The idea of being a housewife, of sitting at home waiting for my husband to come back from work, of bringing out the pipe and slippers, of learning how to cook perfect little dinners, and, worse, of having children and spending the day with babies struck terror in my heart. Imagine my dismay when my mother gave me a book called *A Thousand Ways to Please a Husband*.

I wanted a career. I wanted to be an actress. That hadn't panned out, but I still yearned for an identity, something other than being Mrs. Anybody. I was so confused.

The idea of going from one stupid, boring secretarial job to another was unthinkable. I didn't see that there was any choice but to get married. At least that would give me some sort of position, some place I could be safe until I figured things out.

As we got closer and closer to the date I felt sicker and sicker. We hadn't chosen a church. Episcopal? Presbyterian? Baptist? Neither one of us even knew what we were. The obvious place was the army chapel at Fort Myer, Virginia, where my parents had lived and where my sister had gotten married a few years before. It was not for any religious reasons I wanted to get married in the chapel. It was just that it was, as they say, "the done thing." Where else were we going to get married? It was definitely not going to be a spiritual experience for either one of us. Something was wrong here, wasn't it? Shouldn't getting married be that spiritual experience we were both thinking about? Joining our souls, possibly with God as our witness? I was getting more and more nervous. What was I doing? 'Til death do us part? I couldn't go through with it.

Unable to stand it any longer, one afternoon I gathered all our stuffed animals that we had given each other, put them in a bag, got on the Georgetown bus to downtown Washington, and went to the National Press Building where Warren worked. I marched into his office and dumped all the animals on the torn leather sofa, crying "I can't do this." He began to cry as well, out of relief and desperation. We just looked at each other in anguish. I turned and fled, down the elevator, and back on the bus to Georgetown. I got off at the movie theater on M Street, went in, and bought a ticket to *The African Queen*, starring Humphrey Bogart and Katharine Hepburn. It was almost empty at that time of day. I think I sat through it at least four times crying the whole time, until it was late at night. I was the last one out of the theater. I barely made it back to my apartment. I honestly didn't think I would survive.

My mother came and picked me up the next morning and took me home. I lay on my bed for days in a depression. My father came in one night, three sheets to the wind, and lay down beside me, cradling me in his arms and sobbing as well. Lynda Byrd Johnson got married that week. I watched her wedding on TV, feeling a terrible despair. I would never get married. I would never love again. My life was over.

Finally my parents couldn't bear my suffering, so they put me on a plane for California to stay with my sister, Donna, who was married with two children at the time, two-year-old Christopher and baby Schuyler. They were my salvation, from the moment I woke up until the moment they went to bed. I was sleepwalking through the days.

One night after the children had gone to bed, I took a walk up into the hills in Donna's neighborhood, across the bay in Piedmont. It was a cool California night and the sky was so clear I felt I could reach out and scoop up the stars. I stopped at a point at the top, where a slight breeze was blowing, encircled by a grove of very tall evergreen trees. It seemed a mystical place. I almost expected Druids to come prancing out from behind the rocks, and I could swear I heard chanting. Suddenly I felt a terrible pain in my chest, and I began gasping for air. What was happening to me? I lay down on a bed of pine needles and simply stared into space. Before I knew it I was caught up in a swiftly moving vortex. The stars and the moon began swirling around and, though I was lying down, I had to steady myself from the dizziness.

My body seemed to be lifted up in some kind of embrace. I was being held and coddled and stroked. I felt loved and cherished. I also felt tiny as I gazed up at the universe. There was such power there. I wanted to be part of it. I wanted to be swallowed up in it. I had a real longing for it. I wanted to understand it. Then I realized that I was, I did, I had. I understood that there was something bigger than me. That I would be taken care of. That I was loved. That I would be all right. Some people might say that I had seen God, or at least felt a

presence. I wouldn't exactly put it that way. I would say, rather, that
I had witnessed true mystery. Not for the last time.

· · ·

It was Halloween of the next year, and Warren and I had reconciled
again. Back in "just dating" mode, we were going to a costume party.
We came up with a fabulous idea. I would wear red leotards and paint
squares on them and go as a brick and Warren would wear overalls
and carry a trowel and go as a bricklayer. Get it? We thought it was
screamingly funny.

We got to the party and our costumes were a big hit. We were the
talk of the evening, even though I didn't really feel very glamorous
or sexy. Actually, Warren didn't either. The more I thought about it,
the more I thought we looked really dumb. As the evening wore on,
the lights were dimmed; we all had had a lot to drink and the dancing
began. Suddenly the door opened, and the most beautiful girl I had
ever seen walked in. I knew her vaguely and had always thought she
was pretty, but this night she looked spectacular. She had masses of
lustrous long dark curly hair, almond eyes, eyelashes to die for, high
cheekbones, and lips that were like pillows.

She was dressed as a Spanish dancer with a full swirling skirt down
to her well-turned ankles, an off-the-shoulder white blouse, exposing her alabaster skin, and a wide sash encircling her tiny waist. I felt
threatened instantly. I disliked her because I saw the look on Warren's
face. There was a pain in my gut as my stomach twisted itself in
knots. Somehow I knew what was going to happen. Warren was
going to fall for her and leave me and I couldn't go through another
breakup again. I just couldn't.

Of course she had castanets on her long slim fingers and she knew
how to use them. Which she did. Her date, a tall nice-looking but

very stiff guy, simply stood behind her in the shadows. He was the prop. She began to dance, slowly at first, then faster, twirling around, clicking her castanets, tossing back her hair, rotating her hips, almost as though she were in a trance. Everyone was mesmerized. When she finished, Warren went over to her and offered to get her a drink. The line formed behind him. He spent the rest of the evening by her side, obviously besotted. She led him on, laughing and flirting and batting those eyelashes. She knew we were together but barely gave me a glance, acting as though I didn't exist.

I tried to make conversation, tried to dance, tried to smile. What I really felt like doing was throwing up. I tried several times to suggest that we leave but he was having none of it. He was completely hyp-notized by her seduction. Finally the party broke up. She left with her date, and we followed quickly behind. I watched carefully to see if there had been any exchange of phone numbers but couldn't tell. We drove back to his place in silence, got ready for bed in silence, turned our backs to each other in silence. The next day we both went to work.

The following days were fraught with tension. Neither one of us spoke of her. I didn't know whether he was talking to her or not, seeing her or not. I did know that he was thinking of her because he seemed totally distracted. I couldn't stand it another minute. I had to do something. I didn't want anything bad to happen to her—I just wanted her to go away.

My understanding of hexes had come from the staff in States-boro, but I had never actually seen their voodoo ceremonies. It was important to have a representative or a likeness of the person you wanted to put a hex on. One is supposed to have a lock of hair or something that belonged to that person. It had to be done at night, preferably on a full moon. Writing something on paper about the person and burning it helps. Fire is crucial. Chanting was essential, over and over the same words to cajole the spirits into action.

As a double Cancerian—with a sun sign and rising sign both in Cancer—I am told that I am at the height of powers on the full moon, so that would make a hex doubly effective. I had seen my mother put a hex on our veterinarian, and she had already told me about putting a hex on my doctor from Tokyo. All she had done was tell them to their faces to drop dead. I didn't know whether I believed or not that she had caused their deaths.

I had also known it to work in Statesboro. I think some of the staff put a hex on Uncle Roy Beaver. He didn't last long after Aunt Ruth died. I won't say exactly what I did—even now I think that would be bad luck for me—but I practiced what I learned and observed. I worked on the hex for several days until I felt that it would have some effect. Don't ask me how I knew when it was enough. I just did. I commanded her to disappear.

The worst happened. A few days later I learned that she had committed suicide. The details were vague. I almost died myself. I was stricken with guilt, horrified and sick. Had I actually done this? Was I responsible for what happened? I really couldn't possibly have had that kind of power.

My rational mind told me it was all nonsense. But hadn't I seen and heard my mother doing it? What was I to believe? Belief in the powers of magic was something I wrestled with the way the religious wrestle with their belief in God.

Warren was visibly upset. He also looked at me accusingly. It wasn't that he actually thought I was at fault, but he suspected I was not sad, so he was confused about why I seemed so distraught.

The day after she died, her father called me. I was stunned when he said, "Sally, I want you to know how much our daughter admired you and considered you a friend. Her mother and I will be forever grateful for your kindness to her. It means a lot to us. Thank you so much."

I was at a loss and couldn't understand what he was saying about my relationship with this girl I felt I barely knew. I won't ever get over that call. I never told a soul about what I had done except my brother. He was alarmed and warned me not to do it again.

I vowed never to put another hex on anybody—a vow I was not to keep.

The strange thing was, I actually prayed over it. I prayed to God. Yes, God, whoever that might be. "Dear God," I beseeched, "please don't let me have been responsible for this."

I didn't hear back.

Chapter 10

The word religion points to that area of human experience where one way or another we come upon Mystery as a summons to pilgrimage, where we sense beyond and beneath the realities of every day a Reality no less real because it can only be hinted at in myths and rituals; where we glimpse a destination that we can never fully know until we reach it.

—Frederick Buechner, *Wishful Thinking*

The casting call was for early June of 1969. I had decided to go back to acting. My life, at just one month shy of age twenty-eight, was decidedly unsuccessful and professionally dismal. While Warren was scaling the heights at the *New York Post* and soon to be called back to New York to be groomed as editor, I had gone from one unfulfilling job to another. Never mind the horrible Kelly Girl days in New York where I was constantly getting fired after a few days because my secretarial skills (I still can't file), not to mention my attitude, were decidedly unsatisfactory.

A brief stint as the PR girl for "Murray Zarat's Pet Festival and Animal Husbandry Exhibition" at Coney Island had ended in disaster. I persuaded Murray to put on a Noah's Ark event and trot his animals out on the beach in the spring two by two. The animals ran wild, the cops were called, one of the sheep gave birth to twins, and Murray fired me. I couldn't understand why since I had alerted Channel 4 News in New York and they had covered the catastrophe, complete with my naming the twins after the cops, Al Olson and Bob Mahoney, all of which made the local news.

A short-lived tryout as a go-go dancer (clothed) in a cage in a nightclub in Manhattan was also discouraging. After an audition for the role of the father's girlfriend in the movie *Flipper*, someone in casting offered me the job if I would sleep with him. I said I would have to ask my father. I never got a call back. An interview with the editor of *Newsweek* to be a secretary didn't go well when he told me my job would be to get coffee.

I came back to Washington hoping to fare somewhat better and had a series of jobs. I worked for the secretary of the Smithsonian, Dillon Ripley. That office turned out to be a legendary snake pit.

During this time, I was very social and attended a lot of charity balls and embassy parties, hoping to make more connections. At one point in September of 1970, I was a guest at the Hope Ball in Washington. My parents were there as well, though not at the same table. When the main course arrived, fish, I had a sudden horrible vision of my mother, who had a ticklish throat, choking. I turned to my dinner partner and told him what I had just foreseen. I got up immediately and went across the room to where my parents were sitting. I explained my vision to my mother and begged her, "Please don't eat the fish." Being a good "Scots" woman, psychic herself, and having been the subject of my prognostications before, she agreed not to touch her meal. I left the dance before my parents. Shortly afterward, Mother, who was talking to Mayor Walter Washington, took a sip of wine and started to choke. She turned blue. Evidence of the whole situation was written up in a column in the *Washington Daily News*. A very real psychic episode . . .

Because of the many people I met, I finally landed a great job as the social secretary for the dashing Algerian ambassador and former revolutionary Cherif Guellal. Cherif was extraordinarily good-looking, charming, and madly in love with the former Miss America Yolande Fox, an Alabama beauty queen turned left-wing political activist and widow of movie executive Matty Fox.

Cherif had no clue about embassy social life, and Yolande couldn't have cared less, so I ran the show. It was a pretty big show. Cherif lived in Lyndon Johnson's former estate, "The Elms," and we entertained constantly. He loved parties; Yolande would come when she felt like it. We tried to invite the most interesting people in Washington and beyond. I did the guest lists, the tables, the flowers, the menus, and the seating.

Warren and I became very close to Yolande and Cherif. When we weren't having fancy embassy parties, we were at her Georgetown house with a bunch of hippies, sitting on the floor eating dinner (cooked by the chef) in our tie-dyed tops and bell bottoms, listening to groovy music and talking about the right-wing "pigs" as the smell of pot wafted through the air.

Warren and I were not unaware of the irony of the situation. It was the epitome of radical chic. But it was a lot of fun. Unfortunately, after the 1967 war against Israel, many Arab countries, including Algeria, broke relations with the United States, and Cherif was recalled. That left me alone in the embassy with a bunch of hostile employees until my paychecks finally stopped coming. Those glory days were over.

In the meantime, through my jobs, as well as through my parents and Warren, I had met many people around town. One of them was Phil Geyelin, the editor of the *Washington Post* editorial page. Phil was attractive, debonair, and very bright. We hit it off immediately.

One night at a party Phil was asking me about my plans now that the embassy was closed. I told him I was looking for a job. What a co-incidence, he said, he was looking for a secretary. Why didn't I come into his office the following Monday for an interview? Naturally I did. We had a wonderful interview, and he hired me on the spot. I was to start the very next week.

He introduced me to Ward Just, the brilliant war correspondent turned editorial writer, who asked me to go see the Tom Stoppard play *Rosencrantz and Guildenstern Are Dead* with him that Friday night. Phil also took me into the office of the editor of the *Post* and introduced me to Ben Bradlee.

I was dazzled from the first moment—stricken almost. I had never been so immediately affected by anyone like that before. Ben exuded energy. Dashing, charming, clever, witty, irreverent, challenging, cocky, swashbuckling, he was a life-giving force—and more—yes, he was all those things. His jacket was off, his shirtsleeves rolled up, his tie loosened, and when we walked in, he had his feet on his desk. He rose to greet me, then stood there leaning casually on the edge of the desk with his arms crossed, taking my measure, sizing me up. We only spent about ten minutes in his office, and he and I were already sparring with each other. I don't even remember how I managed to walk out of there, I felt so wobbly.

I thought I had died and gone to heaven. I had landed a great job with Phil Geyelin, gotten a date with a fabulous guy, Ward Just, and had met the Sun King, Ben Bradlee. What more could a girl ask for?

Alas, it was not to be. Phil called the next day to say I was fired. On second thought he had realized that I was overqualified and that we would both end up hating each other. He was not wrong. I already knew that. He couldn't have been nicer or more flattering. Later Ben told me he had advised Phil not to hire me because he was afraid that it would ruin his marriage. (I later accused Ben of projecting.)

The following day Ward called to break our date. He was flying to Spain on Friday to get married. The woman he had broken up with had called to say she wanted him back. I was crushed.

I went back to my mind-numbing job hunt. It was then that I decided I should return to my first love, theater. After all, that was my college major; I was good at it, and I loved acting.

A play—Joseph Heller's *We Bombed in New Haven*—was about to be produced at the West End Theatre in Foggy Bottom, close to the State Department. Wanting the lead, I went to the tryouts. I had no idea how I did. I went home feeling very down. I had given up my apartment and was dividing my time between Warren's and my parents'. I was overcome with the realization that I was too old to be living with my parents, not to have a job, not to be married. I was turning twenty-eight, for God's sake. Whatever would become of me?

A few days later I got two phone calls back to back. The first one was from the director of the play. "Congratulations," he said, "you got the part." I was euphoric. We agreed to meet for the first reading.

The second call was from a voice I recognized the instant I heard it. "This is Ben Bradlee," he said. "I'm the editor of the *Washington Post*." I certainly remembered who he was. "I'd like to talk to you about being a party reporter for the new Style section." Ben had invented the Style section a few months earlier, which was later copied by newspapers throughout the world. I was nervous but excited. We agreed to meet for an interview.

I went to see Ben first, before I met with the director, but not before I had done my homework. I found out he was a Virgo. That made all the difference. If I hadn't known that, I likely would have approached the interview entirely differently. In an interview in the *Washingtonian* several years later I was asked if knowing people's birth signs helped. "Oh, absolutely," I was quoted by the reporter. "I'm not an astrology freak—far from it—but it's certainly more fun than religion. So I laid my Virgo number on them." Actually it was him I laid the number on, and I can't believe I said that to a reporter.

Virgos are dutiful, modest, noble, humble, powerful, achievers, and good communicators. They can see into people and detect their motives. They can sometimes be judgmental. They are decent and cannot stand dishonesty. They are not overly emotional and are not overtly flirtatious.

Armed with this information, my "Virgo number" was in fact not a "number." I was totally honest and straightforward. I didn't brag or exaggerate my background or achievements. Of the latter, I made it clear that I really didn't have any to speak of. I didn't flirt, and I dressed in a very ladylike manner. I wore a pale-aqua silk jersey shirtwaist dress, pale stockings, cream-colored lizard shoes with matching bag, real pearls and pearl earrings, and the pièce de résistance, white gloves. Ladies still wore white gloves in 1969, at least this one did.

My mouth was dry, my heart pounding, my hands perspiring. It wasn't that I was nervous about the job interview. I really didn't have high expectations. Besides, I had the acting job in my pocket. It was Ben.

We probably spent half an hour together; a lot of it was in the form of a dance, a sort of competitive repartee. I was giving as good as I got. Neither one of us wanted to be bested. It was pretty cheeky of me, now that I think of it. After all, he was the editor of the paper and also twenty years my senior. I don't know where I got the courage to go at him the way I did, but he clearly enjoyed it, encouraged it even, and it felt exactly right. (It still did forty-three years later, right up until a few days before he died, when I tried to get him to do something he didn't want to do and he gave me the finger.)

"Can you show me something you've written?" he asked.

"I've never written anything in my life," I replied.

"Nobody's perfect," he said. "You're hired."

Phil Geyelin later claimed he said that, but it's not how Ben and I remembered it.

I started the next day. I covered my first party, the opening of an art gallery. I didn't have a clue what to write. Frantic, I called Warren from my desk about nine P.M. and he told me, "Just pretend you're calling your best friend on the phone and telling her about it. That's what you always do anyway." So I did. I wrote it as if I were talking it through in my own voice. It worked. Everyone seemed to like it. I was on a six-month tryout, but it was clear from the beginning that I had found my métier.

Without hesitation, I called the director and told him I couldn't take the part. Talk about the road not taken. Maybe the gods were beginning to show me the way.

Chapter 11

I am a great admirer of mystery and magic.
Look at this life—all mystery and magic.

—Harry Houdini

It was 1971. The Vietnam War was raging. I was raging. Warren was raging. It was all anyone could think of. Generations were divided. The *Washington Post* was in the early stages of turning around its editorial support of the war, but reporters were near unanimity in being vociferously against it. Nobody could believe that after the antiwar protests of '68 and the years just after that, we were still fighting.

Ben had come around to being against the war, persuaded by his young reporters who were covering it. He went to Vietnam and saw the horror for himself. But so many of his friends had not. His then wife, Tony, and her friends were out on the streets demonstrating against it. All of us journalists couldn't but wanted to.

The caskets and body bags kept returning. So many of my male friends were doing everything they could to get out of going. Some moved to Canada, some got married and had babies, some signed up for graduate school, some faked medical problems. One friend of mine, whose father was in the military, had gotten a low draft number and was called in for a physical. In warm weather he got heat rashes on his feet. The day before the exam his mother wrapped his feet in warm wet towels and changed them every few hours. His feet were so red and swollen that he couldn't walk to the exam. He told them he couldn't be in a warm humid environment. He didn't get drafted.

I admired these friends who did what they did to get out of fighting the war. I also admired those friends I had who went to Vietnam. It was such a wrenching struggle for all of us but particularly for the guys. Those coming back from Vietnam were not recognized as war heroes and some were even demeaned for having been stupid enough to serve. None of us had faced such a grave moral crisis in our lives.

I was as conflicted as my friends—maybe even more so because I had been brought up in the military to be a total chauvinist for our country, believing in the flag and all that it stood for. My disillusionment, however, knew no bounds, not just in my country but in my father as well, at least for a while.

Daddy was appalled at these young men who refused to fight. He was far from willing to admit that the war was a criminal hoax that was devastating America. The whole thing was sickening.

Then, on April 22, 1971, John Kerry, a young, highly decorated navy officer, just returned from Vietnam with a Silver Star, a Bronze Star, and three Purple Hearts, testified about the war before Congress. It was electrifying and profoundly affected everyone I knew.

His testimony was so candid, so raw, so emotional, and so patently true that nobody could deny its authenticity. He talked about the atrocities perpetrated by American soldiers on Vietnamese civilians, the millions of men "who are given the chance to die for the biggest nothing in history," and said, "we cannot consider ourselves America's best men when we are ashamed of and hated what we were called on to do in Southeast Asia."

He spoke of the "attempt to justify the loss of one American life in Vietnam, Cambodia, or Laos by linking such loss to the preservation of freedom, [. . .] the falsification of body counts, in fact the glorification of body counts," and the insanity of losing two platoons trying to take a hill, only "to leave the hill for reoccupation by the North Vietnamese."

His most famous line was the one that galvanized a large part of an entire generation. "How do you ask a man to be the last man to die in Vietnam? How do you ask a man to be the last man to die for a mistake?"

His closing was poignant. "And so, when, thirty years from now, our brothers go down the street without a leg, without an arm, or a face, and small boys ask why, we will be able to say 'Vietnam' and not mean a desert, not a filthy obscene memory, but mean instead where America finally turned, and where soldiers like us helped it in the turning."

That did it for Warren. He desperately wanted to be assigned to cover Vietnam but the *New York Post* wouldn't send him. They had no foreign correspondents, and besides, Dorothy Schiff, known as Dolly, the paper's owner, said he was slated for greater things. I certainly had no desire to cover the war. Very few women journalists were covering it at the time. Having lived through parts of two wars with my father and seen the results up close and personal in the hospital in Tokyo, I had no stomach for it and certainly no illusions about the romance of war.

Warren and I did, however, decide to go to Vietnam—on vacation. Both of us were so crazed about the war that even though we couldn't cover it for our papers, we were writing about it from the periphery anyway and we wanted to see it firsthand. We went in October of 1971, starting out in Paris, then on to Turkey, India, Thailand, and finally to Vietnam.

On our flight into Saigon we ran into a friend, Frankie FitzGerald, who would later write *Fire in the Lake*, a seminal book about the war that won both the Pulitzer Prize and a National Book Award. We were staying with Kevin Buckley, the *Newsweek* bureau chief, and Frankie joined us for dinner that first night. We went to the hangout of all the journalists, diplomats, and officers on leave, the Continental Hotel in the heart of the city. It was an old white French Colonial with a large romantic porch and ceiling fans slowly rotating above us. Slightly jet-lagged, we ate well, drank a lot of wine, and, lulled by the breeze, talked of nothing but the war. It was surreal. Only a few miles away people were fighting and dying—needlessly, it seemed to us. The three of us who had just arrived were emotional. Kevin, who had been living in the midst of the war for quite a while, was hardened and a bit cynical by then. To keep his sanity, we soon learned, he and all our journalist friends had managed to cloak themselves in some sort of defensive covering in order to do their jobs. They were supposed to be objective, which was difficult if not impossible since the war was becoming more and more morally obscene.

As it turned out, Kevin and Frankie fell in love with each other that night and ended up living together for years.

All the publications with bureaus had a researcher/driver/translator, and at *Newsweek* that was Cao Dao, a thin, wiry little man with a goatee who smoked incessantly. He was also whip-smart, cunning, and a seasoned operator. He was a fixer, the guy who could get you in anywhere, get you a meeting with anyone, find anything. He had street cred and nerves of steel. He was someone we were glad to have on our side.

After touring the city and talking to and interviewing as many people as we could, Warren and I decided we wanted to go out to the countryside where the fighting was going on. Kevin told us we were crazy, reminding us that the photojournalist Sean Flynn, son of movie star Errol Flynn, had disappeared in Cambodia with a colleague the year before and was never heard from again. This was not exactly a tourist destination, he pointed out, but Cao Dao said he would take us. I have to admit I had reservations but Warren was insistent and I figured Cao Dao wouldn't have agreed if he thought it was truly dangerous. So off we went.

It was still humid and muggy, even in October, and we were dressed for the tropics. The drive out was relatively uneventful. We saw a few Vietnamese on their bikes and walking carrying bundles. We saw some standing huts and some that had been destroyed—the whole area looked just as it did in the newsreels. We stopped along the road, had a bite, and then headed back. Part of me was relieved, part slightly disappointed. We really hadn't seen that much.

Then suddenly we heard a blast of gunfire, then another. Cao Dao shouted at us to get down on the floor of the car, a command we immediately followed. Before we knew it we were in the middle of some sort of firefight. Whoever was shooting didn't seem to be aiming at us, but they were shooting at something awfully close. Cao Dao put his foot on the gas and began going what must have been a hundred miles an hour as the bullets continued to fly. He was zigzagging the car so as to avoid being the target. It seemed like hours that we lurched along the bumpy road, fully expecting to be killed at any moment. I think I was in too much shock to be scared. Neither Warren nor I said a word. Finally the noise began to subside in the distance, and Cao Dao slowed down. We were on the outskirts of the city, and at last we were safe.

Once we got back to Saigon we thanked him profusely and apologized for putting him at risk. He didn't say anything. He just lit a cigarette, gave us a little bow, and walked away. What a cool customer.

We learned later that he had been unable to get out of Saigon when the Americans left and was killed shortly afterward.

All I remember thinking about at the time were John Kerry's words about the men who were "given the chance to die for the biggest nothing in history."

We could have died as well for nothing. How stupid we were. Yet that experience was seminal for me. In a way that trip was as intense and traumatic as my stay in the hospital in Tokyo. We didn't see anyone die. We didn't get hurt. It was only an hour or so that we experienced the firefight. However, in Tokyo I had not really focused on the moral implications of war. I was concerned for my father, for my own health, for the welfare of the soldiers and the other patients, and missing my mother terribly. Here in Vietnam, it was so much larger than my childhood world.

The few weeks beginning in the middle of June of 1971 when the Pentagon Papers—published first by the *New York Times*, and a couple of days later by the *Washington Post*—burst onto the scene were dramatic and exciting. Of course I had been caught up in the hoopla in the newsroom. The entire place was electrified by the story— and by the threat it posed to freedom of the press. The top editors and reporters were also transfixed for a time until Kay Graham, president and publisher of the *Post*, with Ben's urging, gave the go-ahead to print, defying court orders and risking the financial future of her company, which was on the verge of going public that very week. Everyone in the newsroom was in favor of publishing despite the risks. We devoured the reporting in the newspapers and all over television. It was especially interesting to think back on what we'd heard and read while we were in Vietnam on our "vacation" just a few months later. We were well aware that many people—policymakers and journalists and private citizens alike—had come to the conclusion that the Vietnam War was unwinnable.

I had not studied religion and had never heard of the Augustinian theory of a just war, though certainly Vietnam did not qualify. I didn't pray when we were being fired upon. It didn't occur to me. I didn't pray for those who were being killed or wounded on either side. I was not, nor am I now, a pacifist.

Instead, what I came away with was a revulsion for the Washington power center, for those who had gotten us into what I concluded was this hateful war and then were too cowardly to admit they were wrong and got us in even deeper to protect their own reputations. They lied to the American people, and they lied—in the most cynical way—to those who were fighting. They seemed not to care and tried to make us all believe that we were fighting for freedom and for the good of our country. It's not that I hadn't known this already. Somehow I hadn't wanted to admit it. The reality of it was too painful to accept. After all, I had met quite a few of the people who were responsible. I didn't view them (or at least all of them) as evil, but I was convinced that what they did was evil. That experience changed me as a reporter and as a person. As a reporter, it expanded my world, enhancing my perceptions and observations and adding to my questions. As a person, it focused my attention on the importance of morality in politics and in my life. How to live became much more of a factor in my thinking, more than it ever had before.

Chapter 12

Do not become a mere recorder of facts,
but try to penetrate the mystery of their origin.

—Ivan Pavlov

From Vietnam, Warren went back to the States and I went to Iran where I had been assigned to cover the shah of Iran's two-thousand-five-hundredth anniversary celebration of the Persian Empire in the desert surrounding the city of Shiraz. This was my first foreign assignment and I was terribly excited. I arrived in Tehran for a few days of reporting on my way to Shiraz. It was a whirlwind of intrigue, fascination, and fear. I had done enough research to know that the people of Iran were not all that thrilled about the biggest party ever held.

The shah, in an attempt to put himself on the power map, had invited every head of state, king, queen, emperor and empress, prince and princess on the planet. He had built an enormous tent city on the sands outside of Shiraz and imported everything from France—and I mean everything, down to the eggs, the butter, and the false eyelashes for the female guests. It was costing a fortune while people were starving and the shah and his wife were living like, well, kings and queens, which they were. There was a lot of underground dissent. Nobody dared complain openly for fear of being tortured by the dreaded Savak, the shah's secret service.

My friend Ardeshir Zahedi, who had been the Iranian ambassador to the United States and foreign minister—he was divorced from the shah's daughter but was still on the best of terms with him—had set me up with an interview with the empress, or shahbanou, Farah Diba Pahlavi, which was a major coup. He had also introduced me to a government official who had invited me to his house for dinner with his family.

Meanwhile I had met a number of journalists, both American and Iranian. I had learned early on that no matter where you go, you want to hook up with the journalists first because they are always in the know. That's still true to this day. My first big shock was trying to take a male photographer friend, also covering the celebration, to my room at the hotel so we could have a drink. There was no bar. The all-male desk staff went crazy, and there was a terrible screaming match in the lobby as they at first refused to allow him to accompany me because I was a woman. When I prevailed—I simply refused to stand down—they began yelling at me, calling me a whore and other things I didn't understand but had a pretty good idea of.

The following night I had been invited by a group of Iranian journalists to a secret meeting. If I really wanted to know what was going on in Iran, I was told, I should go, but I had to agree to be blindfolded. It was risky, but I was too curious to refuse.

Once at the meeting I was shocked at what I heard. These people were not just dissidents, they were revolutionaries, and they wanted to overthrow the shah. The celebration, they said, was what had pushed them over the edge. Aside from the shah, one of the things they were most afraid of was the surge in militant Islam. The Islamists were outraged at the shah's flaunting of his secular views and his rejection of their fundamentalist Islamic faith. These dissidents or revolution-aries were terrified that if they didn't try to oust the shah, the Islamists would and they would have an even more repressive state than they already did. This could become a religious war, they said, and Iran could become a theocracy. I was shaken by this information.

The next day one of our foreign correspondents from the *Post*, a friend, showed up in Tehran. I breathlessly told him what had happened. He suggested, somewhat patronizingly I felt, that I stick to party coverage and he would take care of the foreign coverage. However, I remained haunted for a long time by that conversation at the secret meeting.

The following evening I was picked up by the personal driver of the government official whom Ardeshir had introduced me to and I was taken to an expansive and wildly overdecorated house in the suburbs of Tehran overlooking the mountains. When I arrived, I found that the man was there without his family. He explained that his wife had taken the children to the Black Sea for the weekend. I began to feel very uncomfortable.

He offered me a glass of champagne, which I accepted as I talked a lot about "my dear friend Ardeshir," as a way to ward him off. I refused a second glass and we went to the table. One lone servant, very discreet, was there to see to us. It was clear this person knew the drill. The man was beginning to leer and make suggestive remarks. I tried to bring up the subject of a revolution, but he dismissed it out of hand. It was clear he had no interest in discussing politics with me. I was beginning to think that maybe I should leave.

Right at this moment, out came the servant with a tray and a bowl literally heaped with caviar. This was not any caviar. This was the shah's personal stash of golden caviar, the most rare and precious caviar in the world. As it turned out, the shah hated caviar, so he doled it out to his closest advisers.

Caviar is my favorite food. Yet another moral crisis—should I go or should I stay? I stayed. The caviar was beyond delicious. And, yes, even worth the chase around the dining room table. Before he agreed to send me back to the hotel with his chauffeur, I had to threaten to rat him out to Ardeshir if he dared to touch me. I look back on that evening and think how stupid I was to stay. It could have had a disastrous ending. But, oh, that caviar . . .

The following day I had an interview with the shahbanou at her residence. She was beautiful, charming, sympathetic, and very upset. It turned out, as she told me discreetly, that she had been against the party and thought it was an unnecessary extravagance. She was also agonizing over the fact that this celebration was not being used to highlight Iranian culture. She clearly understood that the entire event was only going to exacerbate the already simmering tensions between the shah and the people. The whole thing had been cooked up by the shah's sister Ashraf and her husband, a Machiavellian pair if ever there was one. I left the palace, beyond excited. I had had a great interview, despite the fact that I couldn't use everything she told me or intimated to me. I learned a lot more later to substantiate what I had suspected.

It was true that the shah had done a lot to modernize his country and bring it into the twentieth century, giving women rights and promoting education and economic development. Nevertheless, he was a dictator who could be ruthless. He was so insulated by those around him that he didn't pay enough attention to the religious unrest that was happening on his watch until it was too late.

The celebration in Shiraz was a disaster. It was particularly a public relations disaster and I definitely had a hand in that. I wrote nine stories about it, just writing what I had observed, but the pieces were received as one more damning than the other. The whole spectacle was an egregious display of wealth, power, and ego. The guests included Prince Philip and Princess Anne from the UK, King Hussein of Jordan, Prince Rainier and Princess Grace from Monaco, Ethiopian emperor Haile Selassie, President Tito from Yugoslavia, and Imelda Marcos from the Philippines. U.S. president Richard Nixon had planned to attend but changed his mind and sent his vice president, Spiro Agnew (not quite in the same international luminary category).

It was clear when they got there that they were all wondering what the hell they were doing stuck in their tents in the hot sandy desert in Iran, driving for miles to attend excruciatingly tedious ceremonies and boring dinners, and, even worse, eating French food.

The moral implications were not lost on me at the time. I found it untenable that so much money had been wasted for such a self-serving event, while so many people were living in poverty. At the time, though, I was so wrapped up in the coverage, pointing out the event's extravagance, that I didn't need to editorialize about it. That wasn't my job. I reported it the way I saw it and that was enough.

Later, when I told my brother, Bill, who eventually earned his M.A. and Ph.D. in religion at the University of Chicago, an alumnus of its Divinity School, about the huge, three-day party and the meeting I had had with the dissidents, he was not surprised. He mentioned then that he felt our government didn't pay enough attention to the religions of the countries in which we were represented. By the time the shah was finally overthrown in 1979 by the Islamic Revolution, the worst nightmares of my educated, middle-class Iranian dissident friends had come to pass. Bill said to me then that the government should have an office devoted to understanding religion because it played such a huge role in the lives of the billions of people globally.

In 2001, President George W. Bush had created an Office of Faith-based and Community Initiatives, whose mission, as a report from the Brookings Institution stated, was in part to encourage State Department employees and diplomats to see faith communities as potential allies around the world. In 2013, Secretary of State John Kerry set up a special office and appointed Shaun Casey, a scholar of Christian ethics, as U.S. representative for religion and global affairs.

It was my experience in Iran, and watching the subsequent overthrow of the shah and the ascendance of Ayatollah Khomeini, that first got me thinking in a serious way about the power of religion and the consequences the misuse of that power can have. I began to think about religion coverage and about issues of faith in a way I never had. I started to see that simply because I thought of myself as an atheist didn't mean that I shouldn't try to understand what motivated the vast majority of people in the world. There had to be something there; there had to be. That's when I began paying attention to the role of religions globally, to belief systems, to faith. That's when the seeds of what would become the website On Faith were really planted.

. . .

When I was first shown to my desk in the new Style section, I found that I was sitting next to Phil Casey, a grizzled, hardened, cynical reporter who had been covering the police beat for the *Post* for most of his career. Phil, who happened to be a beautiful writer, had been languishing in the Metro section for years. Ben had scrapped the old women's section "For and About Women" (somewhat to Kay Graham's dismay) for Style. The revolutionary idea was that it would be about people, politics, and culture. Ben brought in writers, men and women, from all over the paper and hired outside renegades as well.

Phil Casey was one of his experiments. Phil wore rumpled suits, his jacket off, shirts unbuttoned at the neck with the sleeves rolled up, and a loosened tie. He had a raspy voice from the chain-smoking. His desk was a heap of littered papers, filled ashtrays, matches, empty food containers and Coke cans, and press releases. Phil was the quintessential tough guy with a heart of gold. He viewed me with a mixture of amusement and suspicion, but he saw how nervous I was. I was assigned to cover parties. He gave me the best piece of advice I ever got as a journalist, which served me well throughout my career and not just in covering parties either. "Remember, kid," he growled, "in every story there's always a victim and always a perp."

Since I had no journalistic training, I simply covered parties and other events in a conversational way, describing what I had seen and quoting what I had heard. I also began doing interviews of well-known figures. I quoted them accurately. They spoke for themselves. The pieces were not always flattering, although I did many more positive pieces than not. Naturally though, it was the "hatchet jobs" that got the attention, and soon I had developed a reputation for being a very tough reporter. I began getting quite a bit of publicity, not all of it good. I also began doing profiles of a lot of famous and powerful people. I wrote it the way I saw and heard it.

I did a profile of Norman Mailer after which he dubbed me "Poison Quinn."

My friends began hiding at parties from those I had interviewed. One woman I barely knew came up to me at a party and said, "I met your mother the other night. She's so different from you. She's really nice."

Part of my reputation may have come from reactions to some of my reporting on social activities and parties, including reporting on the White House. In my powder room at home I have a framed document of abbreviated notes dictated to H. R. Haldeman by President Nixon, dated March 5, 1973. It reads: "Never invite Sally Quinn, violated rules and attacked a guest at church." Nixon had begun having Sunday services in the East Room at the White House, and I was covering one of them. The press was roped off from the "worshippers" and forbidden to talk to them. As people were filing out, I asked one of them a question. That was the end of any relationship I had with the Nixon White House. But the Nixon administration itself had only seventeen months to go.

I did many stories on Henry Kissinger, who once said that Maxine Cheshire—referring to the *Post*'s gossip columnist—"makes me want to commit murder. Sally Quinn, on the other hand, makes me want to commit suicide."

Ben was thrilled. Meanwhile, Ben had hired columnist Nicholas von Hoffman, who was writing vicious columns about everybody and everything. Nick was the most well-read writer at the *Post* and wasn't happy unless the paper got several thousand cancellations after each piece. (They always came back.) Still, he didn't get nearly the kind of opprobrium that I did.

This was a difficult and confusing time for me. I had become quite successful, but I was more feared than admired, more well known than well liked. I have to say that the negative pieces I did write were about people who condemned themselves with their own words and deeds.

Still, it was painful to realize that people had an entirely different view of me than I had of myself, and I began to doubt my own decency, my own worth. I thought I was a good person. A lot of people thought I was not. I had many close friends to whom I was very loyal, and vice versa, and a close family to whom I was devoted. Yet beyond my circle the perception of me was harsh.

I began to wonder if the fact that I was an atheist (though I never uttered that word) and the fact that I didn't believe in God had somehow seeped out of my pores and people were sensing it.

I couldn't help not believing. I didn't choose to believe or not to believe. I felt I was being punished because I didn't believe, and it was infuriating. The idea that you couldn't be a person of values, ethics, and morals because of your lack of beliefs was outrageous. I thought that by writing the truth I was doing the right thing. It turned out that a lot of people didn't think I was doing the right thing. I also recognized that von Hoffman, who was much tougher than I ever was, never had the same reputation that I did. Nick was a man and I was a woman. That was a simple fact of life in our culture then, as it is now.

Ben continued to be shocked by how I was perceived and treated long after he and I got together. The person he knew me to be, he would say, had no relation to my public persona. It wasn't until long after Quinn had all his problems and Ben had died that that view of me began to change. Even today I haven't totally been able to be seen as the person I know myself to be.

Chapter 13

I do not at all understand the mystery of grace—
only that it meets us where we are but does
not leave us where it found us.

—Anne Lamott, *Traveling Mercies: Some Thoughts on Faith*

Back at the *Washington Post* in 1972, I was covering national campaigns. I was on my way down to Miami to cover the Republican Convention, and the *Post* travel office booked my ticket. Nobody flew first class—a Ben edict—so I was in coach. Imagine my shock when I arrived at my seat to find myself sitting next to Mr. Bradlee. He was surprised as well. It seems that the travel person had arbitrarily assigned us seats together. We were both a bit flustered—I because I had been worshipping him from afar since he'd hired me, and he because (as he later admitted) he had been lusting after me from afar as well.

I had always assumed he was way out of my league, not just because of the age difference but also because he had an envied perfect marriage—at least to those on the outside looking in—to one of the legendarily beautiful Pinchot sisters, Tony, with seven children between them. This golden couple had also been best friends with Jack and Jackie Kennedy. Ben thought I was out of his league not just because to him the age difference was daunting, but also because he knew I had a famously passionate relationship with Warren, whom he saw as a dashing, accomplished young journalist. I had started to make a name for myself as a reporter and interviewer and was part of the *jeunesse dorée* crowd of Washington. That's how we saw each other anyway, as we would later learn.

The flight was turbulent, and I'm a terrible flier. We were engrossed in conversation, but when the plane lurched violently, I grabbed his thigh. When things settled down, I kept my hand there. It wasn't deliberate. Really. I just never considered removing it. By the time we landed, two hours later, I was in love.

He asked me to have dinner with him. He was joining Susan and David Brinkley, the legendary NBC News anchor, and would I like to come along. Susan was an old friend, and I had dated David briefly, so naturally, I said I would love to. Ben dropped me at my hotel in a cab. Shortly after I got to my room, the phone rang. "Bad news," he said. His roommate, Howard Simons, the *Post*'s managing editor (editors didn't even get their own rooms), had arranged for the two of them to take a group of reporters to Joe's Stone Crab for dinner. He had to cancel the Brinkleys. Would I like to come along? Disappointed, I said yes. We ended up at a very long table with Ben at one end and me at the other. I tried not to look longingly at him. I tried to make small talk, but the evening seemed endless. We all went back to our respective hotels.

Two nights later, I had had my fill of the speeches and antics on the convention floor and left the center to go back to my room. I was standing on a corner hailing a cab when I heard a deep gruff voice calling out, "Taxi." I looked over to find Ben. Clearly he had had the same idea. "Would you like to get a drink?" he asked. "Why not?" I responded. We got into a cab and headed to the Fontainebleau Hotel. We had no sooner gotten out of the car when we heard a familiar voice. It was Phil Geyelin, who called out, "Benji, Sal, come join us for a drink. We're all going to the Flamingo Room."

We looked at each other in mutual despair and without conferring, both of us regretted. "I'm going to turn in," Ben said. "I think I'll call it a night," I echoed.

That would be the last time we were together for nearly a year.

. . .

Warren had moved to New York by this time and I had gotten a new apartment on California Street in Washington, both of us commuting back and forth between the two cities to see each other. At the same time, he was seeing other people quietly, as was I.

I began to write Ben anonymous love notes. They would come after some sizzling newsroom encounter between us. I would say things like *I don't know how much longer I can stand this*. . . . I later teased him that if he'd had half a brain, he would have figured out who sent them, but he never did. Once, our mutual close friend, national editor Larry Stern, got caught between us during one of these exchanges. After Ben walked away, Larry looked at me, wiped his brow, and said, "Whew! I've never seen such sexual electricity between two people in my life." I just lowered my eyes.

By now the *Post* was in the thick of reporting the Watergate story. We all knew that Ben and Bob Woodward and Carl Bernstein were being watched. Bernstein was even approached on the street by a suspicious character trying to sell him marijuana. He wisely refused. Once when Bob and Carl had gotten an important story, they went to Ben's house, and Ben, afraid that his house might be bugged, met them on his front lawn in his bathrobe to discuss it. The idea that Ben might have an affair was out of the question. It was simply too dangerous. On the other hand, I was so hopelessly in love that I was prepared to throw caution to the wind, and I had a feeling that if I proposed it, he might succumb.

Finally, in desperation, I went to my close friend Paul Richard, then the art critic of the *Post*, and a good friend of Ben's as well. I told him the whole story and asked his advice. "You can't do it," he said. "There is too much at stake. You have to put your country first."

That was the one thing Paul could have said that would convince me to back off. This was about what was best for the country. I made no moves and did nothing.

It was in May of 1973 that Gordon Manning, Ben's dear friend and former colleague at *Newsweek* and then the vice president of CBS News, called me. It seemed that the women at CBS News had demanded a woman anchor. Would I be interested in being the first female anchor for *CBS Morning News*? I knew this would be a revolutionary step, for CBS and for me, but my heart sank. I didn't want to leave the *Post*, I did not want to move to New York, I did not want to go on TV, and most of all I did not want to leave Ben. Nonetheless, I said yes—for one reason: I could not stand being around him anymore without being with him. It was simply too painful.

I asked to see him in his office. I told him about the offer, and I burst into tears. He was livid, furious with Gordon for trying to steal me away, but I could see the anguish in his face. I knew he didn't want to lose me. What I didn't know was whether it was because he thought I was a valuable asset or because he really cared about me. After all, he hadn't made a single move and I couldn't believe that he hadn't figured out who was sending him those little notes.

He tried to talk me out of going. He offered me a raise. Of course he couldn't begin to match the CBS offer, which for that time was an astronomical figure. I told him I was going up to New York to have lunch and an interview with Hughes Rudd, the co-anchor, and Gordon Manning. I would let him know how it went.

They offered me the job at the lunch. I accepted. Apparently Hughes had rejected every woman CBS executives had suggested for the job. I must say I was completely baffled, especially considering I had no TV experience. When I asked Hughes "Why me?," he immediately responded, "'Cause you're meaner than a junkyard dog." At that moment we became fast friends.

I knew that the best thing for me was to leave the *Post* and move to New York to live with Warren. A new career would be good for me. I tried to convince myself I would be happy, but I was dying. I came back to Washington to give up my apartment. I asked Ben to take me for a farewell lunch. He suggested the Madison Hotel across the street from the *Post*. I rehearsed my speech for a week. I couldn't go without letting him know how I felt.

I've never seen so much chicken salad. It was a tower of glutinous white mess. My stomach was churning so I couldn't possibly have eaten a bite. Ben ordered it too. He never picked up his fork. We made polite conversation with lots of questions. When was I moving? Would Warren and I live together? When was the program to air? Finally, I pushed my plate back. I was trembling with apprehension.

"I asked you to take me to lunch for a reason," I began. "I want to tell you why I'm leaving."

He looked at me quizzically.

"I'm leaving because I'm in love with you and I can't stand being near you any longer without being with you." I blurted this out before I had a chance to reconsider. My words seemed to float in the air before they landed on him. He looked stunned and said nothing. We looked into each other's eyes. I could feel mine welling up. I waited.

Finally he spoke. "I can't believe you're saying this. I've been in love with you for the past year. But I thought you were in love with Warren. That's why I didn't try to stop you."

The waiter took our untouched plates away.

Ben had to leave for story conference. "Can we meet tonight?" he asked.

I nodded.

"Seven thirty at your apartment?"

I nodded again. We walked back to the paper in silence.

I was numb with disbelief. I should have been exhilarated, but I could feel nothing. I didn't even focus on the consequences of what we were about to do. I spent the afternoon cleaning out my desk. Around five he came looking for me in the Style section, a worried expression on his face.

"Bob and Carl have come up with a big story," he said. "I may be late. How about eight o'clock?"

For some reason I went into sparring mode.

"How about never?" I said saucily, fully expecting him to laugh.

"I'll be there at seven thirty," he replied and turned and walked off. He was.

We made love that night. Ben was everything I could have ever wanted and more. What I felt for Ben was so transcendent, so sacred, so divine. I had never experienced anything like it. It was magic in the sense that it was otherworldly, life enhancing, life transforming. I had lost myself in another being, another soul. Perhaps a better way to describe it was that I found myself in another being, another soul. Or even more, I merged with another being, another soul. We were one and always were ever after from that moment until the moment he died. For the first time I understood the truly profound meaning of love.

Chapter 14

*Modern views on life and relationship overlook the mysteri-
ous and in so doing dismiss both soul and spirit. . . . Yet fate
and destiny, essential parts of every person's experience, are
largely beyond the limits of our knowing and predicting. How
do you live out a human relationship under such conditions?
You honor the mysterious in the whole of life.*

—Thomas Moore, *A Religion of One's Own*

Ben asked me to marry him (sort of) several days after we had
"gotten together" that first night. We were both besotted. We
were sitting on an ottoman together at a farewell party for me. I'm
surprised that no one seemed to notice we were in a swoon, barely
able to keep our hands off each other.

He didn't get down on his knees. He simply said, "I want to marry
you." I was unable to get my breath to respond. I just nodded. We
never paused to think exactly how that was going to happen. He was,
of course, still married, though he and his wife had virtually no relationship at that point.

Then reality set in and I got caught up in a whirlwind of activity.
Watergate was still going on. Ben was consumed. I was back and
forth from New York for meetings and moving out of my apartment
in D.C. and into Warren's in New York. I still cared deeply for Warren,

but the fact that we were both seeing other people eroded what we had had together. To this day, though, we're the best of friends.

Once I gave up my Washington apartment, Ben and I had no place to meet. We couldn't tell anyone, so we had to behave as though everything was normal. We were frustrated and delirious with happiness at the same time. One weekend we were able to sneak away to his log cabin in West Virginia, where we took a picnic and a bottle of wine down to the river. We made love on the rocks, sunning ourselves in an indolent daze. It was a new kind of magic for me.

. . .

My co-anchor at *CBS Morning News*, Hughes Rudd, and I were sent around the country on a grand promotion tour before the show debuted. Everything was happening so fast I didn't think to ask about rehearsals or any kind of preparation, and I never got any. We were going to be dynamite, everybody said. Hughes and I believed them. We gave speeches together about what kind of show we were going to do. We were boffo, and the audiences responded enthusiastically. The idea of actually doing a live one-hour TV show every morning was a distant blur. What kept nagging at me was that I didn't want to do this in the first place. I didn't want to leave the *Post* and I certainly didn't want to leave Ben.

One of the stops on our CBS tour was in Cleveland. After we had done our TV appearances and Hughes had left, Ben met me and we rented a car and just drove down the highway until we found a huge motel with a restaurant and took a room. We went down to dinner and luxuriated in the fact that nobody recognized us, even though both Ben and I had been in the news for a while. We slow danced, arms wrapped around each other, and even made out on the dance floor. The risky forbiddenness of it all was delicious. Clandestine.

Sometime during the whirlwind of activity, someone from the CBS promotion department called me. Everyone there was ecstatic. Clay Felker, the powerful and charismatic editor of *New York* magazine, wanted to do a cover story on me. Clay was a friend. He had tried to hire me away from Ben and I had declined the offer. He had assigned one of my friends, a former colleague at the *Post*, to do the story. We did the interview, which I felt had gone well, and the cover shoot was scheduled. When I arrived at the studio in New York, the photographer was standing in front of an imposing king-size bed. On it was a man's pajama top. The idea was that I should put on the top and get under the covers, and he would shoot me slithering seductively out of bed. The caption would read something like "Good Morning, New York" or "Wake up with Sally Quinn." I was horrified and scared. I knew I wasn't going to pose that way. It was sleazy, smarmy, and disgusting, and I felt totally exploited. Still, I didn't know what to do. CBS was so excited about the cover story and everyone was counting on it to give the show a great kickoff. What if I refused and Felker killed the story? Finally I summoned up the courage to tell them no. There were a lot of frantic phone calls back and forth to Felker. After much negotiation, it was agreed that I would sit on a pile of steamer trunks and suitcases wearing a pantsuit as if I were the new girl coming to town. That seemed fairly harmless if a little hokey, but I was so relieved that I didn't have to get into the pajama top that I acquiesced.

The magazine appeared on the stands in July with the cover headline reading "Good Morning, I'm Sally Quinn. CBS Brought Me Here to Make Trouble for Barbara Walters." Barbara was a friend and had been incredibly kind to me when I took the job. The piece was a total hatchet job, more fiction than fact. From my reading of the story, I came across as a slut and a bitch. The line that sent me over the edge was, "She once said 'I thought I could get any penis I wanted.'" In my entire life I would be incapable of saying something like that. I thought I would die.

Nobody at CBS knew what to say. Everyone was appalled, including Bill Paley, the head of the company. When I walked into the office, everyone turned their backs on me. I flew down to Washington to see Ben. He sat with me and held my hand and read the piece out loud to me, trying to calm me down. He kept telling me how it wasn't that bad. I was so grateful to him. I had fully expected him to say, "You are not the woman I thought you were," and break up with me. He didn't. He stuck by me. He told me I was strong and that I could handle this. We could handle it together. Warren was wonderful, too, but Warren knew me and knew who I was. He also knew the reporter, and he knew Clay. He understood what Clay was doing. He simply wanted a sensational piece and he got it. It seemed that was all anyone was talking about. Little did they know that Ben and I were together. If they had, it would have been an even bigger scandal.

The show debuted August 6, 1973. It was a complete disaster. I had the flu and was nearly delirious. For some reason I wanted to look serious and had curled my hair in a tight little sprayed do, instead of the long blond look I had had forever. I wore a yellow—my least flattering color—military-style jacket and rimless granny glasses. I guess I was thinking I should look serious. It didn't matter since I didn't have a clue what I was doing because we had not rehearsed the show and I had been up since one A.M. "writing" the intros to whatever script they might have had for me. Also, I didn't know which camera to look into since nobody had bothered to tell me the one with the red light was the one that was on.

I got killed in the reviews, not just because I was so terrible but because, after the *New York* magazine piece, everyone hated me.

. . .

Once I had my disastrous debut on the *CBS Morning News* things became more difficult for Ben and me. He would fly up to New York, meet me at a hotel, we would go for lunch/dinner, then he would fly back to Washington in time for story conference and in time for me to get to bed in order to report to work early. Most days, Hughes and I would have lunch at a Mexican restaurant, get drunk on margaritas, and I would collapse into bed at 5:30 P.M. in order to get up at 1:30 A.M. This was no life. I didn't get to write anymore. I was exhausted all the time and hungover as well. I loathed TV and hated the job but had to keep going.

One day, in early September, Ben and I had a very late lunch on the terrace of Tavern on the Green in New York. It was an unseasonably cold but sunny day and we were the only ones eating outside except for two little old ladies at the other end of the terrace. Because we had privacy we were holding hands and kissing the entire way through the lunch. Ben left and flew back to Washington, and I went back to Warren's to sleep.

Ben was in his office when one of the editors overseeing Watergate coverage came in and closed the door. "So," he said to Ben with a conspiratorial grin on his face, "you and Quinn, huh?" Ben was shocked. "How do you know?" he asked. "My mother was having lunch with a friend on the terrace of Tavern on the Green today . . ."

We both realized then that we had to come out of the closet. Ben had already decided to leave home and a marriage that had been foundering for several years and had moved into the Georgetown Inn. He told his wife that he was in love with someone else but didn't say who. She told some of her friends. My phone started ringing off the hook. Who could it be? Both Washington and New York were wild with curiosity. I even made a few well-placed calls myself, debating the identity of the new inamorata.

We finally told everyone. Warren was the hardest for me because I really loved him. I quickly rented a furnished apartment in a residential hotel on Central Park West and told Warren that night. He was in shock. I moved out and into the hotel where my apartment was immediately broken into and most of my clothes were stolen. This was not a good time.

Ben told a few people at the *Post*, and it went international immediately. Hughes was in shock as well. He was exactly Ben's age, twenty years my senior, and had been like a father figure to me. CBS was also in shock and none too pleased. The last thing they needed on their hands was a new anchor (the first woman in history) with already bad publicity, who also happened to be bombing on TV, and now was running off with a married man.

I lasted on the *Morning News* until December 7, ironically Pearl Harbor Day, when, by mutual agreement, we parted ways and I left the anchor job, leaving the morning news behind, and returned to Washington. I stayed on as a CBS "reporter" for a few months, back in the bureau in Washington. I lived with Ben in a new apartment in the Watergate—yes, the Watergate. It was a large one-bedroom with a beautiful view of the Potomac River and convenient to the *Post*, but the irony was lost on no one.

I detested that CBS job in Washington too, and once again, by mutual agreement, I left. I had no job now.

More important, I still had not forgiven Clay Felker. He had caused me more pain than almost anyone I could think of. I just couldn't live it down, at least in my own mind and imagination. "Where do I go to get my reputation back?," as a once-maligned public figure asked years ago.

I was obsessed with the magazine story and how badly off the mark it was, not to mention its effect on my life. So I decided to put a hex on Clay, which I did. I told Ben about it. He had heard the stories about my mother's hexes and was dismissive of them. But he laughed and said, "Do what you have to do, baby." Some time afterward, Rupert Murdoch bought *New York* magazine in a hostile takeover, and Felker was out. I learned this at a dinner party I was having at my Dupont Circle house. Katharine Graham, publisher of the *Post*, was there. Kay was a close friend of Clay's and had offered to help him buy the magazine but couldn't get the other owners to agree. Clay called in the middle of dinner to tell her the bad news. She came back to the table visibly shaken. I was in disbelief. Was I responsible? Clay never recovered professionally. Worse, he got cancer, which ultimately caused his death.

I was eaten up with guilt and remorse. Had I really done this? Of course I knew intellectually that I had had nothing to do with Clay's misfortunes, but still, my embedded religion and my Southern upbringing made me believe otherwise. I have to say that Ben was a little rattled by what had happened to Clay, even though he thought it was ludicrous. However, he was especially nice to me for a little while after that. I told my brother about this one too. He was adamant that I never do it again. What you put out, he said, will come back at you threefold.

I vowed never to do it again. It was too powerful an emotion. It seemed like sorcery, like black magic. It didn't feel right. I was scared and confused. It would only get worse.

· · ·

After several job interviews and an ill-fated and brief hiring by the *New York Times,* Ben persuaded the *Post*'s managing editor to rehire me as long as Ben recused himself from anything to do with me at the paper. I went back to work at the paper in March of 1974.

It was never the same for me at the *Post*. Suddenly everyone treated me differently. I was the boss's girlfriend.

Then, much to my disappointment, Ben was balking at getting married, even though he had earlier said he wanted to marry me. Marriage now seemed to be off the table.

That year was one of the most intense of my life. On August 8, 1974, Richard Nixon told the country in a televised address of his intention to resign the next day. Several days later Ben announced to me that he was going up to his log cabin in West Virginia to write a book on JFK. Without me. He had signed a contract to do a book on the notes he had taken when Jack Kennedy was president and Ben and Tony were spending so much time with him and Jackie in the White House. He had told Jack he was writing the book and Jack understood. The only ground rules, Jack had insisted, were that Ben wait ten years until after he had left the White House: Ben agreed. Kennedy was killed in 1963 and Watergate was over, so now was the time.

Ben was exhausted physically, mentally, and emotionally after the Watergate years. He needed to get away, he said. He needed to work out in the woods, to empty his mind. He needed solitude. He needed time to process what had just happened. He needed to think about us. He needed to be alone.

I was heartbroken. There was no working phone in the cabin. He said he wouldn't come back until he had finished the book. It could take a month; it could take six weeks. I would be alone in August in Washington in our apartment in the Watergate with no contact with him at all. I understood that he needed to get away. I got it that he wanted to do the book, to focus only on it. What

I didn't understand was why he would want to be away from me all that time. I would have thought my presence would be calming to him, would be soothing, reassuring. I would have thought he would want to sleep with his arms around me at night. I tried to talk to him about it. He was resolute. He got up the next day, packed a few pairs of jeans and some T-shirts, took his research, and off he went.

Naturally I presumed the worst. He would get up there and decide he didn't love me and that he could do just fine without me. He would realize he didn't miss me and that would be that. It was the summer from hell. I was more in love with him now than ever. Could it be that he was not in love with me anymore?

He came back after Labor Day. He was wearing jeans and was clean-shaven. He had stopped off at a barber's to have his hair cut and a shave before he came home. He had grown a beard, which he said was white and scraggly looking, and he didn't want me to see it. His hair was whiter than ever. He seemed a different person. In a way I had the same feeling I had had when Daddy came back from Korea, his hair having turned totally white. I was exhilarated but scared. I wasn't sure who this person I loved so much had become.

We spent many days talking. He had finished the book that became *Conversations with Kennedy*. It would be published the following year and quickly became a perennial bestseller. Ben had spent a lot of time in the woods, chopping down dead trees and clearing brush. He swam off the rocks, our sacred rocks, every day. He had a beer on the porch at night, had a bite to eat, and went to bed early. He was completely refreshed. He had absorbed what had happened in the past two years and had come to terms with the enormity of the *Post*'s role in the Watergate affair.

What Ben had had was a spiritual experience. His time in the woods was and always had been for him, a form of meditation, a form of prayer. He called it mind emptying. He had had a silent retreat, a very long silent retreat. He became a much more thoughtful, deeper, more peaceful person after that. On some level, he must have understood that he had done what he was meant to do. After that he was never as ambitious as he had been before.

I had had exactly the opposite of a spiritual experience. I had been crazed while he was gone. I didn't let him know that. But I was impatient and anxious for him to get on with what else he had been thinking about. *Yes, yes,* I wanted to say, *but what about us?*

We got to that eventually. He had deliberately left it for last. He loved me very much, he said. He was in love with me. He wanted to spend the rest of his life with me. But he still didn't want to get married. He had been a failure at his two marriages, and he didn't want to be a three-time loser. We had such a perfect relationship, he said. Why ruin it by getting married? He definitely did not want any more children. He already had three (and four stepchildren). I had told him, and I meant it then, that I didn't want children either. We were so happy, he insisted. My mother and I had begun to plan our wedding but that had to be scrapped, or at least postponed, I thought, when I was in my most optimistic mood.

Shortly after Ben had finished the book, later in the fall, we were in New York, walking past a small jewelry shop when he stopped and said he'd like to get me a present—very unlike Ben. We went in and they had a series of tiny little rings that were actually chains. Some were plain, some had diamonds, some had pearls. Ben wanted to get me a ring. We chose the plain one. "Let this be our commitment ring," he said to me. "Every year we are together I will buy you another one." He did. I ended up with four altogether, a diamond, a pearl, and another plain. The commitment rings were not enough. We would be together for five and a half years before we finally tied the knot—not without a showdown.

. . .

We went about our lives, both of us getting a lot of attention and a lot of publicity as the "fun couple" from the *Post*'s competitor, the now-defunct *Evening Star*. We moved out of the Watergate. It was too much of a joke. Meanwhile, I used the money I had earned at CBS to buy a house near Dupont Circle. I wanted to own the house myself to give me a sense of security. In case we broke up, I didn't want to be the one to have to leave.

Ben continued to resist marriage, so I started seeing a therapist— one of the best things I ever did—the fabulous Sharon Alperovitz, whom we all jokingly called "shrink to the stars." I think at one point she had half the *Post* newsroom as her patients.

Sharon was brilliant, and also caring, compassionate, wise, and funny. She profoundly helped me understand better the dynamics of my relationship with Ben. After a while, I got him to go with me. He was very anti-shrink, but he loved Sharon. We went around and around about marriage. He wouldn't budge. She taught me that one person really has to change in order to get the other to change. Did I really want to marry Ben? I concluded yes. Was I willing to change? I was willing but I didn't know how to change. What would I have to change? And why? What changes, if any, would make marriage more palatable for Ben, would make him want to marry me? Finally she said the magic words *bottom line*. I had to decide what my bottom line was.

Unfortunately, I didn't put my newfound understanding into prac- tice right away. I kept doing the same things—behaving the same way, pleading, demanding, whining, manipulating, begging. It wasn't pretty. I disliked who I was becoming with Ben, but I also didn't feel good about being the person to whom the man I loved and who loved me didn't want to commit. It was Warren all over again. I resolved to decide on a bottom line. Sharon pointed out that if you have one, you have to stick to it. If I gave him an ultimatum, then I really had to mean it. That was terrifying to me. It meant that I would actually have to leave him if he continued to refuse to marry me. Or throw him out. I owned the house. That was small consolation. For a long time I just didn't have the courage. Then I did. There was a moment when I knew I couldn't live with myself under these circumstances.

The tipping point for me came when Ben was asked if we were going to get married. "I'll marry her when there's a Polish pope," he said, which I thought was seriously ungallant. Then, guess what? Karol Józef Wojtyla from Poland became Pope John Paul II on October 16, 1978.

I told Ben that if he didn't marry me, I was going to start having affairs—and I had a candidate in mind. I actually did. It was 1978, and I was leaving for Israel to do a series of interviews for the *Post* on the Israeli-Palestinian situation. I had heard of Ezer Weizman, the handsome Israeli Air Force commander and war hero, who was the minister of defense. I knew that Barbara Walters had had a brief flirtation with him.

I announced to Ben that when I went to Israel, I planned to have an affair with Ezer. He knew of him and his reputation with women. Ben went crazy. He accused me of everything in the book. I don't think I ever saw Ben that angry or upset. He would hardly speak to me for the next week. I just went along making my plans, whistling a happy tune, packing, doing my research, telling all our friends how much I was looking forward to the trip.

I was leaving on a late plane for Israel when Ben asked me to have lunch with him at Twigs in the Hilton close to the *Post*. I had no idea what it was going to be about, but I had a feeling that he was going to tell me that if I had an affair, he would leave me for good. I was a nervous wreck. I don't think I had been that agitated since I asked Ben to take me to lunch five and a half years earlier.

All I knew was that I had to stick to my guns. We were halfway through an incredibly strained lunch when Ben blurted out, "All right! I'll marry you!"

Needless to say, it was not the most romantic "proposal" a gal could ask for, BUT it qualified as a proposal. I wasn't going to turn it down. "When?" I demanded.

"When you get back from Israel."

"How long after I get back?" I was negotiating.

"Right away."

"Okay." The lunch was over. We kissed each other good-bye. It was awkward. We said restrained I love yous, and I left.

So I didn't stray while I was in Israel. I was sorely tempted one night when, reporting on a gathering, I slept in a tent on the beach in Gaza and the Palestinian leader, an incredible hunk wearing traditional robes, let me know he would be honored to join me in my tent.

Ezer was another story, totally as attractive as his reputation—sexy and smart, with a larger-than-life personality and enormous charisma. Still, I didn't do anything. However, Ezer asked me when I was leaving and when I told him, he arranged to be on that El Al plane back to the States with me, since he was heading to the U.S. to follow up on the recent peace talks at Camp David. He had been a combat pilot serving with the British Royal Air Force in World War II and also a pilot during the 1948 Arab-Israeli War. He was greeted warmly by the El Al pilots who came out to welcome him aboard. At some point in the flight, he came back to invite me to come sit with him in the cockpit while he took over the controls for a while. It was all very romantic, but I was getting married to a man who was even more romantic than Ezer, and I wasn't going to jeopardize it for anything.

On my return, I had to confess to Ben that Ezer flew back with me, but he believed me when I told him it had been very innocent. I got back on a Sunday, and I planned the wedding for the following Friday. I didn't want to give Ben a chance to change his mind, especially since he had really missed me for the two weeks I was gone.

We arranged to be married in the chambers of Judge David Bazelon, an old friend of Ben's. Ben asked *Washington Post* humorist Art Buchwald and establishment lawyer Ed Williams to be his best men. Art had been his best man when Ben married Tony, so there was naturally a lot of joking about that. Kay Graham was my matron of honor. She stopped at a florist on her way back from New York and had a bridal bouquet made, complete with flowing ribbons. She carried the whole creation down on the shuttle with her. I had only told my parents, my brother and sister, and Ben's kids, who were all there. That was it. I searched frantically for a knee-length white dress, but with such a short amount of time, I found nothing I liked so I ended up with a white silk skirt and top, which I feel sad about to this day. I wanted to look like a bride.

Ben was adamant that we not tell a soul except the involved parties. He didn't want to get scooped by the competitive *Washington Evening Star*. He didn't even want to go with me to the Tiny Jewel Box to pick out my wedding ring. Somebody would see us. He didn't want to wear one. He had never worn a ring. He didn't like his hands and felt a ring would draw attention to them. I loved his hands. They were strong and masculine, the hands of a woodsman, which Ben was. I didn't care about the rings at that point, especially since he was making enough of a statement just by marrying me. I asked the *Post* art critic, Paul Richard, to go with me to pick it out. I chose a very thin gold etched band and had our initials and the date, October 20, 1978, engraved on it.

The engagement ring would come later, nine years later to be exact, when I guilted him into helping me design a ring with a matching pair of exquisite emeralds surrounding a diamond of the same size. He complained bitterly the whole time, but nobody was happier showing off the ring than Ben, who spent the next nearly three decades making fun of his other friends for being so cheap they wouldn't buy their wives a decent ring.

The ceremony was short. I stunned everyone, including myself, when I totally fell apart and slumped over on Ben's shoulder, in tears. I hadn't realized how much I wanted this, how much I needed this affirmation from Ben. I was loved. I was cherished. And I loved and I cherished.

I had planned a buffet supper that Friday night and invited about thirty of our closest friends. Many of them had made other plans. Peter and Margaret Jay, the British ambassador and his wife, who were good friends of ours, were having a dinner that night as well. I told my friends that they had to get out of it and come to ours. I said I was calling in my chits, and I couldn't tell them why but it was very, very important. They all came.

As people arrived at the house that Friday night after the ceremony, they were surprised and thrilled to find out it was a wedding celebration. I had the house filled with white flowers, and in the center of the table was a beautiful simple wedding cake. Carl Bernstein and Richard Cohen had brought along a glass, which they put in a paper bag, and as part of the Jewish wedding ritual, Ben, for good luck, stomped on it and smashed it. There were many toasts, planned and unplanned. Mine was this: "Tomorrow you will read in the papers about our marriage: 'her first, his third.' What it should say is 'her only, his last.'"

We scooped the *Star*. Ben was beside himself with glee.

The next day Ben and I drove up to the cabin in West Virginia for the weekend. It was a sparkling October Indian summer day. We took a picnic down to our rocks on the river to celebrate. Ben was happier than I had ever seen him. He was relieved too. He knew he had not made a mistake. He understood he was never going to be that three-time loser he had worried about. He realized that we were more in love than ever and that we would be until the day one of us died. And so it was.

This was not the wedding of my dreams to be sure—I didn't get to be queen for a day—but I had never been so happy in my life.

I've tried to analyze what it was that made me stay those five and a half years before we got married. I know it sounds as though I had been a clingy, whiny, pathetic creature during all that time, someone who had gone from a confident, successful, independent person to a woman who could not function without a man and would take what little crumbs were tossed at her rather than have nothing.

What made me stay was love. A deep knowing that we were truly in love with each other in a way I understood and he didn't at first. It was in my heart, my soul, my bones, every fiber of my being. From the first moment we were together until the moment he died, I never had a single doubt that we were meant for each other. I also knew, and would come to understand more clearly, that I was meant to take care of Ben. Taking care of people was *part* of my religion, though I didn't realize it then. Taking care of him simply added another dimension to my life. I also realized that we had the two qualities in our relationship that mattered most: agape and eros. Agape is the highest form of love and charity. As Thomas Moore writes in his book *A Religion of One's Own*, "agape is the spiritual side of love that asks you to transcend yourself and your needs." Eros is passionate and romantic love.

Agape is also the love of God for man and man for God. What Ben and I had together was actually a spiritual union. And eros, boy did we have eros.

· · ·

Shortly after we married, I bought a ruin in East Hampton on Long Island, called Grey Gardens. It was a well-known house, famous for being owned by Jackie Kennedy's aunt and cousin, Big and Little Edie Beale. They lived alone in the house with thirty-six cats and God knows how many raccoons and the roof was falling down over their heads. The Maysles brothers had made a film of it and had to wear flea collars around their ankles while in the house.

Big Edie had just died and Little Edie was forced to sell. The house was in such terrible condition that the real estate agent refused to go inside to show it to me. Little Edie met me at the door. She had been unwilling to sell it to anyone else because they all wanted to tear it down. I immediately said, "This is the most beautiful house I have ever seen." "It's yours," she replied, and with a little pirouette she danced around and added, "All it needs is a coat of paint."

The next day when I showed it to Ben, who was terribly allergic to cats, he walked out choking after about five minutes and said, "You're out of your fucking mind."

I bought it anyway that August—all cash, with money I'd earned from a book I wrote after the experience at *CBS Morning News*, called *We're Going to Make You a Star*. My mother and I went up to Long

Island in November to close on the house. It was a wild day, over-cast, with howling winds, and the old place was creaking. We were so spooked by it—the rumors were that it was haunted—that we locked the front door behind us.

We were standing in the sunroom in the midst of dead vines, bro-ken glass, and spiderwebs when we both felt a presence. Turning around, we saw a woman standing there. "I came to give you a mes-sage from Big Edie," she said. "She wants you to know she is very happy you have bought Grey Gardens. She knows you will restore it to its original beauty. She's going to watch over the house and make sure everything goes well." Then she disappeared.

Emboldened by the message from Big Edie, my mother and I ventured up to the attic where we found a treasure trove of origi-nal antiques, furniture, silver, linens, mirrors, wicker, and books. I was so excited that I actually started smoking again. Carl Bern-stein bet us a hundred dollars we wouldn't be in the house by the following summer. We were in the next summer and he had to pay up. Everything went perfectly. The house was finished before the contractors said it would be and it came in under budget. Thank you, Big Edie.

The following summer Ben and I were sitting by the pool, where there was a lovely little original thatched-roof cottage just outside the secret garden wall. It was about to be shingled for lack of a thatcher. Suddenly, out of nowhere, a young Englishman appeared in a straw hat and boots. "I say, you wouldn't by any chance have some work for a thatcher?" he asked. We were astonished and hired him on the spot, and he started the next day. Thank you, Big Edie.

Ben wrote much of his memoir in the cottage, and I used it to read palms, tarot cards, and do the Ouija board there. Everything I said then turned out to be true. The August of the summer after our son, Quinn, was born, I used the cottage to nurse him every day. It was so peaceful and serene. Ben called it the "nursing shed." Quinn, Ben's grandchildren, and my nieces and nephew called the cottage the "fairy house" because every night the fairies would come and leave presents for them to discover in the morning. That cottage is a magical place.

Grey Gardens was definitely haunted. The ghosts were not only benevolent but friendly. One was Anna Gilman Hill, a celebrated gardener who had designed the stone wall. When she appeared, she was dressed in her gardening outfit, which I recognized from photos. I saw her once at our bedroom door in the middle of the night. Many of our houseguests saw her as well. One housekeeper was so terrified after a visitation that she quit.

Another ghost was a sea captain Little Edie had been having an affair with, who climbed a ladder up to her bedroom window for their trysts. One week my parents were visiting with Barry Goldwater, and I put him in Little Edie's room where the sea captain was often heard stomping around. I didn't say a word to Barry about ghosts. The next morning I found him asleep on the sofa in the kitchen. "What are you doing in here?" I asked. "There's a goddamn ghost in that room," he said, "and I'm not going back in there." He didn't, for the rest of his stay.

Every year I had a birthday party for Ben in late August at the house—one of the highlights of his year. And the house was always filled with friends and family.

The house, too, was magical. Thank you, Big Edie.

Did I really believe she had made everything perfect for us for so many years? Yes, I did.

· · ·

I was thirty-seven when Ben and I got married, a real old maid. (Doesn't that sound so antiquated now?) It was a long way from our Smith College senior year rallying cry, "A ring by spring." I thought my father was going to expire from relief.

I had told Ben honestly I didn't want children. For a year I was blissfully happy being Sally Quinn (Mrs. Ben Bradlee).

One day, a year or so after we were married, I was walking down Connecticut Avenue near our house at Dupont Circle when I saw a pregnant woman with a baby in a carriage, a beautiful plump, fat-cheeked gurgling baby. She and the baby both looked so content and serene. I clutched my stomach and nearly doubled over in pain. How was it possible that one minute I had absolutely zero interest in having a baby and the next I thought I would die if I didn't? I was over-whelmed with a sense of emptiness. I could actually feel my womb, feel the hole in my body that needed to be filled. It was so visceral. I was in anguish and terrified to say anything to Ben. I knew he would feel completely betrayed. I had made a promise to him. He was so happy with me. His children were almost grown, and he was basking in our life together.

It took me weeks to get up the courage to even broach the subject. Finally, one night at dinner in our kitchen over our second bottle of wine, when Ben was in a particularly great mood, I brought it up. I asked him what he would think about having a baby. He was horrified. He couldn't believe I would even contemplate the idea. I had promised. We had made a deal. It was out of the question. It was the last thing in the world he wanted. It was a deal breaker. He would never agree to it. He didn't want to discuss it ever again. I had expected he would not react positively to the suggestion, but his vehemence stunned me. What was I to do? I had to have a baby. I just had to, and the proverbial clock was ticking.

It was back to Sharon, shrink to the troubled and needy. My take-away from a few sessions with her: I had to decide how important this was to me, what I was hoping to gain and what I was willing to give up. And, most important, I had to have a bottom line. I stopped taking my birth control pills that night. I thought about not telling Ben, but I really didn't want to have his baby if he didn't want it. I didn't want to trick him into it. I had to make him realize that my happiness was his happiness (like the old Jamaican fisherman once said, "a happy wife is a happy life") and that I was going to be totally miserable if I couldn't have a child, our child.

Ben decided to take care of the birth control situation himself. For the next two years, though we were happy and working hard, I had an ache in my gut. It only got worse. I was seeing Sharon once a week. I couldn't bear the idea of losing Ben, but as I got closer to forty I began to panic. I talked it through with my closest friends. Some said I should hold out for a child, that I would never be complete without one, that it was the greatest joy of their lives. Others pointed to so many successful women who had been child-less and had accomplished great things in their lives. I could be one of those.

What finally got to me was that Ben's older son and his wife an-nounced she was pregnant. We went to visit them and took them to dinner. Ben, proud and pleased, toasted the two of them. I'll never forget what he said: that it was so wonderful that they were having a baby because "it was such an important part of the human experi-ence." His words were like a knife in my heart.

I could barely get through the dinner I was so upset, and I really laid into him when we got back to our room. If it was such an impor-tant part of the human experience, I said, with not a little sarcasm, how was it that he was willing to deny that to me? How cruel could anyone be to someone he professed to love? He was pretty much tongue-tied. He really didn't have a good answer.

I hardly spoke to him on the way home and couldn't wait to talk to Sharon the next day. Yep. It was time for my bottom line. Here's what I told him. I said I was going to have a baby and it was either going to be his or somebody else's. He had a choice. I also told him that again I had a candidate in mind and I wasn't talking about artificial insemination, either.

That focused his mind. Again he railed at me, attacking me for betraying him and not keeping my word. He was right, but I was resolute. I meant it and he knew it. I also said I wanted him to be part of the child's life. I didn't want an absentee father. He gave in and agreed on one condition. He was tired. He didn't want to get up for midnight feedings. He wanted us to be able to go out without having to scramble for a babysitter, and he wanted to have some time alone without always worrying about who would watch the baby. He wanted me to promise we would always have round-the-clock help, if needed. He could afford it. He had earned it. I, of course, agreed immediately, not letting on how thrilled I was. I didn't want having a baby to hurt our marriage. Our relationship was too precious to me to let anything change it for the worse. I knew I could do both, be a good wife and a good mother. I wasn't even thinking about my career at that point, I was so focused on my mission.

In reality, I wasn't even thinking about Ben or seeing his side of things. I realize now how terribly selfish I was not to be more understanding about how he was feeling. My God, I was asking a man who was almost sixty, who had helped raise three children of his own and four stepchildren, to embark on another marathon. Of course he had reservations. He didn't want to be an old man for his child. He was afraid he wouldn't be a good enough father or be able to do the things most fathers did with their children, afraid he would die and leave a child fatherless at a young age. He was especially worried about having a son. Ben was so vital, so alive, so energetic. His passion was working out in the woods. His ax, his chain saw, his jeep, and his tractor were his favorite toys. He wanted to share those with a son, if our child was to be a boy. What if he wasn't physically able? He was also concerned about us. He was blissfully content with just the two of us. He knew he had made the right decision by marrying me. What if a child came between us? At this point he was the sole focus of my attention and love. He knew what happened when a woman had a baby. That baby became her first priority. Period. He was really afraid of losing me. I think in some way, once he agreed to have a baby he went into a period of grief, of mourning for our lost perfect relationship.

I wasn't thinking of any of that. My need to have a child was all-consuming, a driving force, the most powerful urge I have ever had. I'm so sorry now that I wasn't as thoughtful about Ben's feelings as I should have been. I wish I had more fully understood his trepidation much earlier. In the end, I had gotten my way, and only later did I see how much he thought he was giving up.

. . .

Prince Charles and Diana's wedding was coming up in July of 1981. I was asked by Style to go to London to cover it, but I said no. I didn't want to be away from Ben and miss a chance to get pregnant. That July we went to West Virginia. We had a beautiful, romantic picnic on the rocks that jutted out into the middle of the Cacapon River. It was a magical day, sunny and dry. We lazed on the rocks for hours, making love, drinking wine, and listening to the sound of the river cascading over the big stones. I never wanted it to end. I felt perfectly happy. I wasn't even thinking of the future, the baby, anything else but the present moment. I just felt so embraced by Ben and his love for me. It was a sense of feeling total gratitude. I was in touch with the divine. It was transcendent—all the platitudes that are so often used were relevant because they were so appropriate and true. This was the greatest experience of agape that each of us ever had.

I also felt a quickening in my womb. Somehow I knew. This was the moment Quinn was conceived.

Chapter 15

My evenings are taken up very largely with astrology. I make horoscopic calculations in order to find a clue to the core of psychological truth. Some remarkable things have turned up which will certainly appear incredible to you. . . . I dare say that we shall one day discover in astrology a good deal of knowledge that has been intuitively projected into the heavens.

—Carl Jung, letter to Sigmund Freud

I am not a student of astrology. I don't know how to read a chart. What I do understand is sun signs and the often stunning accuracy of them from a personal standpoint. The person who really turned me on to astrology was Linda Goodman, who came out with a blockbuster in 1968 called *Sun Signs*. A subtitle on later editions reads: *How to Really Know Your Husband, Wife, Lover, Child, Boss, Employee, Yourself Through Astrology.* The book was thoroughly entertaining and mind-altering in many ways. Never had I read anything that was so detailed and so accurate about those closest to me, never mind myself. (Her later book, *Love Signs,* which explains how various signs relate to each other romantically, has served me well over the years in being able to offer advice to many of my friends.)

One of the amazing aspects of Goodman's first book was that all the verses before the chapters were from Lewis Carroll. This seemed to be quite a coincidence, but although I believe in coincidences, I viewed it more as synchronicity. As I have mentioned, I had always been an *Alice in Wonderland* devotee and had played Alice my senior year in high school. Before me now was Alice speaking to me again in each of the epigraphs, as I devoured every page over and over again. I keep a copy of Linda's *Sun Signs* on my bedside table today and also her *Love Signs* and refer to them both frequently—not just for me but for all my friends, even those who profess not to believe in astrology. For a long time, it was my bible.

Coincidentally, after college my brother, Bill, began taking courses in astrology from the American Federation of Astrologers. Although a skeptic, he was intrigued by it and learned how to erect a natal chart, took exams, and qualified as some kind of purveyor of astrological readings. He met weekly with a group and the leader would pose questions to them. She would give them a time, date, year, and longitude and latitude, and the students would have to create a horoscope account of the person's character. They knew nothing else about the person. She would choose people like Winston Churchill, Elvis, and Gandhi. After going around the room, the interpretations of the charts were almost unanimous every time. Bill says that after this experience he had absolutely no doubt about the legitimacy of astrology. Not only that, he did readings of our family members and found the same thing to be true.

Recently a group of astrophysicists came up with a theory of vibrations, undulations, waves that emanate from the different planets, which Bill and others believe offers empirical evidence that the stars and the planets in fact do affect human beings. The clearest evidence, Bill says, is the moon and its effect on the tides and the human brain.

Bill continued to learn more about astrology, but he would never consider himself a practitioner. He still firmly believes that the

moon, sun, and planets in our solar system give off their own individual electromagnetic energy. According to him, mass affects
mass in space, as physicists would say, and appears as emanations.
These electromagnetic energies have tangible effects on the minds
and emotions and "souls" of us earthlings. The nature of these effects can be argued, but the fact of these effects cannot, any more
than one cannot deny that the moon affects the ocean tides or ampli-
fies the behavior of "lunatics"—from the Latin word *luna* meaning
"moon"—during full moon events. I prefer not to define *lunatic* as
a "mentally ill person" but rather as someone who is "moonstruck,"
or exhibits erratic behavior during a full moon, or is affected with
periodic insanity, depending on the changes of the moon. My sign,
Cancer, is ruled by the moon, and there are actually times during a
full moon when I feel as if I'm about to levitate.

Bill points out that interpretation is the key. Anyone can learn
to do a chart. In fact, most astrologers use computers now to erect
charts. If you have a mathematical mind but not a creative mind,
you may give a completely unsatisfactory reading. That's why it's
important to have a reader who knows what she or he is doing and
has that added understanding to bring to bear on a chart.

Goodman's book is clearly written for the layperson, which makes
it so much fun to read. She writes: "These electro-magnetic vibrations (for want of a better term in the present stage of research) will
continue to stamp that person with the characteristics of his Sun sign
as he goes through life." Note that this latest discovery in 2016 seems
to validate what Goodman was trying to say about electromagnetic
vibrations nearly fifty years ago—and Einstein even earlier.

In fact, aside from having what I considered to have been psychic
moments, I have experienced and even practiced mental telepathy. I
don't see anything particularly controversial about it. It doesn't seem

any more complicated to me than having a very high antenna where certain signals can be picked up. Nobody would have believed in the telephone, the radio, the television, or the Internet a hundred and fifty years ago. I believe it is just a matter of time before we don't have to speak to one another anymore. We will learn how to communicate telepathically. What a nightmare! What will we do about negative thoughts if we can read each other's minds?

I think telepathy works especially with someone you love. I always had telepathic moments between my mother and me and have had (and continue to have them) between Quinn and me. My mother always knew when I was in trouble or in pain and I her. The same with Quinn and me. They say you're only as happy as your least happy child. There are days when I wake up with a nagging sense of depression only to find out that Quinn is having a problem.

I also send loving, happy, and encouraging thoughts to him and others I care about, especially if I know they will be in situations of stress. They say they get them. Some people might call it praying. Maybe I am praying for them. Whatever it's called, it works. When Quinn was young, he was often in the hospital, and all the years he was sick and sometimes near death, I had many friends who would tell me they were praying for me or him or us. Part of me was a bit embarrassed by the overt expression of faith at that time, as I was calling myself an atheist. On the other hand, I genuinely felt buoyed by their prayers or thoughts or wishes for Quinn's recovery.

Studies show that sick people who believe in prayer and are prayed for have a faster recovery time than those who don't and aren't. All I know is that it worked for me. Of course there have been many children at hospitals who were prayed over and died and many parents who prayed and their prayers weren't answered. My feeling is, I'll take all the help I can get.

ABOVE: McDougald plantation house in Statesboro, Georgia

LEFT: Mother, me, and Blitzie in Pineville, Louisiana, 1942

ABOVE: Mother, Daddy, Donna, and me by the Japanese fishpond
at the Imperial Palace Hotel in Kyoto

BELOW: Army brats: me, Bill, Donna, Daddy, and Mother

My debutante year. The Quinn girls:
me, Mother, and Donna, Fort Myer, Virginia, 1959

ABOVE: Daddy and King Paul of Greece at Greek Easter, breaking eggs

BELOW: Daddy being promoted to chief public information officer—
my first brush with journalists—August 1, 1959
Credit: Carl Schneider, U.S. Army Photographic Agency

Heidi? Boarding school in Château d'Oex, Switzerland

ABOVE: Smith College freshman
handbook photo, 1959

RIGHT: The ultimate Southern
party girl, Mother
Credit: Barry Goldwater

OPPOSITE: The modeling-studying-
working-acting-partying-traveling
years; me in Germany

ABOVE: In India with Warren Hoge, a stopover on our way to Vietnam, 1971

BELOW: Covering the shah of Iran's 2,500th anniversary celebration of the Persian Empire, 1971

Ben's favorite picture of me—early years at the *Post*
Credit: The Washington Post

ABOVE: My favorite photo of the two of us, flirting, 1975
Credit: Nancy Crampton

RIGHT: My early days as a *Washington Post* Style reporter

OPPOSITE: Caught swooning by the photographer on our wedding day, October 20, 1978
Credit: Harry Naltchayan/ *The Washington Post*

TOP: Celebrating Ben's eightieth birthday in Turkey—sprinkled with fairy dust

BOTTOM: Sacred table, Thanksgiving, 1989

OPPOSITE: Proud and loving parents at Quinn's christening, October 1982
Credit: Harry Naltchayan/*The Washington Post*

LEFT: Renewing our wedding vows. Twentieth anniversary with a very reverent Tom Brokaw and our wedding party: Quinn Bradlee, Art Buchwald, and Katharine Graham, 1998
Credit: Vivian Ronay

RIGHT: Partying at Grey Gardens, August 2013

BELOW: Great Faiths travels, Potala Palace in Lhasa, Tibet, 2007

ABOVE: Three months before Ben died, on the party boat
at Porto Bello, holding hands as always

BELOW: Placing a white rose on Ben's casket, October 29, 2014
Credit: John McDonnell / *The Washington Post*

ABOVE: Speaking at Ben's yahrzeit in front of the chapel at Oak Hill Cemetery, trying not to cry, October 2015
Credit: James R. Brantley

RIGHT: Ben's mausoleum, amid the cherry trees, Oak Hill Cemetery

Imaging is more or less the same thing. I try to carry positive images with me in my head. When Quinn was in heart failure and we were afraid he wouldn't live, an artist friend of mine, Susan Davis, told me that I had to imagine the two of us sitting on the beach together. She did a beautiful watercolor of the scene and gave it to me. I kept that image in my head all through his illness, during the surgery and afterward. I hung it on the wall in my bathroom where I could see it every day. A couple of years later, he and I were sitting on a beach together laughing and playing. He was totally healthy and happy. So was I. Then I remembered the painting and realized that that image I had been carrying around in my mind had actually materialized for me. When I want something good to happen for me or for someone else, I simply try to imagine it. That could be a way of praying as well. It really doesn't matter what you call it.

. . .

I believe reading one's astrological chart can be at least as valuable as therapy, sometimes more so—assuming you have a good astrologer. Astrology has always helped me in dealing with family, friends, bosses, and coworkers, but never has it been as useful as when I am interviewing people, particularly doing profiles. I always look up a person's sign before I see them and it generally gives me a huge advantage. For one thing, as a theater major at Smith, I practiced the Stanislavski method. What that means simply is that you don't play the character, you become the character. I use that approach in interviewing. I learn a person's sign and then I take on the characteristics of that sign. It gives me a huge affinity for the interviewees because I feel I can empathize with them. It's not fake. I really do empathize with them. It definitely seemed to work for me. People did open up to me in ways that they normally didn't, and I was always being asked how I got people to say the things to me that they did. I never told them I read their signs first. They might have thought I was crazy. Maybe they still will, but I don't care anymore. My motto these days is "whatever works." That's certainly my motto for religious beliefs or the lack of beliefs. I don't call anyone else crazy, including those who don't have any beliefs at all. I expect the same respect for me.

Christopher Hitchens, well known for being an adamant atheist, once confided to me that he actually read his daily horoscope and considered it good luck if he found a penny. Richard Dawkins, also a well-known atheist, told me that he's afraid to step on a crack for fear of breaking his mother's back and that he is terrified of haunted houses and would never spend the night in one.

On my desk I have a framed horoscope, which I had a calligrapher copy and on which is drawn a blue Cancerian crab. It is from the day that I had a meeting at the *Washington Post* to decide and agree to spin off my website, On Faith, and join a start-up in New York called Faith Street. It was a huge and scary decision. Even though I had been associated with the *Post* for over forty years and would continue to be on a part-time level, it was a wrench because I had no idea where it would go. I was about to back out that morning when I picked up the paper and read my horoscope. Here's what it said: "You may feel caught in between two worlds: cut off from what you are leaving behind, but not yet connected to your new future. Step forward in FAITH" (Cancer, May 26, 2013).

I did the deal.

· · ·

Although I find it helpful, I have never allowed astrology or any other area of occultism to determine my life. The readings I have are always very personal, almost like sessions with a therapist, focused on my strengths and weaknesses. However, though not prognosticators of events, these interpretations of my chart are a guide to how I can or might move forward. If I am under the influence of Saturn (not good), I just know that I have a hard time ahead and I can prepare for it. If I come under the influence of Venus, it's a pretty sure thing that I will be feeling loving, or of Mercury, that I will be in a creative and communicative mode. If Mercury is retrograde, I may be a little reluctant to sign a contract during that time or make a major business decision, but I would do it if I had to.

At one point, the story broke that Nancy Reagan had her astrologer determine the exact time *Air Force One* should take off, among other scheduling decisions for the president. She was subjected to an enormous amount of flak and ridicule, and it was a huge embarrassment to the White House.

After the assassination attempt on her husband's life, Nancy was naturally terribly shaken and never really felt safe afterward, according to friends. She would do anything she could to protect him. Although I would never have done what she did in suggesting when *Air Force One* should fly, I totally understood why she would turn to her astrologer and even try to control the flights her husband took if she believed that would help. Astrology is like religion in that way. What Nancy was doing was a form of prayer. She did it in a way that was meaningful to her. She was living magically after the attempt on his life.

I understand why people make bargains with God, why they sacrifice, why they get down on their knees, why they beseech, why they perform any kind of ritual. It helps us get through our suffering and doubt and pain. It's what gets us through the night. And what could possibly be wrong with that as long as it doesn't hurt anyone? What may be mysterious or even nonsensical to some might make total sense to others.

. . .

I love the tarot. First of all, the cards are beautiful. Secondly, they tell stories. They represent the magic and the mystical. The actual cards represent so many different layers of our psyche, and when spread out, they can reveal parts of ourselves that we didn't know or understand. I've found that the tarot is never wrong. But again, it is a matter of interpretation.

A good tarot card reader can look at the cards and create a pattern in your life that makes sense. My favorite card lately has become the Fool, which I wasn't drawn to before. He's about faith. He looks as if he's about to step off the edge of a cliff, as though he expects to land safely with no consequences. I never liked that kind of risk. What I now see is that I can't imagine living without faith. Faith is not concrete. It is not clear, but it's positive. It really is about magic and mystery and awe and wonder. And hope. As I say at the end of "Divine Impulses," my video interviews for On Faith, "we are all looking for meaning in our lives, for a sense of the divine," and I ask the interviewee what gives them meaning, what to them is the divine. I've never gotten the same answer twice.

The tarot works for those with any religious beliefs and atheists alike. What the tarot does for me is lay out the cards with their characters and their situations and let me interpret for myself a story that helps give meaning to my life at that moment. It's intriguing as well as fun. It really works and it always gives me a sense of hope. William Butler Yeats, William Blake, Carl Jung, and Italo Calvino all seemed to agree.

From a very young age, I've gathered and kept talismans and amulets. They are objects that contain magical properties and protect the owner or wearer of them from evil. Most people I know have some sort of good luck charm or habit. For some reason even non-believers tend to believe in them and have them around. I have a friend who goes to Ethiopia quite frequently. When I was there I bought a Coptic cross that I keep on my coffee table. This friend gave me another one recently. He told me about being at an event with President Obama at the beginning of his first term and my friend gave the president the Coptic cross he was carrying. Several years later he ran into the president again and Obama pulled it out of his pocket and told him he carries it with him all the time.

Crosses are an obvious talisman, as are mezuzahs, Stars of David, crescents, the hand of Fatima, a Ganesh (the Hindu god), the evil eye, Greek worry beads, rosaries, St. Christopher medals—anything can be a talisman. I have an evil eye hanging on the chandelier in our dining room. I wear a thin bracelet on my right wrist, given to me by a friend, with a small blue evil eye with a diamond in the center. I never take it off.

When my father was in Korea his nickname was Buffalo Bill, and he sent off for bags of buffalo nickels to give to his troops. Everyone including my father carried one for good luck. The deal was that if you met a Buffalo, no matter when, you could challenge him to see if he was carrying a nickel. If someone was not they had to buy the other one a beer. I wear a buffalo nickel on a chain to this day and I have met many Buffalos over the years. Not one has ever been without his nickel.

Around my neck I have two gold chains. One simply has a beautiful Indian gold Ganesh with a ruby at the top. Ganesh is one of the most famous Gods in the Hindu tradition, though followed by Jains and Buddhists as well. He's sort of an all-purpose God. He rules the intellect, new beginnings, and writing. Most important, he's the remover of obstacles. He is easily identifiable for his elephant head. I first learned about Ganesh's powers when I started the website On Faith for the *Washington Post*. A young Hindu colleague told me about him and I immediately adopted him as the talisman for the website. What could be better than the remover of all obstacles? It was magical. The website was an early success, and one obstacle after another seemed to fall away. I wear another tiny gold Indian Ganesh with little diamonds on the other chain. On that chain I also have my buffalo nickel, a small gold labyrinth, a blue porcelain Fabergé egg with a very small evil eye inside, a gold heart with a small sapphire from my mother, and a gold shell from Santiago de Compostela. I'm totally covered and receive protection from all sides.

On my left hand is the ring Ben gave me nine years after we were married—finally—and a diamond band he gave me for an anniversary, which he picked out and bought himself some years later. On my right hand is my wedding ring and my mother's wedding ring, a West Point miniature with a small green tourmaline in the center.

On my bedside table I have a picture of Ben and Quinn and me on the beach at La Samanna, on St. Martin, a resort Ben and I went to for nearly forty years. We had a ritual of going out to look at the sun disappear over the horizon every evening. We always went for Valentine's week in February, and it was the happiest week of the year for me. It was our honeymoon week. Wrapped around the photo is a set of antique turquoise worry beads I bought on the Greek island of Hydra, one of my favorite places in the world.

I have an exquisite, colorful enameled Ganesh on my bedside table as well, and a tiny white pillow with blue embroidered flowers that was on my mother's bed when she died. On my bed I also have the shirt Ben died in. It's a well-worn blue-and-gray-striped French boatneck, long-sleeve cotton T-shirt—his favorite. I still sleep holding on to it every night. I will give it up at some point—Quinn thinks I should, and sooner rather than later; he wants me to stop grieving, but it gives me such comfort at night when I pray to Ben for strength and courage, as I pray to Ganesh and my mother for the same things.

. . .

Over the course of my life, I had been to many astrologers, psychics, palm readers, and tarot card readers. Many of them, though impressive, were questionable, but when I started seeing Caroline Casey, I really hit the jackpot. Caroline has been my personal north star in interpreting the heavens. She's been at it for forty years. I have never known her to be wrong or off base in her readings. She is brilliant at what she does, smart, creative, and original. Her readings are on a level beyond anything I have ever experienced. She mixes in philosophy, religion, history, literature, mythology, and symbolism, along with her specific interpretation of my chart in our sessions. She speaks my language. Readings with her are riveting and fun as well as informative. They're not crystal-ball gazing. She interprets meaningfully, given the position of the planets at the time and day of birth. In an interview in the *Washington Post* Outlook section in 1984, Caroline described it this way:

> The chart is a map of somebody's task, what they've signed up to do in their life. It's a condensed piece of information, describes who someone is, what kind of family situation they were born into, what the major issues and traumas and talents of their life are and why. Like detective work, you're putting all this information together and saying this constructs a picture, it implies a purpose.

Astrology made great sense to me from the first time I was exposed to it at an early age, and it continues to imbue my life with clarity and confidence. I have had my chart done by different astrologers over the years, but always by Caroline at least once a year to see how things have progressed.

When Ben was editor of the *Washington Post*, the paper ran the daily horoscope. As the *Post* grew in stature, especially after Watergate, he was roundly criticized for it, with some people saying it took up too much space and others, more substantive, asking how the *Washington Post* could be considered a serious newspaper if it ran a daily horoscope. "After all," they would say or write sanctimoniously, "the *New York Times* doesn't run the horoscope."

"Nothin' but readers," Ben would respond, always grinning.

He was right. He knew how many of his "serious" readers actually read their horoscopes in the morning. He never considered not running it, though he would constantly tell me it was all nonsense. It was all nonsense to him, of course, until I came home from a reading with Caroline. His first question was always: "What did she say about me?" I never teased him about it. I didn't want to turn him away from the idea that many people liked astrology and especially reading their horoscopes. He was always grudgingly impressed with what she told me.

When Caroline was asked in the *Post* interview why astrology was so popular, she answered:

> *It represents a voice of the irrational, mystical, spirit domain which says that everything is interconnected and interrelated and that you can't pluck one strand of creation without resonating it all. It corresponds to a very real hunger people have for mystery, for how things are mysteriously connected. Astrology says that cynicism is*

just intellectual laziness. There's no future in nihilism; one has to
believe and have faith in something, a larger process.

. . .

I began documenting my sessions with Caroline in November of
1981, when I was pregnant with Quinn. Ben had been going through
a particularly stressful period. The Janet Cooke disaster had happened earlier that year. Janet was a young *Washington Post* reporter
and had been awarded the Pulitzer Prize, only to have it revoked
a few days later when the *Post* learned that she had fabricated the
story she had written and the *Post* had published. This was a huge
upheaval for Ben and, as a consequence, for me, especially because
of my pregnancy.

Caroline told me in a reading that fall that Ben would see all the
things he valued being destroyed but that he would survive. My role
was to be the grounded woman to give him strength. She tasked me
with being the "village shaman," the wisewoman, and that the most
important thing I could do was to "use my fantastic visualizing powers to imagine my baby circled in light." The baby, she said, was
what was grounding me. He was real and symbolic as well. My creative powers were more concrete than Ben's. He had to decide what
he wanted. I could assist him, she said. I could imagine how things
would go for him.

I took what she said to heart and it really worked. When I suddenly started being "Queen Serene," Ben's demeanor changed
dramatically.

In March of 1982, Caroline wrote to me, "It does seem as though
your true mission is a much more serious one—the reconciliation of
Visionary principles, in a serious fashion, into the grown-up social
world. Recognizing yourself as a powerful imager-visionary, and

holding out that possibility to others. That is the highest calling of a mature woman in these spiritually anemic times."

I have to say that letter surprised me. I hadn't really thought of myself before then as a really serious person. It was only when Caroline articulated this impression to me that I began to think about what I was truly meant to do. I was so obsessed with my pregnancy and about my coming role as a mother that anything beyond that didn't actually penetrate. The idea that I was a serious person was there in my mind and began to grow steadily and helped keep me grounded as I was launched into one of my life's most important roles—one of great joy and great challenge—being a mother.

. . .

Two weeks after we got to Long Island in August of 1981, where we were spending the month, I knew I was pregnant and I was preening around sticking out my flat stomach so everyone would know. I was so happy. Ben would not allow me to tell anyone until I was three months along for fear I would have a miscarriage. When, finally, the woman at the grocery store checkout back in Washington asked me if I was pregnant, I hugged her and went flying back to the house to tell Ben and then got on the phone. That fall was heavenly for me.

When it was time for me to have an amniocentesis, my friend Nora Ephron, who had had two sons, Jacob and Max, went with me for encouragement and to hold my hand. I had been going through the miserable divorce from Carl Bernstein with her and we had become very close. "Just don't look at the needle," she said, knowing from my days in the hospital in Tokyo that I was completely needle phobic.

I was the model pregnant woman. I had actually quit smoking and drinking on my fortieth birthday, knowing that I would try to become pregnant. I exercised every day. I took no medicine, not even nose spray at the end when I couldn't breathe. I drank gallons of skim milk. My one craving was for peanut butter, which I ate by the jar. Unfortunately I ate it on whole-grain bread. That's a lot of bread!

I did gain sixty pounds, which was more than I should have, but nobody seemed worried and I wasn't either until I later tried to take it off. I listened to classical music to soothe my baby and talked to him or her all the time as I stroked my increasingly large belly.

I was determined not to get upset by ANYTHING. Everything I had read said that the pregnant mother's state of mind was a huge factor in the child's emotional development. But I couldn't help worrying about the results of the amnio. In fact I was so scared that I had directed the doctor to call Ben with the outcome so that if it was bad, he could come tell me himself.

When he heard, Ben called me at my hairdresser and didn't even say hello. "The baby's fine!" he practically yelled. "It's a boy!" He was so excited. I don't know why but I thought I had desperately wanted a girl. I think it was spending all those weekends in the country with Ben alone in the cabin while he disappeared into the woods for hours at a time. I thought it would be wonderful to have a daughter to play dolls with.

And then there were the clothes. How I had looked forward to shopping for frilly, lacy smocked pink things. I'm glad I found out before the baby was born. I spent that weekend mourning the loss of my daughter, knowing I would never have another child. We had made a deal. Then we named the baby Quinn, and I began bonding with him immediately. I was in love.

Quinn was three weeks overdue. What a nightmare. I was huge. I couldn't sleep, even though I was floating in a cloud of down pillows buttressing my stomach. I couldn't breathe. I could hardly walk. But by God I was determined to go out every night, just to avoid the stress of waiting at home for something to happen.

Finally my water broke. It was around four in the afternoon. I was totally calm. I just knew everything would be fine. I began having contractions. We were supposed to go to Senator John Heinz's for dinner. Jack and Teresa were old friends of ours. Ben said absolutely no. My doctor said I shouldn't bother to come into the hospital until at least three A.M. I was crazed. I couldn't just sit there and stare at Ben while I was having contractions. We went to the dinner. We were late and everyone was already gathered.

"For God's sake, whatever you do, don't tell anyone I'm in labor," I said to Ben as we walked in the door. We had barely entered the living room when Ben said in a very loud voice, "Sally's in labor!," at which point they all backed away from me as if he had announced I had the plague. Only Jack Heinz walked over to me and gave me a hug. It was a typical Washington seated dinner party with several tables filled with members of Congress, the diplomatic corps, the administration, and the press corps.

Dinner was a disaster. I was seated between Joe Kraft, the distinguished *LA Times* columnist, and the powerful Senator "Scoop" Jackson from Washington State. They immediately began discussing Boeing aircraft. If I had been in a normal state, I could probably have gotten them onto another topic, but I could barely concentrate on what they were saying. Every four minutes or so I would have a contraction and let out a low moan or a little yelp. The two of them were drenched in sweat, their eyes filled with terror as they wiped their brows with their napkins and talked over my protruding and rather active (from all the kicking) stomach.

Mercifully dinner ended and we left, much to everyone's relief. We didn't go to the hospital until Ben finally panicked at three A.M.

and insisted. It was still too early for an epidural, but it was really hurting so they called in a hypnotist. That was a bust. My Lamaze birthing coach showed up. Ben had gone to classes with me, but he threw her out after about half an hour of chanting insipid and New Age mantras.

Finally that evening they gave me an epidural and I was feeling great. I decided I wanted to watch *Dynasty* at ten P.M. I was pushing as hard as I could but I'd had enough of Ben yelling "Pant, pant, blow" and asked him to knock it off until the show was over.

Quinn was born at 12:38 A.M. on April 29, 1982. A Taurus. That was good. Ben was a Virgo, I was a Cancer. Two earth signs and one water. What a copacetic happy family we would be.

Quinn didn't cry out right away, and the nurses rushed him over to a table to suction him out. I nearly fainted from fear. Then came the blessed shriek and they all burst out laughing. He had squirted one of them in the face. She said, "Oh, I'm in love."

There are no words to describe the overwhelming heart-bursting love I felt for Quinn the moment they put him in my arms, all wrapped up in a little blanket. *Oh, it's you,* I thought. His eyes were so alert they just scanned my face, darting back and forth to make sure it was really me, the one whose voice he had heard all those months, singing and whispering and cooing to him. "I love you," I said to him. "You can do anything you want to do in this life." Pure joy.

Before I knew it they had whisked him off to the nursery and I relaxed as Ben held my hand and hugged me. He was so proud of himself. This was the first of his four children where he had actually participated in the birth. It made him feel young again. He was even more cocky than usual.

I sent Ben home to get some sleep and I dozed off. When they brought Quinn back to the room, he was as calm and cool and laid-back as you could imagine. The nurse said they had nicknamed him "Mr. Mellow" because, unlike all the other babies, he wasn't crying. He was just casing the joint. Again, we just stared into each other's eyes, mesmerized.

The next morning was the most heavenly day ever, sunny, breezy, with butterflies flapping outside of my window and flowers, flowers everywhere. The breastfeeding coach came in and barely had to instruct us. Quinn and I took to it right away. I think that nursing him was the closest I have ever come to the divine. I knew there was a God, some spirit, some being that had created this moment, this extraordinary connection to another person and to a larger life.

· · ·

My mother and father came immediately. Everyone was thrilled, beaming, and in incredibly high spirits. Ben and I were bursting with pride. Quinn was the most beautiful baby I had ever seen. No, really, he was.

Dr. Agnes Schweitzer, the "dean" of all pediatricians, arrived that afternoon with a smile on her face. She held him and kissed him and then put him on her lap and pulled out her stethoscope. We were all looking at her with great anticipation.

The smile disappeared from her face. She kept listening again and again, appearing more and more worried. I felt a stab of panic. "Please, God," I whispered. Quinn had a heart murmur. I didn't know what that meant. Dr. Schweitzer called Children's Hospital to make an appointment for me to take him in. She was reassuring. Many babies, she said, were born with heart murmurs and they would eventually go away. My sister, Donna, had been born with a heart murmur—she was called a blue baby in those days—and she was fine. I relaxed.

We brought him home two days later. Bob Woodward had sent a bouquet of the most exquisite pale-pink peonies—to this day, my favorite flowers—which I put on the table across from the bed so I could see them. I nursed Quinn every two or three hours during those dreamlike days, staring into his eyes, hardly believing this magical creature was really there, really mine. Sometimes I would tear up with joy, and there were moments when my chest could barely contain my heart.

We went to Children's Hospital for the appointment. The murmur was due to a tiny hole in his heart. I was told not to worry. The holes often closed up naturally in a few years. I was taught to recognize the signs of heart failure just in case, and I was instructed to get him to the emergency room immediately if any of them appeared.

I tried to put that thought out of my head. I tried to enjoy my every second with this incredible gift I had been given, those tiny fingers curled around mine, that adoring penetrating gaze that just bore through me, which I returned threefold.

My birthday is July 1, and I planned a small dinner for about ten of my friends. We were planning to take Quinn to the cabin in West Virginia for the first time that weekend. I had a premonition that something bad was about to happen. I had been worried about Quinn all that week. He seemed to be losing weight and looked a little pale and scrawny. He wasn't nursing as enthusiastically as usual. Dr. Schweitzer had told me earlier that he was the most breast-oriented baby she had ever seen, which pleased Ben enormously. "Like father, like son," he chortled.

I took Quinn to see Dr. Schweitzer the day of the party, and she was a bit concerned but found nothing wrong. When I brought him downstairs for everyone to see that night at the party, however, I suddenly saw him through their eyes. He looked frail, not thriving. I felt sick.

That night at dinner we were discussing astrological signs and I said how pleased I was that the three of us—Ben, Quinn, and I—were so well matched. A friend of mine went on a tear about how insane and stupid and ridiculous astrology was and how nobody with any sense could possibly believe in it. For some reason I went into a rage. She had challenged my beliefs, and I didn't realize until that moment how strongly I held them. I exploded at her. "You believe in God," I said. "Isn't that just as ridiculous? You believe that Jesus Christ was the son of God. How crazy is that? You believe that Jesus died on the cross, was buried, and then rose from the dead and ascended into heaven. And you're telling me that astrology is ridiculous? As least with astrology you have something you can see. You have stars and planets you can chart. With God you have nothing except your own imagination. Don't you dare tell me what I believe is any less logical than what you believe."

This was an incredibly rare outburst for me. I have practically no temper and am almost phobically nonconfrontational. But I was shaking with anger. Everyone was shocked at my emotional outburst. My friend shut up. The evening ended shortly after and they left, but I was so upset I could barely get my breath. Now that I look back on it, I realize that astrology was a great resource, a solace, a hope for what was happening to Quinn. Where others might have begun to pray, to look at the heavens to find God, I looked up to see what was in the stars.

The next morning Ben and I piled Quinn into the back of the car in his baby seat and headed out to West Virginia. Quinn was fussy and wouldn't nurse. We got out there midday and Ben immediately took off for the woods, ax and chain saw in hand, a happy man leaving me in the house with Quinn who was becoming more agitated by the minute. I walked around holding him, trying to quiet him. Nothing worked. I put him in a Snugli and took a walk, which was a bit better. We went down by the river, and the sounds of the rushing water seemed to soothe him and me. I could hear the whine of Ben's chain saw in the distance. He hadn't been up in the country for about five months. He was always a different person after a day in the woods—happy, in a good mood, never depressed.

On this night, however, I was not a happy woman. Something was terribly wrong with my baby. We went to bed early. I put Quinn in a tiny crib next to our bed and he slept. But it became chilly in the room, and when he woke at about six he had inched up to the edge of the bed rail, clearly cold, even in his flannel pajamas. He began to cry and fuss and I knew then that we had to get back to Washington.

Ben drove as fast as he could, but by this time Quinn was having such a hard time breathing that he could barely cry. He was only able to make pathetic little rasping noises. We stopped once to let me walk him around, but it did no good. We got back to Washington and I called the cardiology ward at Children's Hospital. I had the number by the phone just in case. When I described to the nurse what was happening, there was dead silence. "Get him here immediately," she said. "I think he's in heart failure."

So was I.

That night I sat holding Quinn, hooked to all kinds of monitors, in my arms, in a rocking chair in the cardiology ward. I had told Ben to go home. I was alone with my baby. I thought he was dying. A young male resident came into the room and sat on the edge of the bed. I wasn't in the mood for false hope or platitudes. But he sat there with me in silence for a long time. Then he said, "You know I've seen so many babies in heart failure. Yours will be fine." He said it with such certainty that I believed him. I will never forget that moment of kindness. The medication had begun to kick in. Quinn was able to sleep and even nurse a little. I felt desperate and alone and sad, but I also felt a sense that I was being enveloped in love, that I was touched by some divine hand, that I was surrounded by some kind of magic. Maybe he would be fine. Maybe, maybe he would live. I had to believe it. I had to make him believe it. I whispered it to him all night as I rocked and rocked. "You will be fine. You will be fine." I willed it.

That was on a Sunday. On Monday morning, Ben had to be in court to defend a libel case brought by William Tavoulareas, then president of the Mobil Oil Company, against the *Washington Post*.

The next few days were a flurry of doctors and nurses and surgeons and consultants. The hole in Quinn's heart was much larger than had been detected. He would have to have open-heart surgery. However, he had lost so much weight that he was practically down to his birth weight. He would have a greater chance of survival if we could fatten him up. Those horrid words, *chance of survival*. It was impossible to contemplate losing this person, this person who had only been in the world for a few months, but who I had known since the day I named him eight months earlier, who I loved more than I could ever have imagined loving anyone or anything.

A hospital chaplain showed up, pious and overly sympathetic. "How's Mom doing?" he asked. I lost it.

"Mom is not doing well," I said, seething. "Mom is sitting here in this hospital with all of these sick and dying children, mine included, and wondering why God would allow this to happen." He recoiled. "Thank you, but I don't need your help or your prayers." He backed out of the room and fled. I feel bad about that now. Poor guy. He was only trying to help.

Ben came every morning to visit me before he went to the court-house where he would spend the day. My beloved mother showed up around nine each morning, after rounds, with hot tea for me from the cafeteria and the newspapers. She pretty much stayed with me every day. I had blocked all calls to the room except for my mother and father and Ben. I had told friends I did not want any visitors or phone calls. I just needed to be with Quinn every minute with no distractions. Once again, all I could think of was my time in the hospital in Tokyo without my mother. I couldn't allow that to happen to Quinn. I didn't want him out of anyone's arms for a second, either. I had a shower in the room and a bed. My mother brought me a change of clothes each day.

I was living in a dark tunnel. I didn't care about anything or any-one except Quinn. He wasn't gaining weight and wasn't thriving. By then, at nearly three months old, he had only gained two pounds. The doctors couldn't tell when the surgery would be. They were re-luctant to operate when he was so frail. Ben knew I needed a distrac-tion, so he would insist on taking me out of the hospital for dinner every night. I had our wonderful baby nurse, Diane, "Dee Dee," come and hold him while I was out.

Ben would invite another couple to dine with us. The ground rules were that Quinn's name would not be mentioned. They were to come loaded with gossip and stories. It worked and gave Ben and me a little respite from the relentlessness of our anguish.

I called Caroline Casey after the first week. She did his chart. Caroline is not a fake prognosticator. She said his chart was promis-ing, but she added that he should be operated on sooner rather than later. I talked to the doctors. They wanted to wait until he was at least three months or so. I saw him failing every day. I was getting crazed.

Finally they scheduled a surgery date—a Tuesday. Caroline called on Wednesday, the week before surgery. She told me we had to have the surgery that week, that she didn't think Quinn would make it until the following week. My instinct told me she was right.

I went to the surgery team. They didn't operate on Mondays or Fridays. The other days were booked that week. They had one elective on Thursday. I offered to pay for the family to fly to Washington and put them in a hotel for the weekend if they would switch with Quinn. They refused. They had already made extensive plans. I didn't dare tell anyone that my astrologer said he wouldn't make it over the weekend.

I finally convened all the doctors and threw myself on their mercy. I wept and pled and begged for them to do it earlier. They could sense my desperation. I argued that Quinn was failing rapidly as anyone could see. I told them that they had to trust my mother's instinct. I knew in my heart that he would die if the surgery weren't moved up. I must have been convincing. They agreed to operate that Friday. Caroline and I were both overwhelmed with relief.

I decided on Thursday that I would go to the hospital chapel to pray for Quinn's survival. I hadn't prayed for him, really—not in any traditional definition of prayer. I had whispered "please God" a million times over that month that we'd spent in the hospital, but it was more a mantra than a serious and focused prayer. Now I can see it was a prayer but it didn't feel like it then. This time I was going to reach out to God. I was going to really try to believe in him. I was going to give myself over to him, to trust him, to trust that he loved Quinn and me and that somehow my beseeching would make a difference. I was so desperate. I would do anything, even get down on my knees to a deity I was unsure even existed.

The chapel was empty and quiet when I went in. I sat in the back row. Better not to be too close. You never knew how a first date might go.

I sat there quietly for a long time. I waited for something to happen. I waited for God to show himself to me. "If you're there, let me see you," I said . . . prayed. "If you're there, speak to me. If you're there, help me. If you're there, please save Quinn. Please, please, please God, don't let him die. Please!"

Nothing. I got nothing. I felt nothing. I heard nothing. There was nobody there.

Finally, trying to compose myself, I got up to leave. As I reached the door to the chapel, I turned to the altar. "Fuck you!" I said desperately.

. . .

The night before Quinn's operation he was not allowed to eat after midnight. That may have been one of the most painful nights I've ever experienced. All I wanted to do was hold him in my arms. All he wanted to do was nurse. He kept going for my breast, his tiny mouth puckering up, his hands grasping for me. I had to deny him. He was crying, hungry, needy. I couldn't give him what he needed. I was crying and needy. Nobody could give me what I needed, which was assurance that he would survive.

I kept calling for one of the nurses, asking them to rotate holding him so I didn't have to keep rejecting him. Even then he never took his eyes off me, reaching out to me as if I had totally abandoned him, betrayed him.

Finally, exhausted, he slept in his crib. I hovered as close to him as possible, afraid to wake him. Yet I wanted to spend every moment

I still had left with him in case he didn't make it. Somewhere around dawn I couldn't take it anymore. I was overcome with an animal, visceral, raw need, like a mother lion licking her cub. I carefully took off his blanket and his little nightgown. I leaned down and began to kiss his body. I kissed his head and his little pink ears and his eyes and his button nose and his rosebud lips. I kissed his neck and his arms and his little fingers. I kissed his chest, knowing that the next time I saw him there would be an enormous scar all the way down his front. I kissed his legs, scrawny legs that should have been chubby and dimpled at three months. I kissed his baby feet and his precious toes. I wanted to devour him. I wanted to have his taste in my mouth forever if anything happened to him. The love and desperation I felt for my baby was the strongest emotion I had ever experienced. I was in agony. Later I would do the same thing to Ben the night before he died. I would feel the same way.

Strangely, never have I been so relieved as I was when Ben and the doctors showed up that morning. The anticipation had been unbearable. The ghastly night was over. It was time.

Once we were in the surgical suite, the team, outwardly calm and reassuring, came to get Quinn, but the furrowed brows and worried expressions were not lost on me. I held him one last time and let them take him from me.

As they disappeared with him I sank to the floor in a heap. There was not an ounce of bravery in my body. Ben reached down and pulled me up to him and held me as tightly as he could. "Just think," he said to comfort me, "now he'll never have to go to war."

That may have been the one thing he could have said that would help. It implied that Quinn would live. It meant that with this surgery, he would be 4F, unable to serve for medical reasons. Having seen the results of war, I relaxed a bit in Ben's strong arms. God, I loved this man.

We sat in the hospital cafeteria, Ben and I, drinking coffee and tea, waiting. It would be hours. Thankfully, Ed Williams and Kay Graham showed up to keep us company. By the time the surgical team came out to get us, I was half crazed. The operation, they told us, was a success. They had closed the hole in Quinn's heart. It had been much larger than what they had expected. It was the size of a dime. They were glad they had done the surgery that day and not waited. He may not have lasted until the following week. Caroline had been right.

That afternoon they took Quinn from the recovery room to the ICU. When they finally let us see him, he was still sedated and was hooked up to so many machines and had more tubes running in and out of his little body than one would have thought possible. Again I fell apart.

We were not allowed to hold him. We both put a finger in each of his tiny hands and felt his grip. He knew we were there. I whispered in his ear, "Mommy loves you." Ben whispered to him as well, and his deep growly voice seemed to arouse him.

The doctors swore Quinn was going to be well and insisted we go home. We were both beyond exhausted, but instead of heading home to sleep, we ended up unexpectedly having a party. Coincidentally, the day of Quinn's surgery was the same day that one of the *Post*'s reporters was found guilty of libel in the Tavoulareas case. (The case dragged on for years, through appeal after appeal, until the U.S. Court of Appeals ruled in 1987 in favor of the *Post* that the 1979 story was "substantially" true and not libelous. Tavoulareas appealed that verdict to the Supreme Court, which refused to hear the case and the whole ordeal was over.)

That very night Ben invited everyone who had participated in the trial—the lawyers, the reporters, the editors—to come over for carryout Chinese. In a daze, I ordered the food, Ben got the booze, then I went upstairs to take a shower. Halfway through washing my hair, I collapsed with relief into a pool of water and shampoo, streams of water coming down onto my head and into my eyes and mouth.

I finally pulled it together, got dressed, went downstairs, greeted my guests, drank quite a bit of wine, commiserated about the trial (of course we would appeal), and generally played the part of the hostess. When everyone had left, Ben and I went upstairs and fell into each other's arms. In retrospect, the gathering was a good thing to do. It made everyone feel better, including Ben and me.

. . .

Quinn lived. The next week was a nervous and joyous blur. Amazingly, Quinn was allowed to go home in less than a week, a neat seam from the bottom of his throat to his belly button. I—we—went back to nursing. I had been pumping while he was in the ICU, a very unsatisfactory experience. I didn't want to let him out of my arms or my sight. A week later we were able to take him up to Grey Gardens on Long Island.

I had a telephone reading with Caroline on August 18. She talked about Quinn's "basic, fundamental earthy, hearty soul," saying that it was his own wisdom that made us do the surgery earlier. She said he had been "semihovering," deciding if he wanted to be here. His special connection to me was so strong that she was sure he and I would be great collaborators in this life and that our intense bonding would go on until November. This, she thought, was a time in my life and Quinn's "where we are both creating a strong spiritual family vortex."

On the first of November, exactly six months to the day that I had started nursing Quinn, I was holding him in my arms and we were gazing into each other's eyes, totally connected, as though there was no other human in the world. When he finished, he looked at me meaningfully, took his tiny little hand, now getting pudgy and dimpled, put it on my breast, and pushed it away. He never went for my breast again. I would have thought I would be upset, but I understood completely. He was ready. Even though it seemed as if the bonding was ending, in fact the bonding was just continuing and deepening.

. . .

When Quinn was born, I never even considered having a christening—that is, not until he had his heart surgery and survived.

When I first approached Ben with the possibility, he was stunned that I was even thinking about it. In many ways, I was too. Yet I felt overwhelmed with gratitude and the need to celebrate my child's life. What I didn't know then was how meaningful it would ultimately be for Quinn.

We asked four friends to be godparents. Ben chose his friends Edward Bennett Williams and Art Buchwald, and I chose my friends Nora Ephron and Ann Pincus. We decided to have the christening at a small chapel at the National Cathedral and Ben asked his close childhood friend Paul Moore, bishop of New York, to do the honors. He was one of the most liberal Episcopalians in the country, a man who had lived in the ghetto in New Jersey with his family for years, ministering to the poor, and he had been the first person to ordain openly gay priests. He refused because Art and Nora were Jewish and Ed was Catholic. I have rarely seen Ben that angry. He quickly regrouped and invited Father James Wendt, a liberal priest from St. Stephen and the Incarnation, an inner-city church for which Ben had volunteered for years. We also changed the venue. We would have the christening at our favorite hangout, Restaurant Nora, around the corner from our house near Dupont Circle.

The day came, a week from our wedding anniversary, October 20, and less than a week away from Quinn turning six months old. We set up a makeshift altar on a table with a white cloth. Happily, Quinn was in great health and, though he looked a little scrawny for his age, he looked like a miracle to me in his little white jumper and round collared shirt.

We had champagne in the bar area (somehow I always manage to have champagne at my rituals; no wonder I've come to love them so much) and then moved into the main dining room for the ceremony. A harp was playing. Father Wendt, resplendent in a white robe and long flowered embroidered shawl, read a passage from the Bible about Isaac and Sarah, who bore a child in their old age. He had just returned from the Holy Land and had brought water from the River Jordan "old water." Carefully holding Quinn, he placed salt on his lips and put wine on his hands. He said a blessing and then bent him over the crystal bowl to sprinkle the water on his head. Deeply moved, I—this person who had always been suspicious of organized religious ritual—had turned into a convert in one afternoon.

The four godparents made speeches, then Ben and I spoke.

The pièce de résistance was an armored case brought by Art Buchwald, a time capsule. I had provided pencil and paper for each guest and they were to write a note to Quinn. The case would be sealed, hidden, and opened on his eighteenth birthday. It was a lovely moment as each person, fortified with champagne, took the time to thoughtfully pen their messages to Quinn. People began to leave as he slept in my mother's arms. I was overcome with happiness. If I hadn't been convinced about rituals before, that one convinced me that life without them would be very bleak. I had found meaning in a very powerful way.

When the time came for Quinn's eighteenth birthday, naturally I planned a party to celebrate the opening of the capsule and the reading of the messages and invited all the earlier guests plus newer friends we had made. I had a little booklet printed up with all the notes and a picture on the front of Father Wendt christening Quinn.

I read them aloud at the party, and there wasn't a one that wasn't touching. Ben wrote:

> *My first hope for you 18 years from today would be that you are as alive and as well and as loved as you are today. If I have made it, what a lucky man I will be. You have already enriched my life beyond—way beyond—expectations. If I didn't make it, no grief please. Remember me as you remember and value your friends, and go hard for a life that honors you, me and them. You have already shown me, and your wonderful mother, that you can triumph and that you want to triumph. That's a big edge. Somewhere along the way I have learned to treasure this saying from the Jewish fathers: Love work, hate domination, and don't get too close to the ruling class. It's yours. And so is my love and my admiration. Dad.*

I couldn't live up to that but I had written:

> *You are truly a love child—my happiness. My joy. You are*
> *everything I ever wanted in my life. You fulfilled me in a way I*
> *never knew possible. I love you more than my life. Your mother,*
> *Sally.*

Quinn's birth and his christening marked a major turning point in my spiritual life.

Chapter 16

I don't think that faith, whatever you're being faithful about,
really can be scientifically explained. And I don't want
to explain this whole life business through truth, science.
There's so much mystery. There's so much awe.

—Jane Goodall, in conversation with Bill Moyers,
Bill Moyers Journal, PBS

Nothing reveals to us more clearly that we are dependent on grace and love than becoming a parent—and this is doubly true for parents of children with special needs.

How can I possibly describe Quinn? *Magical* is the first word that comes to mind. He's like a woodland creature, a nymph who appears from behind the trees in the forest or out of a gurgling brook or perched on a rock sparkling in the sun. I told him when he was first born he had "the magic," and I've told him that all his life.

Although my mother had "the magic," as did Ben, Quinn has it in excess. He is a joyous, kind, funny, smart, loving human being, without an ounce of malice in him. He is trusting, too trusting at times. He's friendly and loves to be held, even now in his thirties.

A few years after Quinn was born, I consulted a psychic who was in town giving readings to some of my friends. She told me that Quinn had been abandoned in a forest in his past life and had virtually raised himself. He had chosen Ben and me to be his parents in this life because he knew he would be most cherished by us. He was certainly right about that.

I'm unsure of my views on past lives, but what I do know is that what she said struck a chord with me. I had the sense that this tiny being had come from a place where he had not been loved, that he craved the love he had never had, that he knew he could not survive without it, and that he would now get all the love he needed.

• • •

Svetlana Godillo was a Washington astrologer whom I had gotten to know. She was Polish by birth but had been married to a Russian, then an American. She spoke with a thick accent. She had masses of unruly dark hair, wore scarves and bandanas, large hoop earrings, chains and crosses, many layers of silks and paisleys, and colorful draped clothing. Her apartment seemed decorated to resemble her. She was the queen of fringe. There were always candles and soft lighting. She created an atmosphere of mystery. To her, everyone was "my dahlink." She was dramatic and very opinionated.

I actually started seeing Svetlana before Caroline Casey, and I thought she was pretty good (although once I went to Caroline, nobody could compare to her). Early on, I sent everyone to Svetlana. My mother went. I sent Barry Goldwater. By 1979, she had gained such a reputation that I convinced the Style editor that he ought to ask Svetlana to write a column about Washington political figures. He did and she did and it was an instant hit. She wrote the way she talked, and she did the charts of everybody who was anybody in Washington, laying their lives bare on the page for all to see.

Things were going swimmingly for a while, at least until Svetlana began to believe her own press, bought into her own power, and turned into a kind of monster. She started fudging her astrological findings to conform to her personal and political opinions. I caught on before most people did because I knew what her positions on the issues were. It was malpractice, I thought, and certainly spiritually unethical. I warned her this was not acceptable. Readers began to complain. The editors caught on. Svetlana had to go. They fired her. She went ballistic and blamed me.

In the meantime, I had begun seeing Caroline and had not had a reading with Svetlana for a while. Then Quinn was born and we went through the days and weeks of agony. When I came back from Long Island after that summer, Svetlana called me. She was so sugary I could barely recognize her. "Dahlink," she said, "all is forgiven." She said she wanted to give me a reading for Quinn as a baby present. So I gave her Quinn's information and showed up at her den a week or so later.

What she did was hateful, and I knew halfway through what was going on. She gave me a devastatingly brutal assessment of Quinn and his life. He would never be able to go to school, would never have friends, would be partly "retarded," would never have a job or a relationship, and furthermore, she purred, narrowing her eyes with a feline grin on her face, he was gay. As I got up to leave, she gave me a big hug and a kiss. "So sorry, dahlink, but I must tell you the truth as I see it. It's all in the stars."

Even though I had had Caroline's wonderful reading of Quinn's chart (and by the way everything she ever said about him has been true), I was still undone. What if . . . what if Caroline had misinterpreted Quinn's chart and Svetlana was right? She had managed to create enough doubt in me that I lost my confidence and couldn't stop holding Quinn.

I didn't believe her. She was wrong. She had done this to get revenge on me for getting fired. She was the devil incarnate and misusing her talent and her powers. I went into a slow burn, getting madder and madder. I couldn't stop thinking about her, which made me want my own revenge. I decided to put a hex on her. I felt I had no choice. What she had done was heinous. Consequences be damned—and contrary to my vows and against my brother's warnings—I would put a hex on her.

Again I told Ben what I planned to do. During that time, Barry Goldwater was living with my parents a few blocks away from Ben and me, and we would often have dinner with the three of them. Occasionally the subject would come up about the women in our family being psychic. Daddy was used to it, having spent vacations in Statesboro. Barry didn't disbelieve. He was an honorary Native American, a member of the Navajo nation, and understood mysticism. Daddy and Barry indoctrinated Ben. They used to joke about not wanting to "cross the Quinn girls."

On December 31, 1982, someone found Svetlana's body. She had dropped dead of a cerebral hemorrhage. She was only in her mid-to-late fifties.

I was consumed with dread. All I could think of was the last two hexes before Svetlana. Had that been the cause of Quinn's illness? Had I brought that on him myself? Was I responsible for all his and Ben's and my suffering? I couldn't discount it.

I vowed once again never to put another hex on anyone. Believe me, I haven't, though I have to admit to being sorely tempted on occasion.

Ben found the whole idea of these hexes completely ridiculous, as do most people. However, when he got mad at someone, he'd look at me with a mischievous grin and say, "Go get 'em, Sal."

I still don't know whether I believe in hexes or not. All I can say is that there always seemed to be some cause and effect. If ever there was the slightest chance I had been the cause of someone's demise, I didn't see how I could live with the guilt.

Never have I regretted anything more. I wanted to apologize, to ask for forgiveness of the victims or their families, but I was too ashamed, and I also knew that they would think I was completely nuts. Everything about them still haunted me.

I told my brother, Bill, who read me the riot act. "You have got to stop doing this," he said. He pointed out that on some psychic or spiritual level I probably did have something to do with what happened to these three people. He said one way I could make amends was by some form of reparations, which would be more than simple financial or material reparations. He strongly felt that what was needed was a catharsis, a change of heart and mind, in my psyche if not my soul, so that any and all temptation to repeat these actions would never again occur.

I thought for a long time about what I could do and came up with the idea of donating money to a suicide prevention watch, the American Cancer Society, and the American Heart Association. I know there will never be a way to fully expiate my actions. However, it did help me to better understand the psychological power religion holds over sinners. I finally understood the incredible relief of confession. "Forgive me, Father, for I have sinned." I can't explain how much lighter I feel having told these stories. I have had a catharsis, a change of heart, mind, and soul.

It's still all so mysterious to me.

· · ·

The early years with Quinn are almost a blur to me. It felt like we practically lived at Children's Hospital. It was the only place I really felt safe and secure. At home I was always dreading the next thing that could go wrong with him, the next ambulance ride, the next grim look on a doctor's face.

Every time I took Quinn to Children's Hospital, I would feel sorry for myself. Then I would see a child, hooked up to an IV, completely bald and withered like an old person, being wheeled into the elevator by a parent. How dare I feel sorry for myself? I should feel lucky. I was like the man who felt sorry for himself because he had no shoes until he saw the man with no feet. I didn't want to feel lucky, goddamnit! I felt cheated out of my own misery. I wanted to feel sorry for myself. I've since learned that that doesn't work.

Quinn had a terrible speech impediment early on. He was born without a pharyngeal flap, which is the flap that regulates the air between the nose and the mouth. Because of that he spoke very nasally and was hard to understand. I once took him to the drugstore and he told the druggist he wanted some candy. The druggist realized there was a problem and asked him to repeat himself. Quinn did and the guy still didn't understand him. Deeply apologetic and embarrassed, the druggist asked him a third time. Quinn looked at me with dismay. "Mom," he said, "what is *his* problem?" Regardless of his many problems, Quinn had (and has) enormous self-confidence.

One day more recently, after Quinn had had another disaster at an airport, going to the wrong gate and missing his plane, he seemed his usual unfazed self. "Mom," he said to me rather philosophically, "I think I have too much confidence. It's a good thing I was born with learning disabilities, otherwise I would be a real asshole."

Quinn had constant ear infections with quickly spiking temperatures, eventually leading to ear surgery. He had grand mal, petit mal, and atonal seizures starting at age two and was diagnosed with epilepsy. He had a partially collapsed lung and a compromised immune system, so he had pneumonia and bronchitis constantly, resulting in a tonsillectomy. At one point the doctors thought he had cancer and later cystic fibrosis. Luckily he had neither. His chest was concave due to his heart surgery and he also developed scoliosis of the spine, which caused him to appear bent over. Although he outgrew his epilepsy after four years, he would later develop severe migraines, which caused debilitating pain, vomiting, seizures, and loss of consciousness. His feet were malformed and were eventually operated on when he was in college. He would have four throat surgeries to correct his pharyngeal flap.

Despite all his physical challenges, Quinn was a natural athlete like Ben. Ben was a fabulous tennis player, and Quinn had all his moves. Quinn's coach said he had huge promise and one of the best natural serves he had ever seen. However, Quinn didn't like to play tennis. He admitted that he didn't like to lose, but he didn't like the other person to lose either because it made him feel bad. Not like his father! Early on Ben told Quinn that he would give him a thousand dollars if he could beat him at tennis. Years later, when Ben could barely get out on the court, Quinn would not beat him. He couldn't bear to best his father.

We were told to apply to the Lab School, a school for children with learning disabilities. I drove over to the school and parked across the street to have a look at it. There was a big shuttered and abandoned castlelike edifice with a small, ugly, institutional-looking building behind it that had once been a home for unwed mothers. The director's office was a stone shed. I sat in the car for nearly an hour, in despair, thinking about how this was not what I had in mind for my child. I was dealing with grief from a loss of expectations. Nonetheless, we enrolled him the next week.

At four he was the youngest child to ever attend. He wasn't the best student, but he managed to survive there, with lots of tutoring, until he went off to a special boarding school his freshman year.

Quinn's learning challenges were apparent as early as nursery school, but they were not obviously diagnosable. He was bright, good at chess, and savvy. When he was six, he decided that Ben and I used too many swear words—a hazard of being journalists for both of us and of having been in the navy for Ben. We really did try to tamp it down, but not all that successfully. Quinn told us he wanted us to pay him for each swear word and set the price for penalties himself. We agreed. One night shortly after this pact, a rather conservative couple we barely knew came by for drinks. Quinn came in to say good night. He had a wad of cash in his hands, which he proudly showed off.

"And where did you get all that money?" asked the woman in a singsong voice one uses for children.

"My parents give it to me when they say bad words," Quinn replied. The woman looked a bit askance.

"How much?" asked the husband.

Quinn beamed. "Well, *motherfucker* is two dollars." He had read the room perfectly.

. . .

The year Quinn was eight, he started seeing a new psychologist. I didn't like her from the beginning. I thought she didn't know what she was doing, but she had been highly recommended and I hoped that Quinn might get something out of it. I was willing to try anything. She insisted on testing Quinn. A week later she called to say she had the test results and asked us for a meeting. With no expression she said she was sorry to inform us that Quinn had tested very poorly, terribly, in fact. The sad news was that he would never go to high school, never have a job, never have a relationship—essentially, never have a life. She had taken the liberty of holding a place for him in an institution for the mentally challenged, she told us.

Ben practically had to carry me out to the car. His reaction was that she was full of shit. I didn't get there quite as quickly, but when I did, I was outraged. Ben knew and I knew in my heart that she was completely wrong. We knew this child. We thought Quinn was extraordinary in so many ways. He just had a different way of learning and simply couldn't take tests.

We called the Lab School. This was the first they had heard of the testing and her conclusions and suggestions. They were equally outraged. Needless to say, he stayed at the Lab School and never went back to that psychologist. Even now, though, I get angry just thinking about her.

. . .

Twice I've been visited by someone who has died. The first time was Adrien Lescaze, our friends' young son who died in Children's Hospital at the time Quinn had one of his surgeries. The night he died I was in my bedroom at home when I was awakened by a noise. I looked up at the ceiling in the corner of the room and there was Adrien. He was hovering, as if about to take off. He said he had come to me because I would understand—because of Quinn—what his mom was going through, and he wanted me to tell her that he was happy and that he would be fine. Then he disappeared. The next morning I wrote Becky, his mother, and told her exactly what had happened and the message that Adrien had given me. She took enormous comfort in the letter and she told me that for years she carried it with her wherever she went. I get goose bumps even now just thinking about it.

The only other time this has happened to me was when Ben and I were staying on Martha's Vineyard at Kay Graham's house. Kay had had a dinner the night before, and a lot of our friends were there including Bob Woodward and our mutual closest friend, the national editor Larry Stern, who lived next door to us in Washington. He had just turned fifty. We had all had a lot of wine, and after dinner Larry and I were talking in the living room. At one point Larry, one of the wittiest people I knew, turned to me and said, ominously, "The dark witch's Sabbath has begun." I had no idea what he was talking about. I decided we had all had too much to drink and called it a night.

The next morning, Ben and Kay and some others were playing tennis when I got a call. Larry had just had a heart attack and was being taken by ambulance to the Vineyard hospital. We jumped in the car and headed to the hospital ourselves. It was hot and stuffy, and I rolled down the window. As I did, Larry flew in the window and, as if holding on so that he wouldn't blow away, said he had come to say good-bye. He said he had tried to warn me the night before of what was going to happen. "Tell Ben to be careful," he said. By the time we got to the hospital, Larry had been pronounced dead.

A year later the now famous story by reporter Janet Cooke appeared in the *Washington Post*. It was a story about a child drug dealer named Jimmy, brilliantly written and reported. The problem was that it wasn't true. It wasn't until she won the Pulitzer Prize that the facts came out. Ben was universally castigated by the press and the public. He offered to resign. It was only because he worked for Don Graham that his resignation was not accepted. It was the darkest moment of his career.

. . .

A couple of years before we had that unpleasant report from the psychologist, I had another experience that confirmed my belief in Quinn's special talents. It began when I went to a health spa in California. I was asked the first night if I would like to sign up for a labyrinth walk. I had never heard of the labyrinth; to me a labyrinth simply meant a maze. It was described as a circle where you walk to the center and back, and it is used as a meditation tool. I declined. It sounded too hokey and New Agey for me. However, one of the counselors said that a lot of businessmen had been there for men's week and many of them who walked it swore it had changed their lives. That intrigued me. I signed up for the nighttime walk.

The labyrinth was behind the buildings on a slope in a clearing in the woods, amid a grove of oak trees, their curling branches nearly touching our heads. Torches and candles burned and, as I recall, there was some drumming going on. We were all dressed in pale kimonos. It was very mysterious, and I liked it right away. We were told to concentrate on something important to us, a question or a problem, and then to walk one by one slowly toward the center. Though this labyrinth looked like a maze, it was not one you could get lost in. The path led directly to the center where we were to pause, focus on the issue at hand, and when we were ready, to go back the way we had come, this time more quickly if we felt like it.

I walked it with a number of women, some walking faster and passing others, some taking their time. I don't even remember what I concentrated on; at that moment for me it was more of a game than anything else. I didn't have any particular epiphany, but the walk was pleasant enough. What didn't appeal to me was the group experience. I found it hard to concentrate when others were passing me or walking before or behind me.

I read up a bit on labyrinths and discovered they originated on the island of Crete with King Minos of Knossos. They were a great part of Greek mythology and culture. Later the labyrinth was adopted by other cultures and certain religions. During the Middle Ages, Christians who couldn't go on pilgrimages to the Middle East would often walk the labyrinth as a symbol of their journey, sometimes on their knees. Probably the most famous one is on the floor of Chartres Cathedral in France. It is often used for meditation, but it can symbolize the search for meaning in one's life as well.

A day or two later, before dinner, I decided to go up to the grove alone. The sun was beginning to set, my favorite time of day. It was warm with a slight breeze rustling the branches. The trees were casting their shadows on the labyrinth. It felt instantly mystical to me. I stood for a long time at the entrance and concentrated on Quinn. Quinn was around six or seven at the time and had so many medical and learning problems that I was constantly distraught. I almost never left him, but Ben had been insistent that I really needed to get away and he was right.

Slowly I began to follow the winding path into the center of the labyrinth. When I reached it, the evening was so still that my senses were heightened and I could hear twigs breaking and birds twittering and the wind rustling. I sat down in the middle, cross-legged, my back turned from the entrance, and began to meditate. For a long time I kept my eyes closed. Then I looked up. What I saw astonished me. It seemed to clarify everything that I was wondering about. I hadn't noticed before but right in front of me, surrounded by the oaks, was a magnificent evergreen tree with wide-spreading branches that seemed to be reaching out to embrace me. It was so much more beautiful than all the other trees. Suddenly I saw Quinn as the evergreen tree. He was alone in the midst of all these other trees, but he was the most gorgeous tree of all. Despite all his problems and his differences, he stood out among them as the special beautiful tree. I just sat there in the center of the labyrinth, thinking of my precious child and how unique he was in this world and how much I loved him. It also made me realize that I needn't worry about him so much anymore. He was going to be fine. He was going to be Quinn.

That walk did change my life.

It wasn't over yet. The following year I had a reservation to go back to the California spa. Then we got word that the cognitive testing Quinn had been scheduled for at Children's Hospital had been postponed until the week I was to be away. I decided to cancel, but again Ben insisted I go, saying there was nothing I could do but sit outside the doctor's office and wait. Ben would take him, and I needn't worry. I went.

The day of his test I decided to go to the labyrinth to walk it at the exact moment his testing would begin. Happily, I was alone once more. I concentrated seriously on Quinn's test, praying he would do well. Slowly I began to walk the labyrinth until I got to the center. Once again, I sat in the center and stayed there, focusing on the grand evergreen for the amount of time the test would take. Then I got up and made my way back to the entrance, glancing one last time over my shoulder for good measure.

When I got back to Washington, Ben and I were summoned to the hospital to get the results of Quinn's tests. The doctors looked particularly grim. They went over the numbers with us. They were terribly sorry to tell us, they said, but he had scored miserably on all the tests. However, and they brightened, there was one test on which he had the highest score they had ever seen. "What was that?" we asked. "The maze," the doctors replied.

. . .

It was only recently that I remembered having written about religion in my second novel, *Happy Endings,* and I was stunned to realize that so many of the thoughts that I have today are evident throughout that novel. My main character, Allison, is an atheist who has lost a baby girl and, in one scene, confronts a Catholic priest with her rage at a God who could allow such suffering. "But you must have an answer," she says, "for why a supposedly all-powerful good God would cause suffering. Otherwise you wouldn't have devoted your life to him."

The priest responds quietly: "We are faced with a leap of faith here. Faith is ultimately not the result of a rational conclusion."

To which Allison lashes out: "Bingo! . . . You've just said the magic words."

Reading this again recently, I could see all my questions about faith and God bubbling to the surface at that time. It wasn't until much later that I learned the word *theodicy.* There was actually a word for what I was thinking and feeling.

Theodicy is a theological construct that tries to answer this question of the seeming paradox of a divine being allowing so much suffering in the world. It is best summed up by Greek philosopher Epicurus:

> *Is God willing to prevent evil but not able?*
> *Then he is not omnipotent.*
> *Is he able, but not willing?*
> *Then he is malevolent.*

Is he both able and willing?
Then whence cometh evil?
Is he neither able nor willing?
Then why call him God?

. . .

Quinn was sick so often that sometimes I would just shut down from fear and exhaustion and sorrow. One year in a ten-day period around my birthday I wore the same ugly yellow T-shirt and white cotton pants every single day as they got dirtier and dirtier. I didn't wash my hair. I didn't put on makeup. I was listless and detached. Ben was seriously worried about me. I knew I had to pull it together when he sent me a bouquet of yellow roses for my birthday. I hated yellow. Ben knew this. Subconsciously he must have been thinking of my yellow T-shirt.

When Quinn was a young teenager, he went to Children's Hospital for his regular speech therapy sessions. His therapist began to suspect that he might have a particular syndrome. She had a friend at the National Institutes of Health who was working on a project having to do with a fairly recently discovered syndrome called Shprintzen syndrome, named after the doctor who had identified it. It later became known as VCFS, or velo-cardio-facial syndrome.

VCFS manifests itself in some 180 different symptoms. The most prevalent are heart problems, voice and throat problems, and some forms of facial deformity. Quinn had a bone on one side of his jaw that jutted out just slightly, which had never been explained.

We went to New York to meet Dr. Robert Shprintzen and for Quinn to be tested. When we walked into his office, he took one look at Quinn and told us that he had VCFS. The tests proved positive. Because it is hereditary in 50 percent of the cases, Ben and I were tested too, but both of us were negative. This was a genetic mutation. I was distraught, but Ben did not have to carry me out this time.

If you read the description of VCFS, it is horrifying. As it turns out, Quinn has a very mild case. Some patients actually are admitted to institutions for mental and emotional disorders. There can be terrible facial deformities. There are those who die of heart problems. We were lucky. (There's that word again!)

Despite continuing worries, in some ways I was relieved. At least we had answers. We finally knew why Quinn had been through all this. Most of the medical problems he had had were symptoms of VCFS and manifested in the syndrome. I really had begun to believe that Quinn and Ben and I were under some kind of curse. Was I paying over and over again for those hexes? Every time we turned around something else was wrong with him. As it turned out it was just one thing, one disorder with many faces.

· · ·

When Quinn finished his freshman year at the Lab School, it was clear it wasn't working for him anymore. The high school wasn't as supportive as the lower school had been and he wasn't doing well. He was miserable and cried every day before he went to school.

Much to my dismay, Quinn wanted to go away to boarding school. I couldn't stand the idea of letting him go, but we made appointments for him to look at several schools in New England, including the Gow School for boys, the oldest boarding school for the learning disabled in the country. It was a spectacular campus outside of Buffalo, New York. Quinn loved it. After touring it, we left for Boston where we spent the night. The next morning we were heading down Storrow Drive to see another school on the Cape. I hadn't realized how upset I was at the thought of his leaving when suddenly I had an excruciating pain in my chest; I felt as though a rock had fallen on me. The pain ran down my arms and I was having trouble breathing. I was sure I was having a heart attack.

Just then an ambulance pulled up next to us and stopped at a red light. Not wanting to alarm Quinn, I said to Ben in French, "I think I'm having a heart attack." Without hesitating, Ben put down his window and yelled at the ambulance driver, "My wife's having a heart attack." With that the ambulance turned on the siren, pulled over in front of our car, and before I knew it I was strapped to a stretcher and headed for Massachusetts General Hospital, which just happened to be right in front of us, with Ben and Quinn following in the car. Soon I was hooked up to tubes and Ben was consulting with the cardiologist.

It turned out that nothing was wrong with me—nothing but stress. I was released in a few hours. We never went to see any of the other schools.

Quinn went to Gow that fall. The head of the Lab School told us that it was much too rigorous academically for him and that he would flunk out. The math professor at Gow told Quinn that some people could do math and others could not and that Quinn would have to accept that he was one who could not. Quinn made the varsity tennis team that year as a freshman, and at the end of the year he won the math prize and made the honor roll. Good old Quinn. He never stops confounding people.

One of the happiest days of my life was while he was at Gow. He made a speech to the National Association for Learning Disabilities at the New York Hilton in front of eight hundred people and got a standing ovation. Ben was as emotional as I was. The three of us went back to the Mark Hotel bar and celebrated with a bottle of champagne.

After Gow, Quinn went to Landmark College, the only college in the country for those with learning disabilities. It was not a total success. He needed more structure. He stayed for two years. He then studied film at American University the following year and stayed at home while he was having two foot surgeries. Finally he spent a year at the New York Film Academy, which he loved. We were terribly worried about what he would do, but he got hired by a wonderful film-maker, Mark Muheim, who kept him on for several years.

Quinn is an idea machine. He's managed to create a success-ful career for himself doing many different great projects. He has worked in film, launched a successful website for young adults with learning disabilities (friendsofQuinn.com) that was later acquired by the National Center for Learning Disabilities, and authored a book titled *A Different Life*, which later became the inspiration for an HBO documentary. He and Ben also did a book together, *A Life's Work: Fathers and Sons*.

The only thing missing was a girlfriend. Quinn had never really had an actual girlfriend, though he had dated sporadically. One Christmas about eight years ago I was given a gift of a reading from an astrologer, Gilbert Picinich, who turned out to be very good. I continued to consult him occasionally when Caroline was away for long stretches of time or unavailable. I had him do a reading for Quinn and Ben. As a present, I typed up their readings and put them in an envelope under the tree. The astrologer told me, as had Caroline all through these years, that Quinn was going to be fine. He said he was going to meet someone he would marry soon. He also said he must take yoga lessons. So I called a friend of mine to get the name and number of her fabulous yoga teacher, Pari Williamson, who was known as the best in Washington. I signed him up for six lessons and put that in an envelope under the tree too. Quinn took one yoga lesson with Pari, and they were engaged in two months and married two years later. Quinn adored her, as did Ben and I.

Part Three

MEANING

To find meaning in the mystery of existence is
life's final and fascinating challenge.

—Huston Smith, *The World's Religions*

Chapter 17

There is not one big cosmic meaning for all, there is only
the meaning we each give to our life, an individual meaning,
an individual plot, like an individual novel, a book for each person.

—Anaïs Nin

The death of a parent seems a natural time for someone to raise questions about meaning, purpose, one's own mortality, or the afterlife. For whatever reason, I did not experience the deaths of each of my parents as provoking religious questions but certainly spiritual feelings.

My mother had her first major stroke in early December when she was seventy-four. It was the night of the Kennedy Center Honors, and Ben and I were at the event. Apparently Mother had been standing in the kitchen, spooning her bacon grease into a frying pan, when she collapsed on the floor. Quinn, who was ten, was spending the night with my parents and ran into the library to get my father, who had just turned eighty-five, and he called 911.

Quinn rode in the ambulance to George Washington Hospital with my mother, which totally traumatized him. This had been my worst nightmare. I had been begging her to quit smoking and eating fried foods and encouraging her to exercise.

She went to Pritikin, the rigorous health spa in California and kept the diet for a year or so until she had a bacon relapse. The only residual was that she got a cat and named it Pritikin. She joined an exercise class at the Watergate with friends, which lasted for a few short months until she got bored. I tried to suggest that if she didn't mend her ways she would have another stroke and either die or be permanently impaired.

Mother seemed terribly weak that whole holiday season, though she did make it through her fifty-third anniversary in mid-December. I knew then the big one was about to hit and it did, a month later, at the end of January, shortly before her seventy-fifth birthday. This time she ended up at Walter Reed Army Hospital and couldn't speak or walk for days.

After a few months of rehab, she seemed to be recovering. Daddy spent most of his time at Walter Reed. Ward 72, where Mother was and which no longer exists, was for military VIPs—three and four stars—a kind of palace, very opulent. Daddy actually loved being there, most of all when he wasn't sick. Orderlies served him dinner on a tray when he was in Mother's enormous suite with spectacular views of the city and saluted him and smartly responded to his every command with "Yes, sir, General, sir." He was back in the army.

The day Mother got out in early April, Daddy and I had arranged a dinner to welcome her home at their apartment with all their good friends. Mother was the belle of the ball, a glass of champagne in her hand, ready to party again.

That happy interlude was short-lived. She had another stroke just before Easter, from which she never fully recovered. After a few months of Daddy trying to take care of her at home with the help of a nurse, my sister, Donna, and I moved them both into a Marriott-run retirement community, the Jefferson, in Arlington.

Daddy called it the "land of the living dead." It was pretty grim compared with their former residences. They had a beautiful two-bedroom suite, which we decorated with Mother's best things, but it was never home. She slept in one room with her full-time round-the-clock nurse, and Daddy slept in the other bedroom on the opposite side of the apartment.

My mother had always been my best friend, especially since she was a more constant companion than anyone I grew up with. Now I was her caretaker. My priorities changed. None of what I had cared about so much—writing books and stories in the *Post*, being on TV and radio—seemed as important to me as it once had. I didn't get upset about little things anymore. It used to drive me crazy when I would worry about something Ben thought insignificant and he would say "when the history of the world is written, this will not be in it." Now I could see what he was talking about.

Another change was in how I viewed people. Abraham Heschel put into words one of the advantages of growing older: "When I was young I used to admire intelligent people. As I grow older I admire kind people." I admire people who care about others, who care about their community and their world.

Mother gradually lost her executive function and her sense of inhibition, which, though tragic, was sometimes hilarious. Her mischievous sense of humor would emerge, always at an inappropriate time. We always celebrated Christmas dinner at our house with friends. I would put Mother between Bob Woodward and me because he was so fabulous with her and always made her feel beautiful and charming. One year, when Bob was walking her to the door

after dinner, she turned to him in front of everyone, and with innocent big brown eyes, asked, "Bob, did I ever fuck you?" Bob, as
usual, handled it perfectly, replying, "No, Bette, unfortunately, you
did not." She beamed.

She would visit my brother in Arizona with her nurse once a year.
Bill would always take them out to dinner. One night Mother kept
staring at the man sitting at the next table with his female companion. He was clearly getting uncomfortable as Mother wouldn't even
look at Bill or her food. About halfway through dinner she leaned
over to the guy and asked, in a loud voice, "How big is your penis?"
My brother said the man turned bright red and practically fell out of
his chair, as nearby diners broke up with laughter. That was the last
time Bill took her out to dinner.

My father was seeing other women. We knew that he really loved
Mother and was grieving himself, but he was lonely and deserved
companionship and a sex life. The problem was that whenever one
of her nurses found out about his affairs, he would fire them, making the turnover traumatic for all of us, especially Mother. There
was a succession of terrible nurses Daddy found in the want ads, one
of whom was a self-described Holy Roller who made Mother pray
before meals or she would refuse to feed her. Another was a floozy
with dyed hair who we suspected had been a hooker. One day I went
over and the nurse was gone. Mother was lying in a wet Depends
and Daddy was too ill to get out of his bed. I asked Mother where
her nurse was. "She told me she was going down to the dining room
to find herself a rich Jew," said Mother with no sense of irony. I was
constantly having to let some of these women go and find somebody
else. This was exhausting and expensive. We were all grieving.

Daddy became so sick with pneumonia that I had to call an ambulance to get him to Walter Reed. He never really recovered and

was in and out of the hospital after that. At one point they rushed him to the Arlington hospital and put him on a respirator, which the doctors said he couldn't live without. He had signed a living will. We were talking about unplugging the respirator when he suddenly began thrashing around and making noises. We looked over and he was trying to sit up and kept shaking his head to signify no. Buffalo Bill was not ready to go.

A few months later, after being released from Walter Reed, he was in a terrible black mood. I was worried. It was the worst I'd ever seen him. One afternoon Bernie, the wonderful Filipino nurse who would stay with my mother until the end, called, hysterical, to say that my father had shot himself and had been taken to the hospital by ambulance. They had transferred him to Walter Reed. She thought he was dying and my mother was distraught.

I met them at the hospital. Luckily, he had only grazed his jaw. He claimed he had slipped on a bar of soap while cleaning his gun and had no intention of killing himself. I think he had slipped on the soap and misfired while trying to kill himself. Or maybe he didn't slip on a bar of soap. Maybe he wanted us to think he had tried to commit suicide to get attention and have us feel sorry for him. We'll never know.

Daddy died first. Several months after the shooting incident, he ended up in Ward 72 just a few months short of age ninety-three. He had pneumonia but he was recovering. I knew he was going to die. He wanted to die. Bernie would take my mother to visit him every day. He was listless and had no spark at all. The wonderful Dr. Jones, who had taken care of both of my parents over the years, came in. He talked to Ben and me and to Daddy. "General Quinn," he said, "you're getting better. The medicines are working. The question is, do you want to live? If you do, you can. It's up to you." Daddy listened but didn't respond. I knew the answer. He was done.

I sent Mother home with Bernie that Sunday afternoon. Ben was with me at the hospital, and he and Daddy were watching the football game. At this point my father was somewhat delirious. The (New York) Buffalo Bills were playing, but he thought the commentators were talking about him, and he was so excited and pleased that he kept sitting up in bed and looking at the TV every time they mentioned the name. By the time the game was over he wasn't making any sense at all. Though Ben offered to stay I sent him home. I wanted to be alone with my father when he died.

All at once, extremely agitated, Daddy sat up in bed and began barking orders, clearly thinking he was in battle. He was telling his troops what to do. He told me to call headquarters and give them a briefing about what was going on and order his division commanders to come right away. I picked up the phone and began talking to the imaginary fighters at the other end. "This is General Quinn's daughter," I told them in a very authoritative tone. "General Quinn wants all of his division commanders to report to him immediately. The battle is about to take a turn. That's an order."

Daddy leaned back on his pillow, satisfied, at least for the moment. He began drifting in and out. Dr. Jones and I had agreed it was time to start the morphine. I sat by the side of his bed, held his hand, stroked his head, and told him I loved him. He couldn't bring himself to tell me he loved me, but I knew he did. Then, with pleading eyes, he begged me, "Please don't be an atheist."

"I'm not, Daddy," I said.

He then sighed peacefully. A few minutes later he whispered, "God, Sally, I'm so scared."

Those were the last words of Buffalo Bill, the warrior, who had risked his life in so many battles, who had never shown fear before.

This was his last fight. I held his hand until they came to take him away in a body bag.

I didn't cry then. It was around three A.M. on September 11, 2000. I went home, told Ben, and fell into a deep sleep. When I woke, I called Bernie. I told her Daddy had died that night.

"I know," she said.

"How? How could you know?" I asked.

"Because I heard a noise last night and woke up. Your mother was talking to someone. I asked her who she was talking to. She said, 'I'm talking to Bill. Can't you see him? He's sitting right here on the edge of the bed. He's come to say good-bye.'"

"What time was it?" I asked.

"Three o'clock."

Daddy was buried at Arlington Cemetery with full military honors. The horse-drawn caissons carrying his flag-draped casket, the beautiful plot high up on the hill, the gun salute, the Scotsman playing "Taps." He was buried with his ribbons. Inside his pocket I had slipped the fluorescent cross that I had bought at the hospital in Tokyo when I was so sick and had sent to him in Korea. I found it in his desk after he died.

At St. Alban's Church on the grounds of the National Cathedral earlier that day Ben had given a eulogy. He began by saying, "When I was first brought home for inspection by Sally, the vibes at Connecticut Avenue were not all that favorable. The General was looking for anything *but* a navy man, certainly not a registered Democrat, and never, *never*, please the Lord, a newspaperman." (Ben forgot to mention Yankee.) He went on to list my father's citations for the Silver and Bronze Stars and his valor in battle. He ended with, "What a life! Rest in peace, old buddy."

Too afraid I would fall apart, I had to have Ben read my eulogy, part of which was a story that tells a lot about how I felt about my father:

"When I was little I used to have a recurring dream. There was a terrible earthquake and the ground was splitting open, leaving deep crevasses. Everywhere I stepped huge cracks would appear and I was deathly afraid I would fall in. Suddenly this giant horse with wings and my father's head would swoop down, and I would climb on his back just in time to avoid being swallowed up by the darkness."

I ended the eulogy by saying (through Ben): "I know you're looking down at us, Daddy, and I only hope we pass muster."

. . .

The weekend after Daddy's funeral, I took my mother and Bernie down to Porto Bello, our country house in southern Maryland. A group of us had helped to build a natural labyrinth on the river in front of the house of a friend in her nineties. We put down plastic, then wood chips on top and delineated the pattern with stones. It was beautiful. I would go there most weekends to walk it.

This weekend was no exception. It was early September, hot and still. I began to walk the labyrinth and as I did I concentrated on my father, speaking to him as I followed the path. I was trying to communicate with him, and I asked him to send me a sign that he heard me.

I arrived at the center of the labyrinth and sat down to meditate, sending my father telepathic messages. Suddenly, out of nowhere, a huge gust of cold wind blew up, almost howling, shaking the trees in front of me, sending waves up on the shore, tousling my hair and rippling the water on the beach.

"Hi, Daddy," I said. "You heard me!"

Just as quickly as the wind had come up it stopped, followed by dead calm. He was there. I had chills.

That evening, as Ben and I were getting ready for bed, I opened the windows in the bedroom on both sides of the house so we could get a cross breeze. It was stifling hot on the second floor and the air was completely still. For some reason the air-conditioning wasn't working properly. I decided to tell Ben, the skeptic, about my experience, hesitating a bit, as I was afraid of his reaction. I was right. He just laughed and told me I was being ridiculous.

As soon as he said that, an enormous gust of unseasonably cold wind blew right through the room, practically forcing us against the wall. The noise was deafening. We could hear the branches of the trees outside knocking ferociously against the roof and the curtains were flapping up to the ceiling. Ben tried to close one set of dormer windows but the wind was too strong, and he was pushed back.

"Holy shit!" he said. "What is that?"

"Daddy," I smiled in reply. He just looked at me and said nothing.

• • •

My mother lived for another four years. She developed Parkinson's disease, which made it harder and harder for her to swallow and eat, one thing she always loved doing. She obviously missed my father terribly. At her last Christmas, when she was sitting between the ever-patient and gallant Bob Woodward and me, she didn't say a word. The next day I asked her if she had had a good time and she said no. When I asked why, she replied wistfully, "Because I couldn't hold my own." For a party girl, a hostess, and a sexy woman who was full of life, what could be worse?

That spring she had another stroke, this time a massive one. She was taken again to Walter Reed. It was a weekend and she needed more critical care than she could get in Ward 72. She couldn't move her limbs or speak. Two cocky young residents came in to examine her and clearly decided she was not worth their time. I was infuriated when they walked into her room, looked at her, and announced in loud voices (she was fully conscious) that she would probably never be able to walk again and definitely never be able to speak. The following day they came back and, in a condescending tone, asked, "How are we feeling today, Mrs. Quinn?," thinking she wouldn't respond.

"Like shit," my mother replied, a big wicked grin on her face.

Out of the hospital again, Mother came up to Long Island in August to visit us. It was a painful time, with her sleeping most days. At some point, she must have decided to die, because when we got back to Washington in early September, she announced that she was going to stop eating. I talked this over with Donna and Bill, as well as her doctor and Bernie. We all agreed we should let her do what she wanted. I was the only one of the three of us with her. I held her hand and told her that I loved her and we all loved her and gave her permission to go. Donna and Bill did the same thing over the phone. She didn't want to do it gradually. She wanted to go cold turkey. Bernie offered her food every day. She refused. She took only a bit of water. I wanted to bring her home to my house, but Bernie didn't think that was a good idea. She felt Mother was more comfortable in her own surroundings so I went there.

About two weeks into her fast, I walked into her apartment to see her eating a pulled pork barbecue sandwich.

"Mother!" I exclaimed. "Why are you eating?"

"Because," she answered simply, in her slow Southern drawl, "I was hungry."

She was clearly fading a week later. I had the hospice kit with the morphine. Except for the pork sandwich she hadn't eaten anything or drunk anything but sips of water in close to a week. Bernie and I were brushing her lips with a wet sponge.

The day before she died I decided to come over and stay to the end. I brought a bottle of Perrier-Jouët champagne, her favorite, and put it on ice. She was still alert but uncomfortable. I started the morphine, giving her little syringes by mouth every few hours, which seemed to relax her. She wasn't talking but I got into the hospital bed with her and lay there telling her how much I loved her and stroking her hair.

I got out the champagne and two flutes, poured them for us, and held a glass to her lips. We toasted each other. I told her she was the greatest mother in the world and that I loved her to pieces. She told me she loved me. I told her Daddy was waiting for her. I told her that we admired and understood her decision to leave. I told her I would be fine, Ben and Quinn were fine, and that though we would all miss her terribly, she needed to rest.

She drank almost half a glass. I'm surprised I didn't finish the whole bottle. She seemed really happy and at peace.

Donna caught the red-eye from California as soon as I told her Mother wouldn't last long. I slept in the bed with Mother on and off all night, weeping and clinging to her with all my might. I didn't know how long this would go on but by dawn it was clear she was going.

Donna's plane landed around six A.M. When she called, I told her Mother was barely alive and to get the driver to go as fast as he could. I told Mother that Donna was on her way and she had to hang on until Donna got there. She nodded and smiled. Donna made it.

Mother died about fifteen minutes after she got there. Donna was able to hold her and tell her she loved her.

After she died, we decided to bathe and change her and make her up. We were both amazed at her body. She didn't have a line on her face, her skin was soft and supple, and her breasts were round and firm. Her legs, of course, were fabulous. She had never looked more beautiful. She looked like the Bette Quinn we knew and loved before she began to have the strokes. She looked like my mama again. I'm so lucky to have been able to see her then so I can always remember her that way.

Her funeral was different from my father's. For one thing, she wanted to be cremated. She also wanted her ashes to be put in a magnum of Perrier-Jouët, which she had given me, empty unfortunately, about fifteen years earlier just for that purpose.

Donna and I took the bottle to Gawler's funeral home. These people are consummate professionals, but you can imagine their faces when they saw the bottle. Nonetheless, they were very accommodating and didn't blink. Mother was to be buried with Daddy in his grave at Arlington. As we all—only family and a few close friends—gathered at the gravesite, two uniformed white-gloved soldiers were waiting. When the Gawler's sedan pulled up, they ceremoniously reached into the sedan and gently pulled out the champagne bottle with my mother's ashes.

In lockstep they carried it to a platform set up under the canopy next to my father's grave and placed it in the center. The bottle was surrounded by white gardenias, her favorite flower. We were laughing and crying at the same time. My mother's favorite shoes were a pair of black velvet Stubbs and Wootton shoes I had given her with red devils embroidered on them. In fact, I had given them to everyone in the family for Christmas one year so we all wore them. I wore a black sweater I had bought for her in Paris with big red lips and a smoking cigarette embroidered on the front.

The poor army chaplain didn't know where to look, glancing nervously at the champagne bottle as he continued to refer to it as "Mrs. Quinn." He didn't know her, but his brief eulogy was beautiful about how military wives were the unsung heroes.

After the ceremony, we went back to the house to prepare for the memorial service that evening. I had placed small round tables with chairs in different rooms and had a buffet of all her favorite recipes, including chicken and dumplings, butter beans, pickled peaches, black-eyed peas, her famous spaghetti dish (Johnny Marzetti), and ambrosia. As guests, including about one hundred of her friends and mine, arrived they were served a glass of Perrier-Jouët. A gigantic poster of a photo of her (taken by Barry Goldwater) holding a glass of champagne with her leg wrapped around a lamppost in London was hung on the living room wall. Bottles of champagne graced the mantels like sentries. A combo from her favorite orchestra played the romantic music she loved. Members of the family and her doctor spoke and toasted my mother. I spoke last and somehow managed to remain completely dry-eyed. I don't know how I got through it but I did. At the end we all sang the song that was played at my parents' wedding, "Because of You," which ends "Because of you my life is now worthwhile and I can smile because of you," leaving everyone in tears. I drank so much champagne that I collapsed in the front hall and the caterer had to carry me up to bed.

. . .

My mother was dead, but all that love wasn't gone. Somehow it seemed to flow into me. I felt an almost physical infusion. Where does that abundance of love come from? How does it multiply the way it does? How is it possible that it grows and never runs out? Sometimes when I feel I can't possibly fit any more love into my brain or my body, I'm filled up again. I'm never on empty. Never have been. In the end it's the only thing that matters. I really think how you love is what defines you.

What did I do, what have I done with all this love that keeps coming at me? I pass it around. Give it away as fast as I can because I know it will be replenished.

That makes me happy. That knowledge gives meaning to my life. It took me a long time—too long—to learn love's lessons.

I also figured out the big question. Where does it come from, this never-ending waterfall of love? It was still mysterious to me, but I was increasingly aware of a meaningful spiritual presence much greater than myself. There was a larger force guiding me, but I wasn't quite ready to call it God.

Chapter 18

*Faith consists in being vitally concerned with that ultimate reality
to which I give the symbolical name of God. Whoever reflects
earnestly on the meaning of life is on the verge of an act of faith.*

—Paul Tillich, *A History of Christian Thought*

I always thought that my marriage was perfect, that our love was inviolable and eternal, but on January 8, 2003, Ben and I sat in the waiting room of a highly respected Washington psychiatrist named Steven Wolin. We were miserable. Our once glorious marriage was tense and strained. Neither of us understood what was happening, and it is only now, nearly fifteen years later, that I can more fully understand the why of it all.

My incredulity in 2003 at Ben's behavior is quieted now that I can see the picture as a whole. Retrospectively, I see how each piece of life's puzzle, each stone in the path toward enlightenment, is strategically placed, which led me toward a revelation—for me it was the road to finding faith. The key to finding meaning is the awakening that allows us to finally see these nudges, synchronicities, and opportunities for what they are—invitations to meet the divine. We can choose to ignore them for as long as we like, but eventually, the persistence of the invitation will become so obvious, so earth-shatteringly loud, that it refuses to be ignored any longer.

As unlikely a place for me to wake up—in a therapist's office—
and as late in my life as it came, I am now incredibly grateful for the
struggle between Ben and me that led us to couples' therapy that day
and to Steven Wolin, in particular. This was one of my life's biggest
nudges. One that, finally, I was unable to ignore.

But on that cold January day, I was devastated by Ben's change in
attitude and behavior toward me. His personality had always been
sunny and optimistic. Now though, where he had been affectionate
and loving, where he had been funny and insouciant, suddenly he
had become moody, downbeat, and in some instances outright hostile. Nobody else saw that side of him. It was only directed at me. I
was crushed by the changes in him. They had come on gradually, but
now it was clear that this behavior was intensifying and not going
away.

I always loved the way he called me "Sal," as though he had slath-
ered honey all over each letter. I had recently read an article in which
a group of children were asked to define love. A little boy, age four,
responded, "When someone loves you, the way they say your name
is different. You just know that your name is safe in their mouth."

My name didn't feel safe in Ben's mouth anymore.

Steven Wolin was welcoming right away, and Ben and I both
trusted him immediately. This was not Ben's favorite thing. He didn't
like the idea of being "put on the couch." He also didn't like to be on
the defensive, which he definitely was once I described the situation
from my point of view. Ben seemed a bit confused when he heard me
relate our problems, as though I were talking about somebody else,
not him. Steven put him at ease by his friendliness and empathy. As I
recall, Ben kept saying things like, "I can't believe I said that or used
that tone. That's not who I am." He would say, "But I love her. Why
would I talk to her that way?"

Ben admired Steven, but he didn't like going to see him with me. I could tell that he ended up feeling embarrassed and humiliated in our disquieting sessions, never actually able to refute what I was saying but not owning any of it either. We finally decided to see Steven separately and Ben enjoyed their sessions enormously. He wouldn't talk about what they discussed except to say, "It was quite good fun." For me, going to see Steven alone was one of the most enlightening experiences of my life.

He made me think in a different way. I was never particularly introspective before that. I had been fairly cynical of my friends who were "in therapy," especially those who seemed to me perfectly healthy and normal. Now I see that nobody's ever really normal. From my point of view then, they just enjoyed going to talk to somebody once a week. I asked one friend in New York, where therapy was all the rage, what he was getting out of this. Without missing a beat, he explained why he went: "It's the pause that refreshes." Being "in therapy" meant talking about yourself all the time and it just seemed like narcissistic, solipsistic navel-gazing.

Sharon had been different. I went to her to work on a specific problem. Quite belatedly and sadly, it began to dawn on me that learning about oneself, understanding oneself, might actually lead to becoming a better, kinder, more empathetic person. I had bought into the public impression of me as an ambitious, superficial, self-centered person. I didn't like the caricature I was seen as, and I didn't like who I seemed to be becoming. I came to understand, thanks to Steven, that I wasn't that person. I was a good person and also an authentic one. I was true to myself.

It was in therapy that I came to see the wisdom in the words of Socrates that "the unexamined life is not worth living." It was also in therapy that I began to recognize that throughout my life I hadn't understood what it was that I actually did or did not believe. It was in therapy that I became fascinated by religion and struck by the confluence between psychiatry and religion. It was in therapy that I first read William James's book *The Varieties of Religious Experience*, which altered my whole attitude toward living, opening my eyes to the idea that there were many different avenues to faith and spirituality and religion. It was in therapy that I actually began to discover myself.

Steven is an observant Jew. His closest friend, Jim Anderson, is an Episcopal priest who had been in analysis for several years and who became a mentor to me. They were both therapists, priests, shamans, wise men. They both pushed me to take an inward journey of self-discovery. I accepted the challenge.

I never met with them together, but when I told each one of them separately that I was an atheist, they both had the same reaction. They laughed. "No, you're not," both insisted. At first I was insulted and annoyed that they weren't taking me seriously. Then I began asking questions. "Why don't you think I'm an atheist?" was the first of many. The answers they gave stunned me, especially in revealing the superficiality of so much that I had thought important.

I felt as if I were back in college, sitting up all night discussing the meaning of life. This time, though, it was for real. This time I had lived more than half my life and I knew how high the stakes were. I had experienced pain and sorrow, which had caused me to stop blithely designating myself as one thing or another. I would come to conclude much later that what I was looking for was the god in myself, the good, the *imago dei* in which I had been created. I felt compelled to really examine who I was, what I believed, what I wanted, what I valued, and what, in fact, gave my life meaning. It became this woman's search for meaning, in the Viktor Frankl sense—not that any pain and suffering I had experienced was in any way comparable to what Frankl had seen and experienced himself.

Ben and I continued to see Steven separately. Although the hostility I felt coming from Ben persisted for some time, I used the confusion and sadness to push me further toward self-discovery.

. . .

Part of that self-discovery had been my experience walking the labyrinth at the spa and, later, for a number of years at my friend's across the river in southern Maryland. Long ago I had decided I wanted one of my own. I viewed labyrinths as a spiritual tool. Ben planned to have a labyrinth built for me at Porto Bello as a surprise for my birthday, a copy of the one on the floor of the nave of Chartres Cathedral. Mine is on a high slope at the edge of the woods, overlooking the St. Mary's River, on Indian sacred ground.

Naturally I had to have a dedication. In July of 2003, we invited friends to join us in the country for the ceremony. The path to the labyrinth was lit with candles and the sounds of drumming could be heard from behind the trees. Not only that, we had a full moon. It was absolutely magical. One friend read a Native American poem. After a reading I did, dedicating the labyrinth, Ben ended the lovely evening by reading a quote from the Bible, Jeremiah 6:16: "Stand at the crossroads, and look, and ask for the ancient paths, where the good way lies, and walk in it and find rest for your souls."

Then we all walked into the woods to a bonfire, took out pads and pencils, wrote down what we wanted to let go of in our lives, and threw the messages into the flames. When it was over, we walked quietly down the hill arm in arm.

The labyrinth is like having my own private chapel. I walk it every day when I'm in the country, no matter what the weather. Sometimes

I will sit in the center for hours and meditate, lost in concentration, often astonished at how long I'm there. I look at the river, listen to the waves lapping along the shore, watch the birds dart from tree to tree, and follow butterflies as they flutter around me. I take notice of the trees and watch the sailboats drift by dreamily. Time slows down. The pace of the whole place is so congenial, lending itself to contemplation. Noise from an occasional speedboat reminds me that we are often too much in a hurry.

My labyrinth walk is a form of prayer. There are moments when I feel as if I'm on the verge of being let in on a great mystery. Walking the labyrinth always makes me feel better, even if I'm starting from an already good point. During and after my walk, I often feel calmer, more content, more loving.

The labyrinth is outlined with small river stones within a slate frame. Underneath the stones I have buried gifts I've asked for from many of my friends and family. They are small, never expensive. Their value comes from the real meaning to and from the givers, so when I'm walking the labyrinth I feel surrounded by a loving community of friends and family who lift me up and support me.

Some people go regularly to religious services. I go, from time to time, to services of many different faiths, but for me walking the labyrinth is equally as powerful and transformative as most experiences I have had inside of a church or temple or any kind of structure, no matter how beautiful.

I love this quote about the labyrinth from the short story "The Garden of Forking Paths," by Jorge Luis Borges: "I thought of a labyrinth of labyrinths, of one sinuous spreading labyrinth that would encompass the past and the future and in some way involve the stars." Mine does. *Ad astra per aspera*—to the stars through difficulties . . .

. . .

One day I was having lunch in New York with my friend Jon Meacham, who was managing editor at *Newsweek,* soon to be promoted to editor in chief. The subject of religion came up. I brought it up, actually. I sort of eased into it. I was so absorbed with the topic because of my sessions with Steven that I could barely think of anything else.

I found myself challenging Jon, testing him on his thinking about my self-labeled atheism: "I'm an atheist," I announced, with, looking back, not a huge amount of conviction.

"No, you're not," he said without hesitation. There it was again.

"Yes, I am," I insisted.

"No, you are not," he repeated emphatically, and he proceeded methodically to lay out his argument as to why I was not. "You are not a negative person," he began, "and atheism is negative. Atheism is about *not* believing in anything. It's about denying the existence of God." It was Jon who pushed my thinking to the point where "atheist" suddenly felt like a silly, fatuous word, an inappropriate and ill-considered label I had slapped on myself.

He also pointed out—fairly—that I knew nothing about religion. If I were to call myself an atheist, then I should have some idea of what I was talking about. He suggested I do some reading about religion, see what some of the great thinkers had to say, and embark on a study of the subject. Then, when I had learned something, I would be in a better position to speak intelligently about it, to frame my views in a cogent way, even to reappraise my own beliefs or lack of beliefs.

At the end of our three-hour lunch, my head was spinning. I was even more confused. Jon helped me out. He gave me a list of books to read, a starter library of religious literature, the titles of which I jotted down on the back of an envelope. Jon's list: *The Resurrection of the Son of God*, by N. T. Wright; *The Confessions of St. Augustine; Jesus of Nazareth, King of the Jews*, by Paula Fredriksen; *Leaves from the Notebook of a Tamed Cynic*, by Reinhold Niebuhr; *Moral Grandeur and Spiritual Audacity: Essays*, by Abraham Joshua Heschel; *Death on a Friday Afternoon*, by Richard John Neuhaus; and *Orthodoxy*, by G. K. Chesterton. I ordered all of them and began to read—and think.

I had my work cut out for me. I took the project seriously. I read them all. I wasn't looking in their pages to find Christ, to be saved. I was simply asking questions, especially those that would surely add understanding and dimension to my search.

The most important thing I discovered is that, for me, there are few answers, but homing in on the crucial questions might help fill in the gap between uncertainty and doubt on the one hand and meaning and belief on the other.

We all have our own questions and should. Once armed with the ideas, beliefs, values, and perspectives of others—and our own—we simply have choices. What I did find, after this reading and all the subsequent reading I did, was that I had achieved a measure of clarity—an understanding that I needed to find my own path to leading an even more meaningful life.

. . .

By now we were well into the first decade of the new millennium. Where was I and what was I feeling? I had Ben, with whom I remained deeply in love, but whose new disturbing behavior was a constant source of anxiety. I had Quinn, whom I adored more than anything, but whose problems continued to overwhelm me. I had lost my parents, but I had my work, writing for the *Washington Post* part-time, which I was finding increasingly unrewarding.

At this point in my life, it seemed that nothing was working for me.

Around this time, too, I went to New York to interview Karen Armstrong about her new book, *The Great Transformation: The Beginning of Our Religious Traditions*. Despite my constant reading, I was still a total neophyte in the area of religion, but Karen knew me and I could be open with her about the fact that I had little to no idea what I was doing.

The Spiral Staircase, an earlier work of hers about falling away from her faith after leaving the convent, had had an enormous personal influence on me. It was as if she were talking directly to me. I totally identified with her and her story. She called herself an atheist at that time. "I used to hate religion," she told me. "I loathed it in my angry days." Yet she became (and remains) one of the preeminent religion scholars of her day.

By the time we did the interview, she no longer called herself an atheist. "I call myself a freelance. I can't see any one of the great religions as superior to others. . . . I'm seeking to make sense of life, looking for its meaning and how we can have a better humanity." She told me then that her own religious beliefs were a "work in progress" and over the past decade they had continued to evolve.

She said that it was through the act of writing her books that she found out what she actually thought about religion and that it was in her study that she felt most spiritual. In *The Great Transformation*, she compared four religions that emerged concurrently during the Axial Age (900–200 BC)—Confucianism and Taoism in China, Hinduism and Buddhism in India, monotheism in the area of Israel, and philosophical rationalism in Greece. She reveals her surprise at their similarities even though they didn't have much contact with one another. For one thing, she said, they did not seek to impose their own views on the others. "What mattered was not what you believed but how you behaved."

It is interesting to me now how much the thinking of those in the Axial Age reflects a lot of what is going on with so many of our country's people today. Those referred to as the "nones" have rejected institutional religion for a more personal spiritual path, turning to a practice that the Chinese called "jian ai," or concern for everybody, not just your own group.

Karen believed then, and still does, that it's a mistake to define God. "I gave that up a long time ago," she said.

My habit has always been that when I do interviews with people about their faith, I ask them to tell me what they mean when they refer to God. Their responses are never the same.

The most affecting thing that Karen, whose mother had died recently, talked to me about was sadness, pain, and grief. "Being spiritual means allowing your heart to break," she told me, adding, "In the end, death is the great mystery, the terrible mystery."

What really resonated with me was her invoking the Sanskrit word *dukkha*, an important Buddhist concept, with which I was unfamiliar at the time, that means suffering. Karen elaborated: "Buddha would say that life is suffering. There is no why to it. Suffering and unsatisfactoriness. Indians say start with the pain of life and let it crack you open."

Somehow I had always felt that you were weak if you allowed yourself to even admit to suffering. I was constantly trying to avoid it and deny suffering a foothold anywhere close to me—very unsuccessfully I might add. Steven Wolin once said to me that I had absolutely zero capacity for denial. No wonder it was so hard. It didn't work. I was not capable of denying suffering.

There were times after Quinn was born, my mother had her stroke, my father got sick, and Ben started becoming confused that I didn't think I could bear the pain. It was really only after Ben died that I accepted *dukkha*, that I let the pain crack me open. That was the way I survived.

Surprisingly, unsatisfactoriness—or dissatisfaction with life— was never my problem. I always had an unsurpassed capacity for joy. Ben used to call me a "joyous creature." In order to deal with the pain, I always turned to joy, embraced it. I was always filled with hope. I became more grateful, too. Gratitude was something I miraculously developed throughout all those difficult times. As trite as it may sound, to this day gratitude sustains me. I don't know how this happened. It just did, and for that I am eternally grateful.

When I first heard the song "Dayenu"—one of the most beloved Passover songs in the Jewish faith—the words were a reminder to never forget all the miracles in our lives. The word *dayenu* is repeated and translates to if I only had this much, "it would have been enough." I find that I will often whisper "Dayenu" to myself, when I'm feeling especially grateful.

Sometimes I find it hard to believe how fortunate I am. Why? I have no answers for that. I realize that this book is written from a privileged point of view, of an educated and richly experienced life. How can I possibly tell others less fortunate to "find magic" when their lives are so filled with despair? But then I think they might look up at the stars and see something beautiful. They might cradle a new child in their arms. They might feel the love of someone. Something allows them to live and accept their suffering. Could it be faith? I have found that those who suffer the most and have the least are often the most faithful. That could be magic.

. . .

As I began reading and studying more about religion, I started going to a conference, the Faith Angle Forum, for journalists to discuss ways to bring faith into their reporting on and coverage of national and global politics. I also began to pay more attention to the role religion played in the world. Some of the books that left a huge impression on me were *The World's Religions*, by Huston Smith; *A History of God, The Great Transformation*, and *The Spiral Staircase*, all by Karen Armstrong; *Mere Christianity*, by C. S. Lewis; *The Age of Reason*, by Thomas Paine; *The Gnostic Gospels*, by Elaine Pagels; and *The Denial of Death*, by Ernest Becker.

As I was reading I was becoming even more aware of how much influence religion had on our national politics and our foreign policy. Although Jon had pointed this out to me in his usual diplomatic way, I was also shocked and ashamed at how little I knew about religion and how uninformed I had been about something that suffuses the lives of such a huge percentage of the world's population.

I felt the *Post* wasn't covering the stories surrounding all aspects of religion as adequately as we should. I wrote several memos to the editor suggesting that we beef up our coverage, but my notes fell on deaf ears. Religion just wasn't on most people's radar at the paper.

Finally, partly out of frustration and partly because I value his ability to listen and his always thoughtful insights, I asked the *Post*'s owner and chairman of the Washington Post Company, Don Graham, if we could have lunch. When we met, I voiced my concern about the lack of religion reporting in the paper. He wholeheartedly agreed and had an idea. He suggested I start a religion website for the newspaper. I was floored.

"Don," I said, "I don't know anything about religion and even less about the Internet. I can barely do e-mail."

"Well," he said, echoing Ben's comment from three and a half decades earlier when I had admitted at a job interview with him that I hadn't ever written anything, "nobody's perfect."

I laughed and said yes, and the *Washington Post* website On Faith was born.

. . .

The first thing I did was tell Don that I felt I couldn't even begin to tackle this task if I didn't have Jon Meacham, soon to be the editor of *Newsweek* (which was also owned by the Washington Post Company at the time), by my side as co-moderator. Don gave me his blessing to ask Jon.

I had turned to Jon for so many reasons. Beyond being my friend, he is brilliant, a beautiful writer, an inspiring editor, and a religion scholar. He's also one of the most thoughtful people I've ever known, on any subject. He has an elegant mind, maybe the most dazzling mind I have ever come across. It's not just that he's a true intellectual, it's the way he processes information and expresses himself. He has a wry, even wicked and self-deprecating sense of humor. He is humble but not apologetic. Wise beyond his years, he never takes himself too seriously.

When Jon became a child managing editor at *Newsweek* magazine at age twenty-nine and then editor in chief at age thirty-seven, he was referred to as the youngest geezer on the planet. Now, in his late forties, he's too old to be a young geezer, but not old enough to be a real one either. He seems to get wiser every day. His perceptions, insights, and judgments are flawless. He has an enviable quality of being able to step back and observe with equanimity even the most outrageous and absurd situations, which makes his reporting, his writing, and his worldview so invaluable. He is universally admired and respected.

The difference between Jon and so many others in the political, journalistic, and academic world is that he is a truly kind person. He is sincere, thoughtful, and generous, not only with his advice and attention but with his time as well. No matter how busy Jon is, he is always there when you need him.

As I have been lucky (and happy) to get to know Jon well over the years, especially since I began studying religion, I understand better now what makes him unique. It is his profound sense of faith, his belief in God and the tenets of Christianity—without apology—and his total acceptance of everyone of every faith and no faith. In 2006, he had just published (to universally rave reviews) his book *American Gospel: God, the Founding Fathers, and the Making of a Nation*. This may have been the book that had the biggest impact on me. In it he wrote "Belief in God is central to the country's experience, yet for the broad center, faith is a matter of choice, not coercion." He quoted George Washington as saying America is "open to receive . . . the oppressed and persecuted of all nations and religions. . . . They may be Mohometans, Jews or Christians of any sect, or they may be atheists." "For many," wrote Jon, "reverence of one's own tradition is not incompatible with respect for the traditions of others."

Jon and I and the Founding Fathers were clearly on the same page. From the point of view of the founders, Jon would be the most exemplary of Americans. He represents exactly what this country stood for at its inception and should stand for now.

. . .

When I approached him about co-moderating the new site, Jon immediately agreed with the important and necessary caveat that he did have a day job and that this would be my baby. He would write occasional pieces and help me put together a large group of thinkers and writers, religion scholars and theologians. He had the street cred that I was sorely lacking. He started calling me "Mother Superior," a sobriquet I felt I had to earn, and I called him "Your Holiness," a title I felt was well deserved.

The *Post* had recently started its own website, housed across the Potomac River in Arlington, Virginia, seemingly on another planet. This was in the digital dark age of 2006. With Jon on board, though, I whipped across Key Bridge every day to a completely new world, new culture, and new language: eager young people, concrete floors, a Ping-Pong table, jeans and casual clothes for everyone, whiteboards, free coffee, bagels with cream cheese and peanut butter, computer nerds, URLs, traffic. It was exhilarating.

To my mind newspapering has always been the most exciting profession because there's a different story every day. Especially for me as an army brat, where I thrived on change, it was the perfect profession. The Internet took it to a new level. It wasn't a different story every day, it was a different story every minute. You could post things in real time. There was also no bureaucracy over the river. It was like the Wild West. We could do almost anything we wanted to. Seemingly everything was possible, experimenting was encouraged, new ideas were embraced and applauded. A religion website? Sure, let's do it.

We had a great team from the start. The idea was to have a group of between twenty and fifty people in our stable of experts, and each week we would pose a question to a panel pulled together from a few of the commenters on religion and faith. Their responses would be our content. Although this was not my world, I did have four friends I was able to call on initially who all helped us jump-start the site. One of them was Archbishop Desmond Tutu, a South African religion leader and Nelson Mandela's close friend. Others were Karen Armstrong, whose work I had admired for years, Martin Marty of the University of Chicago Divinity School (and a former adviser to my brother when Bill was doing his graduate work there, along with his other doctoral advisers, Mircea Eliade and Wendy Doniger), and Elaine Pagels, another well-known religion scholar. Happily, they all said yes.

Jon had a lot of heavy-hitting friends in the religion field and he added many panelists to our gathering of contributors. With great bravado I announced that I would get the Dalai Lama to write a piece for the launch. Everybody died laughing. I got the Dalai Lama.

An example of one of our early questions was "Does Satan exist? Where do you see the devil (literally or metaphorically) at work in today's headlines?" One answer from Christian Scientist Phil Davis was eerily prescient. "If you want to know if the devil exists, look at today's headlines. It sure seems that way, doesn't it? Genocide, corruption, disintegrating economies—well, the list of the bad and the ugly goes on and on."

Mark Tauber, publisher of HarperOne, responded, equally relevantly: "We may want the devil today, but do we really need a Satan when we have such horribly real folks as Robert Mugabe, Omar al-Bashir, and Than Shwe? . . . In the end, of course, one's idea about Satan depends a lot on one's idea about God."

What I had envisioned for the site from the beginning was a safe and sacred place for conversations about the most important issues in the world. I wanted a place where people could come to discover and learn and have a dialogue about what informed their lives and the lives of their friends and families and people around the globe. I wanted a site where there were no "others," where everyone was accepted for what he or she believed or didn't believe and felt supported and understood.

As it turned out, this is what we created. I found as I went along and continued to write about religion and study and learn, my focus became more spiritual and less news oriented. This happened over time.

We hired a fabulous religion editor, Dave Waters, who totally got what we wanted to do. With him at the helm and Hal Straus as producer, and of course Jon being always available albeit from a distance, the site took off. It surprised nearly everyone but me—I was sure people needed and wanted an outlet for sharing their own thoughts and faith. Soon our traffic was over 100,000 page views per month. Here's where Ganesh, the Hindu god known as the remover of obstacles, came into my life. A colleague of mine, Amar Bakshi, had told me about this god, and I immediately made him our talisman. He seemed to be doing the trick.

One of the first things we wanted to do was to explore Islam. I had long felt it was seriously misunderstood as a religion, and especially after 9/11 Muslims had become objects of suspicion and distrust. We formed a partnership with Georgetown University and arranged to have a forum on Islam there called "What It Means to be Muslim in America." We focused on four categories or groupings of Muslim identity: Islam as a moral compass, a political agenda, a spiritual journey, and a culture apart. We ended up with a distinguished panel, which Jon and I moderated. We had Eboo Patel, a dynamic young Muslim leader from Chicago; Ingrid Mattson, from Harvard, then the head of the Islamic Society of North America; Imam Hendi, a Muslim religious leader at Georgetown; Sherman Jackson, a Black Muslim leader; and Pakistani Salman Ahmad, a Sufi rock star, leader of the band Junoon. The panel was a smash.

What was so exciting about it to me was that everyone present learned something. It was an eye-opener for the packed house of students as well as the media. The Internet can be so remote and distancing, but this live event with real people made me realize what a powerful tool the website could be to educate, inform, and open people's minds. The reaction and reception were even greater than we'd hoped for. I was ecstatic and encouraged about doing more.

What I did right from the beginning was write some columns for the website. One of the first pieces I wrote was about saying grace at Thanksgiving, shortly before my mother's debilitating stroke.

> *When I was 13 . . . I announced to my father that I was an atheist and that I would never say grace again. I thought it was stupid, I told him. It nearly broke his heart. I wasn't able to articulate clearly what I thought was stupid about it. It was only later when I read about St. Thomas Aquinas's objections to petitionary prayer that I understood what was bothering me. And then Immanuel Kant's take on Aquinas made total sense to me. "Praying," he said, "thought of as an inner formal service of God and hence as a means of grace, is a superstitious illusion (a fetish-making), for it is no more than a stated wish directed to a Being who needs no such information regarding the inner disposition of the wisher: therefore, nothing is accomplished by it."*
>
> *. . . When I got my own house and began having Thanksgiving and Christmas dinners here I would ask my father to respect my*

wishes and not say a prayer at the table, and for years we did
nothing. So I have no explanation for why, that Thanksgiving,
. . . I sat at the opposite end of the table and asked my father to say
grace. There was stunned silence for a moment, and then without
a word, we all held hands and my father began, "Lord, make us
truly thankful . . ."

. . . What was I feeling? Truly thankful. I had a wonderful
loving family and many blessings. Why, I asked myself, had I
been so against allowing my father to express those feelings in a
way that was meaningful to him? . . .

This year, though, I'm going to say grace. I haven't become
a believer, but I do feel overwhelmed with gratitude for all the
wonders of my family and friends and the gifts I have been given.
After all, what is grace anyway, what does it mean but gratitude?

Here's what I'm going to say: "Let us be truly thankful for these
blessings which we are about to receive. Amen."

Another column I wrote that has stayed with me over the inter-
vening years was one that we titled "What My Son Taught Me About
God." Quinn was twenty-four at the time and I actually didn't know
until a few days before I wrote the piece that he believed in God.
When we sat down to talk, he began by saying, "My image of God
is what Michelangelo painted on the ceiling of the Sistine Chapel."
He continued:

God is a man stronger and more powerful than everybody else.
I also believe that if you think about God, if you say his name
all the time, then you will believe in him. He will be in your
subconscious. . . .

I had always struggled with what to tell Quinn about God. I didn't know enough to actually teach him about different religions and beliefs, but I wanted to expose him to religion so he could eventually choose for himself. When as a child he went to spend the night with my parents, they read him Bible stories and talked to him about God. For myself, I didn't want to lie to him, so when he was old enough to take it in, I told him I didn't believe in God, but I added that believing gave many people a lot of comfort.

He told me that although he didn't know what *atheist* meant, he thought it was "a harsh word, a very ugly word." He had decided that his own medical and learning problems had taught him that everything happens for a reason and that "maybe it's God's plan for me to go through this because I can handle it."

Our mother-son conversation ended with me asking him if he was angry with Ben and me for not giving him a real religious education. His response was poignant and telling:

> *Not at all. I'm happy with the way I was brought up religiously. If you had taught me there was only one thing I was supposed to believe then I wouldn't have options. You taught me I could believe in anything. . . . I could choose what I wanted to believe in. In a way, believing in God is like having a girlfriend you love and care about. You feel safe with her. You feel safe with God, the way you would with your girlfriend. When you get married she will be with you in sickness and in health. That's what I believe God will do when I'm going through the hard times of life.*

Finally, I asked Quinn what he thought about my new venture in religion as a moderator of On Faith. "Well," he replied quickly, but with a mischievous grin, "you started out as an atheist. Now you're a freethinker. I think you're on your way to believing in God."

. . .

The hour-long video interviews I began to do with prominent people about their faith were especially exciting to me. I also persuaded the *Washington Post* to change the name of its Saturday religion page to On Faith and started writing occasional columns that appeared in both the paper and on the website.

In the interviews, every one of the people I spoke with was interesting and thoughtful and eager to talk about their faith in any and all its manifestations. I called the series "Divine Impulses" because I believe that we all have them and I wanted to know what they are. I have to think that one of my most important and personal divine impulses was being involved with On Faith.

The first video interview I did was with Archbishop Desmond Tutu. I recall him talking about loving God and yet getting angry with him: "I get very angry with God, but I rarely remonstrate him and don't say, 'For goodness sake, how in the name of everything that is good, can you allow this sort of thing to happen?'" I also remember the power of his message: "God loves me. God loves you. God is incredible. Actually, sometimes it's mind-blowing to think that I, with all of my foibles and my weaknesses and my sins, am loved."

Actor Richard Gere, a serious Buddhist and close friend of the Dalai Lama's, told me that he didn't see God as a creator, as some outside entity or puppeteer who is somehow making things magically happen, assigning roles to everyone: "You are going to be happy, you are going to jail, you get a good parent, you don't. . . . No, no. I don't believe that," Gere said emphatically. "I believe that we are totally responsible for our experience, we ourselves. Ultimately completely fully, we are responsible, and I find that very liberating. I can change my experience. I don't have to beg someone else to change it. . . . I have the resources myself. My mind is vast, my heart is vast, and I am really responsible for my being."

Another person I interviewed as part of "Divine Impulses" was my good friend the late Tim Russert, then the moderator of *Meet the Press*. Tim was a practicing Catholic and talked thoughtfully about the influence of his faith: "In the end there is a reason it's called faith, it's something you believe in. . . . I absolutely know for certain that this is exactly what happens, you hope and you believe and it gives a sense of purpose and meaning which I find very helpful." The Jesuits believe, he went on to say, "we have an obligation to help people who are less fortunate, who are needy. That is where you see the presence of God in others. That's the central piece of my faith that I think is more important than any other."

Also I spoke with my friend the late Christopher Hitchens, a well-known and outspoken atheist. Christopher was dying of cancer. When I asked him whether it might be nice to believe that there was someone up there in the heavens looking after him, he answered at length:

> *No, which is why I say in fact, very deliberately, that I'm not an atheist, I'm an anti-atheist. In other words, I'm not just one who's concluded it's not true, or rather that there is absolutely no evidence to think that it is true. I'm glad there's no evidence for it, because if it were to be true, one would be living under a permanent surveillance, around-the-clock celestial dictatorship that watched you while you slept and could convict you of thought crime, could indict you for things you thought in the privacy of your own skull, and sentence you to quite a long stretch—namely eternity—of*

punishment or alternatively dangle a not to me very attractive
award of a life of eternal praise and groveling and sprawling
and singing the praises of someone that you are ordered to love,
someone you must both love and fear. That [concept] used to distress
me when I was little as well. How are you supposed to love someone
you're afraid of?

. . .

I've always liked the idea of Pascal's wager, which essentially offers a rational reason for believing in God: in light of the impossibility of knowing unequivocally if God exists, one should live as though God does, because that path leads to potential gains if indeed God exists and there's nothing to lose if not. Pascal's is a pragmatic approach to thinking about and deciding on one's beliefs. If you gain, you gain a great deal. If you lose, you lose little to nothing. An added benefit is that it's possible that living as if one has faith could actually lead to faith.

For Leon Wieseltier, the whole idea of faith hinges on Pascal's belief, advocated by William James, that "if belief in religion is going to change your life for the better, then you have every reason to hold that belief because what matters is its practical effect on how you live."

. . .

Some years later, and only a few months before he died, I sat down with Ben for a video interview at the *Post*. Especially as he aged and his faculties faltered, Ben never wanted to talk about religion or spirituality or his beliefs. I knew he wouldn't answer my questions in private, but to my surprise he agreed to sit for an interview and have it be public. I started by putting the question to him, "If I asked you today if you believed in God, what would you say?" His answer came right away: "I believe there is a force for right, that is called a hundred different things, but whatever it's called I believe in it. And if I couldn't believe in the force, then I wouldn't be an honest person."

In a part of the tape that was lost he also told me he thought God had saved him in World War II when his destroyer was being bombed. I asked him if he ever prayed, to which he answered, "I don't know what you call it, but, yeah, sometimes I do." When I asked him if he thought God had a plan for him, he replied: "I think he had a plan for how to handle my life."

Finally I asked him what gave his life meaning. He pointed to me. I lost it.

. . .

What shocked me about the Internet—then and now—were the vile comments on columns or transcripts or commentaries that appeared. Many of them seemed to have been written by crazy people, sitting in their pajamas (or underwear) in their basements, sending out hate-filled screeds at all hours of the day and night.

As part of my Muslim outreach I was able to get Queen Rania of Jordan to write a piece for the site about the role of women in Islam. Her piece came in, and we ran it along with the queen's picture, which was beautiful. Everyone involved with the site was thrilled. However, the day after it ran, I got a call at three A.M. from the palace in Jordan. All officialdom was going crazy. I was sound asleep and at first didn't understand what was being talked about, what seemingly several voices at once were saying. Then I realized they were upset by the first comment that ran after her story went up. Apparently some sensitive guy had written, "Boy, would I like to bang her."

That was the last time she wrote for On Faith. It was years before the *Post* could get a handle on how to control some of the worst comments. I refused to read any about me and my columns. My editors did, though, and others monitored the comments and passed this one along: "I hope you get in an automobile accident and the gasoline spills out and catches on fire and you burn alive and end up in hell."

That one was from a self-described evangelical Christian. Interestingly, most all the negative comments came from Christians. The second worst were from atheists. I never got a hostile comment from a Muslim, Jew, Buddhist, or Hindu that I know of.

This gave new meaning to the question "What would Jesus do?"

• • •

One of the most controversial and still ongoing events in Washington is the National Prayer Breakfast, held every February, when the president, vice president, and more than three thousand people—many of them in positions of power, turn up to show their religious bona fides. The original idea of the prayer breakfast was to build relationships among the business, social, and political communities. Recently, it seemed clear that the prayer breakfast had devolved into something that it had not started out to be.

I was there one year when Darrell Waltrip, former NASCAR driver and the keynote speaker, told those assembled, including President Obama and the Dalai Lama: "Let me tell you something: Good guys go to hell. If you don't know Jesus Christ as your Lord and Savior, if you don't have a relationship, if He's not the Master of your life, if you've never gotten on your knees and asked Him to forgive you of your sins, or if you are just a pretty good guy or a pretty good gal, you're going to go to hell."

One can only imagine what the Dalai Lama, a Buddhist who does not believe that Jesus was the son of God, thought. Hearing this in a traditionally nondenominational setting was, for me, the moment of the end of the prayer breakfast as it was originally meant to be.

As President Obama would say when speaking at the same breakfast: "We see faith driving us to do right. We also see faith being twisted and distorted, used as a wedge—or worse, sometimes as a weapon."

Author and senior fellow at the Brookings Institution Leon Wieseltier once remarked: "One place where prayer is certainly not possible is at the National Prayer Breakfast. It is an annual institution for the degradation of prayer."

Of course, there are prayer groups and circles meeting all over town, in Congress, in the White House, in the military and the diplomatic corps. The churches and synagogues and mosques are filled on holy days with observant families. There is "one nation under God" and "in God we trust" and there are Senate and House chaplains who begin the sessions with prayers. The president rarely speaks without ending with "God bless you and God bless the United States of America." But, boy, when the starting bell rings, all bets are off.

· · ·

Five years after I had founded On Faith, I wrote a piece looking back over those rich, full years, concluding that I had been enthralled with the entire subject of religion and spirituality and had learned a great deal across a range of issues. Never had I been so fulfilled by a subject. I summarized five lessons I had learned about faith:

1. Nobody knows.

2. Religions are the same—and not.

3. Everything is about religion.

4. We are all looking for meaning.

5. Why there is suffering.

My ultimate conclusion to that fifth lesson is that there is certainly no one answer—and perhaps no good answer, but certainly no "right" answer—to why there is suffering. Even some of the great theologians have simply "thrown up their hands."

At the end of this column I asked myself the question "Do I believe in God now?" Certainly, as I wrote, "Where I am with this question has changed many times since I began On Faith." A final thing I learned is this: "God is what you or I or anyone else thinks God is."

I would find as the years went by that I agreed with this concept of God, but it turned out to be a lot more complicated. I still think this is the case.

Jon Meacham believed that On Faith was a success in the beginning because it gave "unlikely scholarly and expert voices a big audience to talk about unlikely things." He felt it was also a time when the subject of religion had real news value and a moment when religiously charged issues were particularly sulfurous. It was a moment when the topic of religion, especially after 9/11, was very much in the public square. It was also a time when the United States was experiencing what Jon called "the rise of atheist chic," a significant intellectual struggle in the country about issues of beliefs and disbeliefs. He felt that climate was essential to the success of the conversations of On Faith.

Jon also felt that what I contributed to On Faith could be summed up by thinking of my contributions as three tributaries: my inherent curiosity, deepened by my years of working as a journalist; my competence as a social convener in the tradition (according to him) of Dolley Madison and Katharine Graham, both of whom were lower-case republicans who created social spaces for public life to unfold; and my own restlessness about my personal faith journey, which he once characterized to me as my "inability to be satisfied with a given moment." (He may be right about this last one.)

Jon described what we tried to do with On Faith from the beginning: "It's that we threw the most interesting party about religious beliefs in the first decade of the twenty-first century. And when people get together things happen. Ideas are exchanged. Friendships are formed. Affairs begin. Wars end. Everything that happens in a human context comes onto the radar. On Faith created that context where one did not exist before." It became almost a form of participatory religion.

By the time On Faith was launched, I realized Jon was my road to Damascus. He provided illumination along the way to my own transformation of attitude and belief.

Chapter 19

The quest of the human heart for meaning
is the heartbeat of every religion.

—Brother David Steindl-Rast, *Gratefulness, the Heart of Prayer*

At the beginning of 2007 I received a brochure in the mail advertising a trip around the world. It was called "Great Faiths: A Journey to the World's Sacred Places." The starting date was in a few months, still in the early months of On Faith. The places to be visited read like a Grand Tour of the Holiest of Holies of many important world religions, including Rome and Vatican City; Jerusalem and Bethlehem; Varanasi, India; Kyoto, Japan; and on to Ethiopia, Egypt, Armenia, and Turkey. I didn't hesitate.

"Travel with world-class scholars," the brochure read, "walk in the footsteps of pilgrims, explore some of the world's holiest sites and gain insights into humankind's search for meaning." I knew I was ready to walk in pilgrims' footsteps and signed up immediately. I thought it was a godsend. I was never fully aware of the significance of the word until that brochure dropped from the mail slot onto my floor.

Not only was it a fabulous way for me to learn about religion, a real crash course, but it was also an escape of sorts, a way for me to get some distance from Ben and try to understand what was happening to him, to me, to us.

Perhaps if I were gone for three weeks, it might help Ben change his strange behavior or I might come to some greater understanding of the cause of it. We had never been apart longer than two weeks in our entire marriage and then, only twice, for reporting trips I took. Since he had stepped down as editor at the paper in 1991, we had not been apart for more than a day or two. This would be a huge departure, literally, from our normal lives.

He was terribly upset when I told him I was going and for how long I would be away, and especially dazed when I said I had already bought my tickets. As that reality took hold, I began to realize how uncharacteristic it was for me not to have talked with him about this whole new part of my life. He seemed so uninterested and lacked any curiosity about it that I found his attitude surprising and hurtful. He even made fun of me about it. What an upheaval this entire period had been. We were moving into new territory separately and together.

I was scared but exhilarated, which fed my thinking that I needed this. I felt that something momentous was about to happen to me. I wasn't thinking that this would be a big step in my serious search for meaning. I wanted to know much more about religion and the faiths and beliefs of others, and I also needed and wanted to rediscover the magic that had always been such a central part of our lives together.

. . .

Rome, a city I love, was our first stop on the tour. I'd been there many times. In fact, I was there just the year before with Ben. We had a private tour of the Sistine Chapel. It was breathtaking. For one brief moment I felt a presence larger than I was. The art and whole experience were transcendent.

The Vatican, however, is surprisingly one of the least spiritual places I've ever visited. It seemed like a big bastion of bureaucracy, secrecy, and dogma.

The only real emotional moment I had in Rome was the walk through the old Jewish ghetto and learning some of the history of how the Jews in Rome had been persecuted.

I'm sure others visiting Rome on the trip had a different experience, but to me this visit didn't represent at all what I hoped to discover about religion. This first stop didn't manifest itself spiritually. Never once did I have the slightest intimation of the divine.

. . .

From Rome we traveled to Israel where we stayed in Jerusalem. I had been enthralled by the city on my first trip to Israel as a reporter. The last time I was there I stayed in the old part of Jerusalem, the Arab part, and I was always transported by the magical sounds of the muezzin calling to prayer throughout the day. This time we were at the King David Hotel in the more Jewish part of Jerusalem, which is not as quaint as the older part and is now and was then quite modern and filled with bustling world travelers.

On our visit to Bethlehem, we were struck by the wall that the Israelis built to keep out the Palestinians and to protect themselves from attack, the wall that has become a symbol of intolerance and persecution to many around the world. What was really shocking was how run-down Bethlehem was. The visit to the Church of the Nativity was even more disappointing. Dark and dusty, it looked as if it had been abandoned years earlier. There were bare lightbulbs, debris, piles of ladders, holes in the walls that our Palestinian guide said came from people having stolen pictures, cheap wall hangings, a torn canvas Bible, water damage, dead flowers, broken oil lamps. The entire church smelled musty, like old shoes.

Most unforgettable were the priests—Armenian, Orthodox, Catholic, Syrian—who were fighting among themselves over territory, not vast acres of land as in the old days, but areas within the sacred spaces themselves. Inside the church, a priest from one religion had placed a chair in the middle of the room to define his territory and dared another priest to move it. Yet another priest was sweeping the floor with a broom and swept the dust and dirt to another priest's side causing a rift. "Welcome to the Holy Land," our guide said with a laugh and an air of resignation.

There was little peace to be found here—far from the picture in many of our heads of the "little town of Bethlehem, how still we see thee lie." Since that visit I haven't been able to sing that classic Christmas hymn with the same feelings I once had.

We did hear an enlightening talk by a rabbi about Judaism. He focused on how important the Torah was to Jews and suggested that there was no greater religious duty than to study it. It reminded me of the famous Rabbi Hillel story. A gentile, a potential convert to Judaism, asks the rabbi if he can teach the whole Torah to him while he, the prospective convert, stands on one leg. Hillel replies, "That which is hateful to you, do not unto another: This is the whole Torah. The rest is commentary—go and study it."

Our speaker talked about Jews being the "chosen people." "Chosenness is a responsibility," he said, "and you must dedicate your life to God and the world, to live an ethical and moral life. Being chosen is never much fun."

As we approached the Wailing Wall, the first thing I saw were the thousands of pieces of paper stuck in the cracks of the mortar. This wall is such a good example of a ritual that invites participation. Visitors write notes, full of wishes and prayers, and stick them in the cracks of the wall. Even Pope Francis left a note at the Western Wall during his visit in 2014, putting his note in the cracks as he prayed. It was later revealed that his note was the text of the Lord's Prayer written in his native Spanish.

This place has been the subject of a lot of anguish, especially by Jewish women because they are not allowed to pray with the men. There is a small separate section where the women are allowed. (After a number of near riots and demonstrations since I was there, this is beginning to change.) The day that we visited there was a bar mitzvah going on, naturally on the men's side. A makeshift curtain was drawn between the two sides. The men were dancing and laughing, praying, and davening—reciting the traditional liturgical prayers—most of them rocking back and forth rhythmically all the while. On the other side of the curtain the women in the family, including the mother of the bar mitzvah boy, had brought chairs and were standing on them on tiptoe, trying to see the boy celebrate the most sacred day of his life. It was heartbreaking and pathetic. This was a religious site?

On this trip, it became clearer to me how women get short shrift in every religion.

. . .

What I came away with in the Holy Land was this: There has been and is so much pain, so much anguish, so much suffering in the world. From Christ dying on the cross to six million Jews being slaughtered in Germany during World War II, to the Palestinians living in an occupied territory that is slowly being taken away from them, treated like second-class citizens in a no-man's-land. It never seems to end, yet for all three of these Abrahamic faiths, so much of what believers of each faith go through is either self-inflicted or inflicted on one another. The Golden Rule is preached in all these religions and yet in none of them do many of their followers seem to practice what is preached. From the quotidian pettiness to the monumental atrocities they—we—are all guilty.

Leaving Israel I felt bereft, overcome with a sense of hopelessness. What was the point of any religion if its adherents didn't abide by the moral tenets? The idea of a God I could believe in felt even more remote and unrealistic. It was ironic that some of the places considered to be the most holy in the world left me feeling so empty.

. . .

Varanasi, the spiritual capital of India, provided a very different experience, partly because I was determined to distance myself from the physical environment and dwell only on the spiritual. We first went to Sarnath where Buddha attained enlightenment and gave his first sermon twenty-four hundred years ago, a place that is sacred to both Buddhists and Hindus and where they both go for pilgrimages.

Listening to a lecture on both faiths, I was struck by how different the two faiths are, despite having sprung up so close to each other. In Buddhism, there is no God, in Hinduism there are many. Buddhism is austere; Hinduism is colorful. Buddhism is one story; Hinduism is many stories. Buddhism is cool; Hinduism is hot. Buddhism centers on the one follower; Hinduism, many. Buddhism is neat; Hinduism is cluttered. Buddhism is solemn; Hinduism is joyous. Buddhism is quiet; Hinduism is noisy. Being around both faiths made me feel schizophrenic, but they do coexist.

Examining these contrasting ways of looking at the world got me thinking. That's when I began to consider the notion of cherry-picking—pulling my favorite thoughts about different religions, and latching on to what resonated with me personally. This idea might be anathema to the orthodox followers of different religions. To them, an adherent must commit to the tenets of one faith. That doesn't work for me. I like the idea of meditating silently on a mat in a plain cotton cloth robe and then going out dancing in the streets in a shocking pink and gold sari with dangling earrings.

Did I have to adhere to some orthodoxy to find meaning? No. I could adopt the elements that appeal to me from any and all faiths and create a religion of my own, to paraphrase the title of one of Thomas Moore's bestselling books, *A Religion of One's Own,* whose subtitle speaks exactly to this idea: *A Guide to Creating a Personal Spirituality in a Secular World.* I didn't have to declare myself any particular denomination or label. I could and would and do have access to it all. What a liberating idea! At that point, I thought if I got nothing else out of this trip—which was certainly not the case—that was it. And it was still early on. I couldn't wait to see what more I would learn and how much I might change by the time the trip was over.

. . .

The Ganges is a filthy river. The banks of the Ganges are strewn with trash and garbage, steeped in mud, animals wandering around the bodies waiting to be cremated, dried cow dung piled up for the poor who cannot afford to pay for the sandalwood to burn their relatives. Guides tell observers and sightseers not even to put your hands in the water when you go out in a boat. Yet you see hundreds of people bathing in the river, washing their hair, doing their laundry, even drinking the water, as dead animals and even a dead baby float by. Apparently the price of cremation is so high, people will often put dead children in the water to be carried away.

I was not prepared for what we saw that evening as we glided out into the river on small boats at twilight to cruise up and down the Ganges. All along the banks, hundreds of ghats, or funeral pyres, were burning. Bodies clad in brilliant colors were submerged in the river, then brought up to dry, wrapped in white, and laid on banks of wood and covered with bark as well so that the body would not sit up when the flames began to engulf them. Only male relatives, usually the eldest son, dressed in white, head shaven out of respect, were allowed to participate. Women were not allowed as they were thought to be too emotional. Only when the skull cracked open was the soul released from the body to attain nirvana or even moksha, the liberation from the cycle of death and rebirth.

As we floated down the river and the darkness descended, the flames took on a magical quality and I could almost feel the souls wafting out of the bodies and hovering above us in the atmosphere. In the moonlight the sight of the squalor disappeared and one could only behold the mystery of life and death in its most raw form. Ashes to ashes, dust to dust became a reality.

I thought of how we Westerners deal with death and our hands-off approach to embalming and even to cremation, which is all done out of sight. I couldn't help but wonder if what I was witnessing first-hand in India wasn't a better way. You can't deny grief when you see a person you love going up in flames. I knew I couldn't bear to watch that, though, and I couldn't bear the idea of being cremated myself. Was it because I was a woman and "too emotional" or was it because of my cultural upbringing?

Ben had asked to be cremated, but I certainly knew I couldn't stand to have him cremated, especially after watching those bodies burned and their ashes dumped unceremoniously into the river. The first thing I did when I got back from my trip was to beg him to change his mind. I wanted to know that he would always be with me in some way. I wanted to be buried with him. I wanted to have his funeral where he would be in a casket in front of me so that I could touch it and feel his presence there. He did change his mind. Besides Quinn, it was one of the greatest gifts he could have given me.

Varanasi did that for me. It was worth the whole trip.

. . .

Kyoto took me back to the Japan of my childhood. This part of the trip, though, was not one of discovery or of many spiritual insights. Kyoto is the capital of Zen Buddhism, an imported religion, not established in Japan. I felt there was something antiseptic about Kyoto this time: the shrines, the Shinto religion, the atmosphere.

A number of things our guide said helped me comprehend some of what I was feeling. When he talked about nature and beauty and gratitude, those concepts resonated with me. This was the Japan where I had had some truly spiritual experiences. This was the mysterious, mystical, and magical Japan of my memories.

What had appealed to me about Zen was the practice of meditation, and zazen, sitting, or as my brother, Bill, who has been practicing zazen since the 1970s, would say, "put your fanny on the cushion and do it every day." The idea, as our lecturer told us, "is to empty the mind, enter a state of peace where you have no delusions, no angst, no fear. The mind turns in on itself without distortion. Nothing bothers you. You laugh out loud. You see your own true nature and it is the nature of the universe." That sounded good to me.

I have meditated every day since my trip, and have found it really does work for me. I feel calmer and more centered because of it.

· · ·

Flying from Chengdu, China, to Lhasa, Tibet, over the Himalayas was one of the closest things I can imagine to dying and going to heaven. The views from the plane were achingly beautiful, divine even, with the perfect white peaks jutting out from the equally pristine white clouds. My eyes and the rest of my senses couldn't get enough of what I was seeing and feeling.

I stared at the views knowing that, except for the return flight, I would likely never see such glory again. In terms of impact, it was probably the most memorable sight of the trip. After seeing those mountains, it would be hard not to believe in a creator or at least something bigger than oneself and one's own world.

Lhasa itself is a Potemkin village. It's Disney World. It's a sham of a place, using real temples and colorful people as a backdrop. It's chilling. Chinese police were everywhere, even if you couldn't see them. They were there to destroy Tibet as it once was. Here was the home of the Dalai Lama until he was forced to flee by the Chinese after their takeover. For reasons I still don't understand, they see him and Buddhism as a threat. What on Earth have they been thinking? Tibet is certainly a draw, even without the Dalai Lama, and even for people like me who know what is really going on. Imagine if they actually had the Dalai Lama and his entourage, the monks and supporters and pilgrims, there. What a huge attraction the country would be. Instead of the fake plastic imitations and representations of a "quaint" Tibetan village—never mind the Tibetan monks who periodically self-immolate in order to draw attention to the free Tibet movement—this mystical place would be the end goal of many pilgrims, not to mention a PR dream for travel companies.

Our guide was an adorable and very naive young Tibetan who spoke to me privately about the Han Chinese domination of his country. He was also quite funny, though he didn't know it. His name was Dogshit. I was startled when he translated it to me. "Ah, what an interesting name," I said, diplomatically. "How did you come to be named that?" It turns out that his parents named him Good Luck. Unfortunately, because he was sick for most of his early childhood, his parents decided that they had tempted the gods by naming him that. They changed his name to Dogshit so the gods would not be jealous and it would bring good luck, which in fact it did. Once his name was changed, he said, he was never sick again. This happens a lot, he said. One family had only girls and they wanted a boy so they named their last girl Stop in order to stop having girls, and, presto, the next child was a boy. Call it superstition, call it faith, call it what you will but it works for them. Who are we to say?

One of the most vivid sights in Tibet was seeing pilgrims prostrate, sliding along the cobblestone streets on their stomachs, praying. Everywhere one sees white scarves or prayer scarves and these are given out in front of temples to make an offering to the Buddha. I still have one. Among my most cherished possessions are two large antique thangkas, paintings on cloth, both of the goddess of compassion. Compassion wasn't a word I often used before this trip. It is now. It follows the Golden Rule. I hadn't thought of that before.

I don't want to suffer—*dukkha* again. I want to be enlightened and compassionate. The compassionate part I can do—most of the time. Ultimately, though, I can't not want what I want. I can't not love whom I love. The only real way to end suffering and attain enlightenment is to eliminate all attachments. If I eliminate all attachments,

I will suffer. Loving all sentient beings, including ants, just ain't the same as loving another person. Besides, it would be really boring. That would cause me to suffer. It's a catch-22, or as the Buddhists might say, a koan or riddle.

Though he travels tirelessly around the world promoting his cause, the Dalai Lama is never coming back, never returning to his rightful place, his native land. His picture is not allowed to be shown in Tibet, which is ironic since the Dalai Lama, even in his absence, is its biggest celebrity.

I've often wondered about his conundrum as a Buddhist. He writes books about how to be happy and he certainly is a jolly soul in person, laughing and giggling constantly. Yet, as we know from Buddhist philosophy, the only way to alleviate suffering is to not want, but since he left Tibet, he has spent his life wanting to return, wanting Tibet to be independent from the Chinese, wanting Tibet to still be the center of Buddhism. If that isn't a cause for suffering, I don't know what is.

· · ·

Heading west now, on our way to Ethiopia, we stopped in a different part of India. The Golden Temple in Amritsar is the spiritual and physical home of the Sikh religion. What appealed to me about this belief system was the idea that all are equal, regardless of caste or sex or color. The Golden Temple, on an island in the midst of the holy Pool of Nectar, is the embodiment of that idea. Goodness and purity are what people strive for and the one God is everywhere and unknowable. It is important to do the right thing and stand by your deeds. Sikhs broke off from Hinduism because they could not support the caste system. Those who are baptized must wear an iron bracelet, men must not cut their hair but wear it in a turban—after

9/11 many Sikhs in the United States were vilified because people thought they were Muslim. Often, they must carry a wooden comb and a small dagger and must wear special underwear. They must not indulge in antisocial activity and are not allowed to commit adultery. They believe that when your heart is pure, you will see miracles. If you pray with a happy heart, your prayers will be answered. Happiness and sadness are both part of life. Meditation is imperative.

. . .

In Ethiopia, we were supposed to go to Lalibela, a world-famous site—in fact a UNESCO World Heritage site—full of churches carved out of red volcanic rock, with caves, crypts, grottoes, and galleries. After breakfast we boarded buses to the Addis Ababa airport for an Ethiopian Airlines flight to Lalibela. At the airport we were taken out to the plane, only to be told that the plane had mechanical problems but we were not to worry, everything would soon be fixed. I looked around the airport. I didn't see any other planes that looked like they were about to fly. It was empty. We all got out on the tarmac next to the plane. The pilot and the flight attendants were standing there arguing with some mechanics, all with a lot of hand gestures on both sides. I could swear somebody was kicking the tires. The Ethiopian guide was talking animatedly to somebody who apparently was the airport manager, who was extremely agitated. We waited and waited, interrupted only by frequent assurances that the problem would soon be solved. Meanwhile the pilots continued their harangue with the mechanics. I and several others began to get cold feet. Suddenly my mouth went dry, my heart started pounding, my palms were sweating. I'm not the world's greatest flier to begin with, but this situation seemed dire and a flight out of the question. I had absolutely no confidence that this plane would or could take off, much less get us to and from Lalibela in one piece. All I could think about were Ben and Quinn. What if the plane crashed? I couldn't die and leave them alone. Who would take care of them? Eventually, still sweating, I bailed out, as did about half the group. Those who came across to me as either foolhardy or full of faith boarded the plane as those of us who had decided against the flight drove back to the hotel. We were given the choice of lounging by the pool and having a long lunch in luxurious surroundings amid the palm trees, or taking a van and touring the city. I chose, as did a handful of others, to tour the city.

Although I know Lalibela would have been spectacular—and we heard that night from those who had gone (they came back alive) that it was indeed fabulous—I remained glad that I had stayed behind and seen Addis Ababa in all its realities. The contrast between the plush atmosphere at the hotel and the dilapidated houses and squalor and disease we saw in those hours was astonishing. It was Palm Sunday and many of the Coptic Christians were about in the city with wreaths on their heads to show they had been to church, many wearing their best clothes. The most horrifying and revealing part of the impromptu tour, as well as the most touching, was driving through what we were told was Africa's largest market, teeming with thousands of people, a mass of humanity, many of the people plainly and visibly miserable. Along the streets we saw a man lying in the gutter, covered with huge lumps all over his body, being walked over by pedestrians, child beggars with stumps for arms and legs, old people stretched out on the pavement with flies circling their glazed eyeballs. There was a man beating donkeys and goats, tied up and unable to escape the lashes. Extreme poverty was evident everywhere we looked. Tin huts lined the roads, with hardly room for one person, let alone large families. The contrast to our opulent environment at the hotel with the elegant French restaurant couldn't have been more stark.

Once back inside the fence separating us from the masses, I couldn't help feeling guilty, wondering what I had done to deserve my good fortune. And yet, so many of the people I saw outside the fence were the religious ones, not me. I was overwhelmed with gratitude. Uneasiness and gratitude.

I was missing Ben and Quinn. I called home. Quinn, in particular, was so happy to hear from me. He had had a terrible nightmare about me the night before. According to Ben, he had dreamed that I had died in a plane crash. He had gone into Ben's room sobbing, threw up, got into bed with Ben for the first time in years, and cried all night.

I had chills up and down my spine. What if I had taken that flight? Would it have gone down? What did it all mean? What I do know is that Quinn and I were communicating telepathically. Not for the first time, or the last.

. . .

I had never been to Cairo before, so I was really looking forward to seeing the pyramids and the Sphinx.

What a disappointment. . . . These structures, so magnificent in photographs and from a distance, were disintegrating from lack of care. They were dirty, littered with trash and garbage, surrounded by beggars, and overrun by tourists. A man was urinating on the side of one. Stray animals wandered about untethered. One could only imagine how these once grand religious monuments, tombs for the greatest pharaohs, had looked, polished and reflecting the glittering sun, symbols of resurrection as the fiery orb died each night and then rose again in the morning.

I was shocked that the Egyptians had let the pyramids and the poor old Sphinx, both wonders of the world, go to ruin. One of the most potentially magical places on Earth had become completely devoid of magic. I wondered what the sun gods were thinking.

. . .

By the time we got to Armenia, I was exhausted. Severe jet lag had set in and the early wake-up calls had gotten to me. I was tired and lonely. I wanted to go home immediately, but I had Armenia and Istanbul and then back to Rome yet to go.

No matter where you are in Yerevan, the capital, you can see the breathtaking peaks of Mount Ararat, which is the sacred mountain of Armenia. Mount Ararat is said to be where Noah's Ark ended up after the great flood. There have been a number of archaeological expeditions to find the ark, which some say simply is a myth, while others swear there have been pieces of it found. Mount Ararat is covered year-round by snow, and many Armenians believe that the ark is buried there, preserved in the snow and ice and will one day be found. Unfortunately, though Mount Ararat is the holiest of sites for the Armenians, it is actually in Turkey, a fact that has been and continues to be disputed by the Armenians.

I don't believe the story of Noah's Ark, but it captivates the imagination like few other stories. Looking out at Mount Ararat one can see how it could be an inspiration and how, even if you didn't find the story credible, the idea of it could connect you in some way with the divine.

. . .

Nearing the end of the trip, I passed out a brief questionnaire, asking for certain opinions from my fellow travelers. One thing I asked was what moved them the most about this experience. Almost to a person, they responded that it was Chet's lecture. Chester Gillis is a Catholic theologian and dean of Georgetown College, along on the trip as a guest lecturer, which probably wouldn't have resonated as it did if we hadn't seen the mystery and beauty of the sights. He had given a talk as we traveled from Tibet to India, which he'd titled "On the Plain of Unity," and it turned out to be one of the most enlightening talks I had ever heard. It was about pluralism, and I'm embarrassed to say that this was a new concept for me, particularly in relation to religion. Today it is a common topic, but a decade ago it was not.

"What a perfect setting to discuss it," he began, "on a world tour of faiths in which we encounter Christians, Muslims, Jews, Sikhs, Buddhists, Hindus, and others—to talk about Christianity and the world religions."

He stunned us all by beginning with the idea that the scandal of Christianity is its divisions and disunity: "We cannot help but see a pluralism of belief and practice that transcends Judeo-Christian confines." Chet went on to quote from *God Has Many Names* by the contemporary philosopher of religion John Hick:

> *We have been like a company of people marching down a long valley, singing our own songs, developing over the centuries our own stories and slogans, unaware that over the hill there is another valley, with another great company of people marching in the same direction, but with their own language and songs and stories and ideas; and over another hill yet another marching group—each ignorant of the existence of the others. But then one day they all come out onto the same plain, the plain created by modern global communications, and see each other and wonder what to make of*

*one another. You might think that the different groups would then
simply greet one another as fellow companies of pilgrims. But in
fact that is made difficult by part of the content of our respective
songs and stories.*

Chet went on to say:

*It is obvious that we have emerged from the valley and entered the
plain. The plain is wide and broad, and we have several options.
We could regroup our company of pilgrims and return to the
relative security and absolute isolation of the valley from which we
emerged. We could politely bow to the other companies of pilgrims
and move in our own direction. We could approach them for a
closer look, get to know them a bit, but then make a friendly exit
from them. Or we could stop in the middle of the plain with them
and tell them from whence we have come. We could try to learn
about their religion and they about ours, so that we could discern
if indeed we are on the same journey of faith, moving towards
the same Divine One who beckons us from the valley to plain,
to perhaps a new mountain where together we will see the route
ahead.*

He concluded by suggesting: "But perhaps we are headed in the
same direction. Perhaps there is for all of us the same eternal one
who beckons us. Perhaps the journey would be easier and more enlightening together. Perhaps the discussion must begin before the
journey can go on for any of us."

What was so fascinating to me was that Chet had articulated what
I wanted On Faith to be, I just hadn't been able to formulate it in
my mind or properly put it into words. I wanted to take it further

though. To me it wasn't just about religions. It was about faith and spirituality and people with different beliefs, including those who had no religious beliefs at all. Most people believe in something. The important thing is to try to understand and respect one another. It's interesting how difficult that is for many people. If I could have some part in changing that, I thought then, that would be tremendously satisfying. There is a Jewish saying, "Tikkun Olam," a concept that encourages acts of kindness in order to "repair the world." That would be a goal I could aspire to.

I had gone on the trip almost as a student or reporter—to learn about religion generally and certain religions specifically. In a way it was a business and educational trip, as well as a chance to have some distance from Ben in both time and space, to try to process what had been happening to us. As it turned out, I was totally and happily distracted and absorbed by the trip and really hadn't focused much on my life with Ben except toward the end when I was missing him and Quinn so much.

I certainly learned a lot about religion, which is what I had hoped for. I saw that there are so many ways to practice one's faith, and that they should all be respected. One of the things many religion scholars detest is to hear people say that all religions are the same. Yet almost to a person, those on the trip were astounded by the similarities in the basic tenets of the religions we had studied, even though the rituals might be different.

Though most people said they were clearer about their religion or their beliefs after the trip, I was more confused. It was a little bit like the graduates at the military academies throwing their hats up in the air after the ceremony. I always wonder how they find their own hats after it is all over. I had for so long worn my atheist hat and had always thought it quite a good fit. Now I would have to go around trying on other hats to find one that better suited me. Maybe I'd find mine again or maybe not. Maybe if I got the old one back, I wouldn't want it anymore. Maybe I'd find someone else's hat that fit me better. There was something frightening and hopeful about that possibility.

. . .

Finally we arrived in Turkey. We had celebrated Ben's eightieth birthday in Turkey in 2001 with twenty-three of our closest friends and their kids. Talk about magic. . . . Now here I was in Istanbul, only this time I was alone. I had had it. Two more days to go, another day in Istanbul and then back to Rome, and I couldn't be away another minute. I went back to the hotel and booked the next flight to Washington and was on my way home that afternoon.

When I arrived at Dulles, Ben was there with a bouquet of flowers in a rented limousine to pick me up. We held on to each other the entire ride back. I loved him so much and he loved me so much. I was so happy that he had come by himself. It was romantic and gave us a chance to be alone together. I knew I could never be away from Ben for that long again. I never was.

I also knew in my heart—both before and after the trip—that love was at the center of my life and that nothing could ever be more important to me than the ones I loved. That was the transcendent, that was the divine, and, yes, that was the magic.

Chapter 20

Love is our true destiny. We do not find the meaning of life
by ourselves alone—we find it with another. . . . The meaning
of our life is a secret that has to be revealed to us in love.

—Thomas Merton, *Love and Living*

After I returned from the Great Faiths trip, things between Ben and me improved considerably. According to everyone who had been around him, he had been especially bereft, almost desperate, lost really, without me. He couldn't keep away from me, constantly holding me and kissing me and telling me how much he loved me and that he couldn't live without me. He didn't want me out of his sight and, though he was still going to the *Post* every day (for shorter and shorter times), he wanted me to be home when he got back and would be upset if I wasn't there. The few times I had to go to New York for work, almost always only for a night, he would be so morose that I would call him constantly to check in.

It was around this time that people were beginning to notice Ben's lack of affect, his distance, his forgetfulness. It was clearly time for Ben to be tested. Much against his will, he agreed. He knew—dreaded—and so did I, what the diagnosis would be. We were right. Dementia. Frankly, I didn't care what the label was. It was what was happening to Ben that I cared about. I told nobody.

. . .

Quinn's wedding in 2010 was the happiest day of my life, except for the day he was born. He was twenty-eight. He was marrying a beautiful, kind young woman, full of life and full of love. My darling Quinn, whom we had been told would never finish high school, never go to college, never have friends, never have a job, never have a relationship, was getting married to Pari, someone he and we adored. Ben and I kept pinching ourselves. How could we be so lucky? This was beyond anything that we could have imagined. He was so happy. We were so happy.

They both wanted the wedding to be at the Washington National Cathedral. I was fascinated to see that Quinn (Pari was raised Catholic) wanted the highest, most religious ceremony possible. He had rarely been to church himself. His church was with his father in the woods. Yet the idea of this ritual was deeply important to him as it was to Pari and of course to me.

The day was 10/10/10, a Sunday of Columbus Day weekend, chosen by the three of us for its magical date. And it was magical, from beginning to end. The weather was perfect—eighty degrees, dry and clear with just the slightest breeze. The black-tie ceremony started in the evening with the radiant pink sun about to slip down over the horizon. The cathedral was filled with candles and the lights were low. The main illuminations came from the last streams of sunlight shattering the dimness with shards of brilliance from the multicolored stained-glass windows. A harp played in the background as guests were seated.

When Quinn stepped up to the altar, he was in full Scottish regalia, wearing his kilt, the Sterling family tartan complete with shawl and pin. I know, I know, I'm the mother, but he looked so handsome he took my breath away. I held it together until I saw Ben and Pari.

There was something so deeply touching about Ben as he walked down the aisle, gently holding Pari's arm to give her away. Their walk together was spirited and exuded happiness.

Pari looked exquisite. Quinn was spellbound. He looked so young and vulnerable and scared and proud and happy. Ben didn't cry often, but this time he barely made it through.

It was the most beautiful wedding I had ever seen. One of our guests would later say that the whole thing made him forget for a time that he was an atheist.

At the reception Ben and I decided to speak early on so we could drink. I insisted on going first. I began by saying, "This is the happiest day of my life." When I had finished, Ben made his toast and began by saying, "Sally just stole my lead. This is the happiest day of my life."

The evening was very multicultural with food from different lands: Persian (Pari), all-American (Quinn), Southern (me), and Yankee (Ben). Salman Ahmad, a Pakistani rock star and good friend of all of ours, played and sang a dizzying song from his band, Junoon. Christiane Amanpour (Iranian) and Salman's wife (Pakistani) performed a Middle Eastern ceremony for the bride. Bandleader Peter Duchin had everyone on their feet until midnight.

When I think about magic and its effects on the mind and body, I see clearly that Quinn and Pari's wedding had it all—the sacred ritual, the beauty, the mystery of the marriage vows, the wonder at the flowing of life and the changes we go through, the awe that we somehow experienced together, bonded in that holy place filled with grace, the sense of community it inspired. Most of all there was heightened magic in the profound love Ben and Quinn and I had for one another and the opportunity to add Pari to the inner circle of our family. Who could ask for more than that?

Somehow it seemed like a metaphor for our lives. It was all there that night. The memories live on. I still cherish them and all that they meant.

. . .

Ben's confusion accelerated. A reporter called to interview him about something sensitive that had happened at the paper. His secretary, Carol, put him through. Ben was very forthcoming—in fact, too forthcoming. He told the reporter much more than he should have, much more than he knew. He opined about whatever the subject was, naming names and not being very flattering. After the piece came out, I went to Don Graham and suggested that it might be time for Ben to stop going to the *Post*. Don, the kindest human being on the planet, refused to even consider it. However, we did work out a plan. All the secretaries and assistants on the floor were advised never to put a call through to Ben without checking with Carol or Don or me. Everyone was told to turn down all interview requests. Ben never knew about it. When we went to dinner parties, I would make sure we arrived late so we didn't have to make a lot of conversation beforehand, and then I sat with a knot in my stomach, watching Ben from across the table to make sure he wasn't saying or doing something to embarrass himself. I began making excuses for him. When he would forget something, I'd make a joke and deflect the worry and concern of others by saying something that could be taken as funny or at least lighthearted, like "you're having my problem, when you're the one who's supposed to have the good memory."

Ben became more and more dependent on me in social situations and on Carol and Don at the office. Almost every day he went down to the *Post* cafeteria for lunch and would be immediately surrounded by a coterie of reporters and admirers and that seemed to perk him up. There was always a group conversation and as long as Ben gave somebody the finger or told somebody to "fuck off," people didn't seem to notice the forgetfulness that much.

I organized a lunch group at the Madison hotel across from the *Post*, where I had a running tab. Ben's secretary, Carol, had a sign-up sheet and up to five people could join. It was always full. We called it "Tuesdays with Ben."

One night we went to George Stephanopoulos's and Ali Wentworth's house for a party. We were all standing around having cocktails when Ben, suddenly pale and weak, collapsed on the sofa and proceeded to have what looked like a seizure. His eyes rolled back in his head, his mouth dropped open, and he blacked out. I asked somebody to call an ambulance, and within minutes we were speeding to George Washington University Hospital where we were met by our doctor, Michael Newman. Within a half hour, Ben was alert and talking. He was agitated and telling anyone who would listen to "get me the hell out of here." He was fine.

It was the consensus that he had had a vasovagal syncope episode. Within hours we were home and in bed as if nothing had happened. It was only a day or two later that I realized he was behaving differently. He wasn't as sharp. He had lost something. In fact, he had had a mild cognitive impairment, sort of like a ministroke, or TIA. I was the only one who noticed.

· · ·

By now, our psychiatrist, Steven Wolin, and I both knew about Ben's dementia, which explained everything about his behavior, especially the recurring bouts of hostility aimed at me and only me. I also had read enough about dementia by this time to know that the patient usually takes out his feelings of anger, frustration, and fear on the one closest to him. That was me. With everyone else, he was still fabulous Ben, but there were times when he would be sarcastic, contemptuous, and even verbally abusive to me. I understood why, but it was still unbelievably painful. I wanted to get back what Ben and I had had together. By this time, Ben was no longer seeing Steven.

At one session with Steven I told him about a poem I had discovered in high school, "Maud Muller," by John Greenleaf Whittier. I thought it was one of the most poignant things I had ever read. It's about a young country maid and a judge who comes by on his horse and asks her for a drink from the stream. They chat for a while and then he rides away. She can't help wishing she could be his bride and he can't stop dreaming of her. She marries a poor, uneducated man and has a passel of children. He marries a cold, social-climbing wife. They each live out their days longing for the lives they might have had with each other. The poem ends with the line "Of all the sad words of tongue or pen, the saddest are these, 'it might have been.'"

Nothing could be sadder, I thought even at the time, than to have regretted not doing something you wanted to do, not taken that road, opportunity, risk, adventure, that leap of faith. I vowed I would never be the one to say to myself wistfully one day *it might have been*.

Yet here I was with my beloved Ben seeming to turn on me, and me not knowing how to deal with it. I couldn't bear the idea of having him die and be left with a lingering sorrow, thinking I could have done something differently.

Steven found the poem, read it to himself, looked up, and sighed, then asked me to read it aloud. I told him I couldn't. He insisted. I started to read and only got through the first few lines before I broke down, barely making it to the end. He told me it was up to me to make sure that I would never have those regrets. I needed to keep loving Ben as much as I could and would. Stroke him. Cherish him. Be grateful for him. It worked.

Not that there weren't episodes after that, but the unconditional love I showed him and he returned to me really changed things. After that, I never had to say or even think to myself *it might have been*. I had him and all the love I could ever want or need.

• • •

At one point, PathNorth, a group I belonged to, was having a meeting in New York. PathNorth was started by AOL's Steve Case and Doug Holladay, a hugely successful businessman who had also been to Princeton Theological Seminary. It's a group for leaders, CEOs, and executives who get together in informal settings and talk about the meaning of life. Doug would ask questions like "What makes you feel alive?" "What truly matters?" "How can we be better versions of ourselves?" "How can we do well by doing good?" There is a spiritual but not a religious component in the sharing of new ideas and connections to become deeper people.

Doug and Steve invited Ben to participate in a conversation with Jon Meacham in front of about 150 CEOs. I wasn't sure it was a good idea, but Ben wanted to do it. I explained to Doug Holladay, the head of the group, that Ben had become somewhat forgetful and I also discussed it with Jon. They thought it would be fine so we scheduled it.

We went up to New York two days early to see friends and go to galleries. The day before the lunch we were walking up the wide steps to the Metropolitan Museum of Art when Ben started to collapse. I got him off to the side of the stairs where he sat down and blacked out, his eyes rolling back in his head, his mouth open as had happened at George and Ali's. I didn't panic right away but held him for a few minutes until he came to. We sat there for about half an hour until he said he felt okay, then got up and slowly walked to the street, hailed a cab, and went back to the apartment where he slept the rest of the afternoon.

I told him we could cancel the event the next day but he insisted he wanted to do it. Even as we were getting dressed that morning to go to the lunch, I could see that he wasn't in full Ben form and again suggested canceling. Again he insisted he was fine.

We got through the lunch somehow. Ben was at a table with me and everyone was talking to him and he appeared to be having a good time. It wasn't until after the lunch when we went into the next room for the talk that I began to feel nervous. Ben and Jon were seated on a platform in front of the packed house. I was in the first row. From the beginning I was worried. Jon started by asking Ben questions about his navy experience in World War II, and Ben had a hard time articulating his responses. Jon kept trying, bringing up the Pentagon Papers, Watergate, the state of journalism, anything he thought Ben might respond to and be able to talk about. Ben, however, was shifting in his chair and looked anxious. I could see Jon's concern.

Finally Jon asked Ben another question. Ben looked down at me and said, "Help me, Sally." I prompted him. Jon looked at Doug, Doug came up to the platform, thanked them both, and started the applause. Ben stepped down and was immediately surrounded by people.

I told Jon I had to go to the ladies' room and rushed into a stall, afraid I would throw up. As I was there a group of women came in and began talking about Ben. To my surprise they exclaimed excitedly about how wonderful it was to get to hear Ben Bradlee.

. . .

Happily, Ben had recovered from the blackout as he would from others and went back to being his old self, though still confused at times.

We continued to live our lives as normally as we could. He continued going to the *Post* every day.

One of the things I learned from the doctors was that these lapses were unpredictable, infrequent, and unexpected, which made them particularly alarming. Between episodes, Ben was alert, insightful, and aware. The awareness made the lapses all the more painful. What was so compelling was that I never knew when I was going to have the real Ben as opposed to some stranger.

By that fall, though, I knew it was time to come clean. I was going to have to tell people that Ben had dementia. This was one of the hardest things I ever had to do.

Ben was in his office and I stopped by. The phone rang and Carol picked it up. It was our old friend, British editor and publisher Harry Evans, the husband of editor Tina Brown. They had actually gotten married at our house, Grey Gardens, on Long Island years earlier. Harry was twenty-five years her senior. I took the call. "Harry," I said, "Ben can't take calls anymore. He has dementia." There was dead silence on the phone and then Harry plaintively said, "Oh dear, I'm afraid we're all going to end up that way at some point, aren't we?"

It was done. We were heading into a new life, a life I was dreading, and yet a life that would be fulfilling in a way that I never could have imagined.

Once people—family and friends, everyone at the *Post*, and those who knew Ben only by reputation—found out, our lives changed, as I knew they would. The *A* word is a killer, which is why I always said "dementia," even though it was never clear which he had. Somehow Alzheimer's sounds like something one could catch. Dementia sounds tamer, more like gentle aging. At dinners, I would ask my friends to seat me next to Ben so that I could protect him when we did go out. I'd make sure the person on his other side was aware of Ben's situation.

Again, Don Graham was amazing. I suggested once more that Ben give up his office. Again, Don wouldn't hear of it. He was resolute. Ben's office was there for him until he died. Everyone on the ninth floor was clued in. Ben was welcomed and embraced with open arms.

. . .

The geriatric psychiatrist recommended a fabulous support group called "The Friends Club" that met in a church in Bethesda, Maryland. There were twelve men at various stages of dementia who met three days a week from 9:30 A.M. until 1:30 P.M. I thought I was in for a big fight with Ben, that he would never agree to go to some "candy ass" program. I never described it as a club for men with dementia. I told him it was a group for old navy men and foreign service types and journalists (all true) to get together and hang out several times a week. Sandra Day O'Connor's husband, John, had been in the group and so had Sargent Shriver. In fact, they apparently got into a pissing match one day when John told Sarge he talked too much.

At a cocktail party during that time, at Walter and Cathy Isaacson's, I saw Sandra, who had been a close friend of my parents through the Arizona connection with Barry Goldwater. She took me aside, put her hands on my shoulders, and with glistening eyes, said, "I just want you to know this is horrible, horrible, horrible."

For reasons that I will never understand, Ben agreed to go to the support group. On the first day, I took Ben to "school," which is what he called it. I hadn't been that nervous since I first took Quinn to nursery school, knowing he was learning disabled and had a speech defect and terrified he wouldn't be accepted by the other kids. I sat in on the whole session, next to Ben. The people who ran the group were brilliant with the men. The men were clearly at different stages. One man sat quietly, not participating at all. There were others in the group, the newer ones, who seemed quite normal until, after an hour or so, they began repeating themselves. Every once in a while, one of them would stop in the middle of talking and say, "I can't remember shit!" The others would totally crack up with appreciation. Ben did too. He began to relax.

I found myself holding court, keeping the conversation going around the table, telling stories, basically standing on my head. I was trying so hard to entertain them all so that they would like Ben. All I could think of was all those years I tried to attract friends to Quinn when he didn't have any by being funny and talking too much, trying too hard. It was emotionally exhausting. I had become Ben's protective mom. Ben held my hand during most of the meeting. I could see how dependent he was on me. He was so nervous and looked lost. I had never seen Ben like that. It killed me. Any hostility he had been showing to me simply disappeared. He had never been so loving in his life. As I drove him home he just put his hand over mine and said, "I love you, babe." It was like a miracle. It *was* a miracle. I felt in some way that God had given me Ben back. He loved me that way until he died.

· · ·

I was beginning to have to help Ben get dressed and undressed, to help him shower and shave and brush his teeth. At night I laid out his clothes for the next day. He had forgotten how, and I wanted him to look well groomed and sharp.

At this point I rarely left him. I moved my office from the third floor of the house and turned an old pantry next to the library into a little retreat for me so I could be near him all the time.

One day I had to go to New York and stay overnight for work. Carmen, our fabulous house manager, had also become a caretaker of Ben's. She said she would sleep on the sofa in our bedroom because I was afraid he would try to go downstairs and hurt himself. He refused to let her, so she kept the bedroom door open and slept in the room across the hall. The next morning she came in to wake Ben up and was shocked to find that he had completely destroyed my dressing room. He had turned over the chairs, torn the skirt on my dressing table, taken all the clothes out of the closet, trashed the medicine cabinet, cracked a mirror, broken a metal lamp with his bare hands, and knocked over the TV. He was sprawled across the bed dressed in my clothes, sound asleep. She couldn't get him up for school. She called me frantically, and I came home immediately. According to the doctors, this was a psychotic episode. He had absolutely no recollection of it. It would be the first of many. Oh, Ben, oh, Ben, where have you gone?

I tried to protect Quinn from as much of this as I could but still let him know that I needed his help. I didn't want him to be afraid of his father. He worshipped Ben. There were some things, though, that I thought would be too hard for Quinn to confront. Happily, Quinn and Pari were living in the house attached to ours, a house we had rented out until he came back from school with a group of roommates. Sadly, they were about to separate amicably. We never told Ben.

When things began to get really bad, Quinn and Pari were an enormous help to me and wonderful to Ben. There wasn't an evening they didn't come over to give him a hug, have a cocktail with us, and watch the news. This was his favorite part of the day and mine too.

They and Carmen, as well as all my wonderful friends and family, sustained me.

. . .

Still, I needed to get away again. I was losing myself. As it happened, PathNorth was having its annual silent retreat at Holy Cross Abbey, a Trappist monastery in Berryville, Virginia, acres and acres of rolling hills on the Shenandoah River.

I drove to the monastery on January 7, 2013. I had no idea what to expect and I was particularly self-conscious about going. We were to spend nearly three days in absolute silence. Even at meals. No phones, no TVs, nothing.

I could feel the tension dissipate as I drove in and saw the old manor house where meetings were held, the chapel next to it, and the retreat house to the right, sitting up on a rise overlooking the wide flowing river.

Steve Case and Doug Holladay had arranged for twelve of us to be together for these few days. My friend Tim Shriver, author and chairman of Special Olympics International, was also a participant. The entire group met first to talk about our expectations before we began our silence. This was not necessarily meant to be a religious exercise. For some it was, for others it was simply a time for quiet. That was what drew me in.

The discussion we had that afternoon was stunningly candid about why each of us had come. I talked about Ben and the exhaustion of taking care of him. One man talked about how he had gotten a very harsh letter from his wife, which ultimately led to a divorce. Given that everyone there was considered an extremely successful, privileged person there was a lot of pain in that room. After the meeting, we did not speak.

Our rooms at the center were comfortable but spartan. A window, a single bed, a chair, a dresser, and a lamp. No locks on the doors. I had brought a few religion books to read and there was reading material available and even a small library. The "dorm master" was a monk who lived in the building. Right down the hall from my room on the ground floor was a beautiful small simple two-story-high chapel with a cross at the altar and a stone font in the front. I went in there just to look around and found myself sitting silently for a long time just looking at the cross. My mind was a blank. A rare blissful blank.

The monks prayed the "Divine Office" or "Liturgy of the Hours" five times a day: vigils at 3:30 A.M., lauds at 7:00 A.M., midday prayer at 2:00 P.M., vespers at 5:30 P.M., and compline at 7:30 P.M. I decided I wanted the full experience so I went to all the services. I went to the first one at 5:30 before supper. The services—short, maybe half an hour, with readings and chanting and prayers—were in the main chapel attached to the monks' quarters and the manor house up the road. I liked being there alone but not alone. I felt comforted. It was already dark and freezing cold and we trudged through the ice and snow back to our quarters. A simple supper—meat, vegetable, and a starch—was self-served at a long U-shaped table. No alcohol of any kind. I didn't really feel like a drink. We ate in total silence with the strains of monks chanting over the sound system. The silent meals were my least favorite part, in fact the only thing I didn't like about the experience. There is something unnatural to me about sharing a meal, breaking bread with others, and not communicating with them. A meal is a ritual. It should be sacred. It should be a holy communion of sorts. There should be wine and candles and laughter and joy and shared experiences.

I finished eating in about fifteen minutes, washed my plate, grabbed an apple to take back to the room, and left. It wasn't long before the 7:30 compline. We had to take flashlights to guide us through the pitch-black to find the chapel and get back. Nobody spoke. I went to bed immediately, knowing I had to get up for the 3:30 A.M. vigils. I was surprised at how many of us actually showed up for the 3:30. Again, it was a calming experience. Back we went with our flashlights and fell into bed. The 7:00 A.M. lauds was the hardest to get up for. I felt I had barely slept. I came back, got some oatmeal, and fell back into bed, not to awaken until lunch. After lunch I went to the 2:00 P.M. midday prayer.

I decided to take a walk. With twelve other guests at the monastery, I expected to run into someone but didn't see another soul. I headed down the long road to the entrance and turned toward the river. I went past the open-air chapel where services were held for the Cool Spring Natural Cemetery overlooking the Shenandoah River. At Cool Spring bodies are covered only with a shroud and lowered into the ground with a river stone as a marker. I rushed past the cemetery. I didn't want to think about death.

I found my way to the riverbank. The sun was getting lower and it was very cold, but I came upon a thick log right on the edge and sat down, leaning back against a tree. The water was dark and frigid, the sound of it rushing was urgent yet oddly soothing. Maybe because it seemed alive. I thought about Ben and was shocked to realize that it was the first time I had thought about him since I'd been there. How was that possible? He consumed me.

I don't know how long I was there. Maybe two hours, staring at the turbulence below me. I had unconsciously picked a pointed branch off a small tree near me, covered in dead leaves. Slowly, methodically, almost meditatively, I began to pick off each leaf until it was completely bare. It was only after I had finished that I understood what I had done. Each leaf represented something in my life that I had had to give up or was about to give up in order to care for Ben the way he needed to be cared for and the way I wanted to care for him. I had divested my life of all the nonessentials and I was happier for it. I felt free instead of burdened. I felt content instead of agitated. I felt gratitude that I was able to do that and to devote myself to him. He wouldn't be with me for long. I was losing more of him every day. I wanted, no, I needed to concentrate on Ben until the end. Only then would I be able to deal with what I knew would ultimately be my great loss.

I made it back in time for vespers, supper, and compline, after which I went into the tiny chapel by my room and lay on the floor in front of the cross, my arms spread out on either side of me. I completely lost myself. At some point I managed to get back to my room and sleep for a few hours until I plunged out into the icy darkness with my flashlight to go to the 3:30 A.M. vigils. That morning was like the last. When I had first arrived, I marveled at the idea of the monks living thirty, forty, fifty years like that, doing manual labor, speaking rarely, waking at all hours to pray. How could anyone choose that life? At first it seemed so mindless. Now I was beginning to see it was mindful. Exhausting but mindful. On some level I envied them. There was truly a sense of peace there, a peace I craved and had just caught a glimpse of.

Before we departed, we all gathered in the library to talk about our experiences. Everyone had a deeply personal story to tell and everyone had been profoundly affected in some way by their short stay there. I brought my bare branch with me and explained what it meant.

I also brought it home with me and am looking at it now as I write. It rests in a tiny Chinese vase hung on the wall above my desk. It reminds me to be aware always of what is really important and meaningful in my life. That's a gift.

. . .

It was during a kind of twilight zone period when Ben was on and off in terms of understanding what was going on with him. He had good days and bad days. During that time I got two requests for him to do interviews. Both of them were from close friends, but after the PathNorth interview episode with Jon Meacham, I didn't want anything like that to happen again. I refused them both at first. Robert Redford, who played Bob Woodward in *All the President's Men*, was doing a film about the making of the movie. Andy Lack, now the chairman of NBC News, was producing it. Andy was an old friend too, and they convinced me that they would protect Ben. They felt they couldn't do it without Ben, so I finally relented.

Tom Brokaw wanted to interview Ben for a special he was doing on Jack Kennedy. Again I said no. Tom was a trusted friend and persuaded me that he would protect Ben as well. Ben was thrilled to be doing the interviews. He was excited and the whole thing seemed to make him feel vital.

As it turned out, the interviews were both difficult for Ben and very little of what he said was used, but Andy, Bob, and Tom were true to their word. When both films came out, Ben looked and sounded like his regular old self, but he wasn't. Those were the last interviews he would do.

It broke my heart. How could this be happening to this brilliant, charismatic man? All the tectonic plates of my life were rearranging themselves. I had to come to grips with it. Few things have been harder.

. . .

In August of 2013, Jay Carney, then Barack Obama's White House spokesman, called me to say that the president was going to award Ben the Medal of Freedom but that it was to be kept a secret until it was announced some weeks later. Ben was ecstatic, although I'm not sure at that point that he really understood what was happening. That night we had people for dinner, a number of journalists, and Ben announced to everyone that he was getting the Medal of Freedom. He had forgotten it was a secret. I made them all swear they wouldn't say anything, but I lived in fear he would answer the phone or the door and blurt it out, which was exactly what he did. Somehow the story kept out of print for a while, but I did have to tell them that Ben was the leaker.

The ceremony was to be in November, and Ben was obsessed. Night after night he would get up at all hours and try to dress for the ceremony. I would have to convince him it wasn't going to be until November, but at that point he had lost track of dates. The night before the awards I invited all his children, his grandchildren, his stepchildren, his step-grandchildren, and his nieces and nephews for a family party. Ben was in his element as he sat on the sofa surrounded by a rotating group of adoring kids cuddling, holding his hand, embracing him, and telling him they loved him.

I have to say that I was surprised at how important this medal was to Ben. Public affirmation of his achievements was something he had never really cared about. Actually, he had always been a bit uncomfortable with personal accolades. Especially in his later years, he was constantly being asked to be celebrated at various events. He almost always declined. "But for the honor of it all . . ." he would scoff. Yet, here we were, as Ben was about to receive the highest civilian honor an American can get and he was beside himself with excitement and anticipation.

It was less than a year away from his death. He must have known that he was coming to the end of his life. He had been reminiscing more than usual about his past with me and his friends (his long-term memory was still good, his short-term memory not so good). It occurred to me that in some way this medal represented to Ben so much that had given his life meaning. He had served in World War II, defending his country and its values. He had worked as a journalist for nearly sixty years, devoted to finding the facts and exposing the truth, defending the Constitution and the First Amendment and all that it stood for. He had fought the good fight, he had finished the race, he had kept the faith.

Now, surrounded by all the people he loved, he would be recognized for that in a truly American ritual by the president of the United States. For Ben, I believe, it was a highly spiritual moment in his life.

The plan was for me to go early to the White House for the rehearsal to stand in for Ben and he would come later. There was no way he could stand around for hours beforehand.

Among those who were being honored that day were Bill Clinton, Oprah Winfrey, and Gloria Steinem. The irony was that during Clinton's presidency, some fifteen years earlier, Ben's name was on the short list for the award. Unfortunately for Ben, it was shortly after the Monica Lewinsky story had broken and I had just written a particularly scathing piece in the *Post* about the president, quoting many prominent members of the establishment community excoriating him for his behavior. I was told that the president was seething mad and kept the story on his desk for weeks, ranting about it to anyone who would listen. So it was a surprise to those who gathered to go over the final list for the medal recipients that when Ben's name came up, he spoke up enthusiastically, saying that Ben should definitely get it. He was asked why, considering the piece I had written about him. According to John Harris's 2005 book, *The Survivor: Bill Clinton in the White House*, the president's reply was "Anyone who sleeps with that bitch deserves a medal!" As you might expect, Ben didn't get the medal that year.

Now, there we all were, Ben and Bill being honored together, one big happy family. I had walked through the drill along with the other recipients. They had to walk up the aisle of the East Room to the podium, get up the stairs, wait for their citation to be read, walk up to the president, receive the medal, get back to their chairs, and then get back down the stairs. I was frantic. I knew Ben couldn't do it by himself. He was particularly out of it that morning, probably out of nervousness and excitement and lack of sleep. He had his good days and his bad days. This was a bad day.

Since the medals were awarded in alphabetical order, Clinton was directly behind Ben. In desperation I went to him and asked him if he would help Ben get through it. He couldn't have been more gracious. He took Ben by the hand and guided him up the red carpet to the podium and helped him to his seat, signaled him when he was to get up, helped him over to the president, guided him back to his seat, and then took his arm and led him out of the room when it was over. I was so grateful to him.

At the reception the former president came over to me laughing. "Do you know what Ben asked me? He said, 'Did I ever piss you off?'" "No," responded Clinton, "but that's only because by the time I became president you had already stepped down as editor." I thanked him profusely. We kissed and made up.

Ben went home and slept the rest of the afternoon. Miraculously, when he woke up, he was himself again so we were able to go to the president's dinner for all the honorees, present and past, celebrating the fiftieth year of the medal itself.

We were lucky. Normally there is no dinner afterward, just the reception. We were all seated at a long rectangular table and President Obama made a point of going around the table and greeting everyone who was there. He spent an especially long time talking to Ben who held his own in the conversation, laughing and joking with Obama. It was as if he had had a giant bolt of energy come down from the sky and infuse his body with his Ben-ness. I couldn't have been more proud or loved him more that night. I know how hard it must have been to rally but rally he did.

I told him how proud I was as we drifted off to sleep that night. He was truly happy. Around three in the morning he woke up and tried to get dressed to go get his medal. He continued to do that until he died a year later.

· · ·

Ben and I started going to La Samanna on the French side of the Caribbean island of St. Martin the year or two after we got together. It was the perfect place, for us, a paradise. Ben was very good at vacations. He worked incredibly hard and he relaxed really well. We would stay for a week, take a suitcase full of books, and never leave the hotel. Our days were a haze of relaxation and dreaminess. The hotel was a Moroccan-style villa on a high point overlooking the sea, surrounded by lush vegetation, bougainvillea, and shaded by palms. A short walk down a slope were small individual villas right on the beach, simply furnished with bamboo sofas, white cushions, and hand-painted tiles.

Our daily routine was the same. Breakfast, croissants, and apricot jam on our little terrace a few paces from the water, reading on *chaise longues* on the beach under a thatched umbrella, swimming in the iridescent sea, lunch with rum drinks, long naps, more reading on the beach. Another swim, more reading, tennis for Ben, a long walk on the crescent sand for me.

It was my meditation walk. It took nearly an hour to get to the end, collecting beautiful shells as I went. I would find the perfect large stone to lean against. I would stare out to sea, across the water to a tiny rock island called Saba, a gray point against the landscape if it was hazy, a ghostly blur if it was not. Saba was my sacred touchstone. Each time I rested there I would relive the year behind me and contemplate what lay ahead. I never visited the island. It was too mystical, too magical to want to acknowledge its actual existence. I prayed to Saba. I talked to Saba. I wanted it to be there in the clouds, where I could hear nothing but the insistent rush of waves as I pondered about what it all meant. Often I would stay for an hour or so in my silent reverie before I headed back in time to watch the splendid sunset with Ben, just the two of us, knowing that it would rise the next day and we would still be there together.

We would go up to the hotel for cocktails at eight in the Moroccan bar, a romantic dinner on the terrace with a fabulous view of the twinkling lights from the cruise ships floating by, stars, moonlight, the soft sounds of the waves licking the shore, wonderful long dinners, more wine, and then to bed. Talk about magic.

We led hectic lives at home and this was always a time to regroup and reconnect. We never failed to come back more in love than ever. I said every year and I say it now, that was the happiest week of the year for me. Ben and I did this for forty years, always the week of Valentine's Day.

I was seven months pregnant with Quinn there, sunbathing in the nude on a second-floor private terrace. After he was born, we took him there every year, first with a nanny, then with a friend, then with a girlfriend, then with his wife, Pari. When he was old enough to understand, we explained that this was our annual honeymoon week, but we missed him too much to leave him at home, while at the same time needing time alone. He totally got it and was almost apologetic about bothering us while we were there. He was happy to come in, give us hugs, and then run out to the beach or the pool, have dinners in his room watching movies and go to bed.

The February before Ben died, Quinn, Pari, and I collectively decided that it was best for them not to go. The past several years had been difficult for all of us because Ben was less and less engaged and more and more needy. Besides, I had a feeling this might be our last year there—which turned out to be the case—and I wanted to be alone with him the way we were in the beginning.

I hired a nurse to simply be there for him so that if I wanted to go read on the beach or swim or walk, he wouldn't get confused or scared or wander off. He slept most of the day, had a late breakfast, came out to sunbathe for maybe half an hour, had no lunch, and napped for the rest of the afternoon. The nurse left at six.

At seven the first night, I gave him a shower, got him dressed, and we walked up the steep slope for dinner. He made it without complaining. I was dreading the dinner, anticipating a lifeless, monosyllabic Ben and me staring wistfully, tearfully out to sea, remembering the golden days. How wrong I was.

Every night, like the Nutcracker, Ben miraculously came to life. Once we had gotten to our favorite table for two on the edge of the terrace and ordered our bottle of wine, it was as though we had gone back in time. I have to admit I did most of the talking, laughing, gossiping, telling him funny stories, but he responded with enthusiasm and excitement. We would hold hands walking down the hill, fall into bed, and hold on to each other all night. It was the same each day. Ben was out of it until dinnertime and then rose to the occasion.

The last night was the most special. We held hands and kissed all through dinner and just stared lovingly at each other as if someone had sprinkled us with fairy dust. At the end of dinner Ben took both my hands and looked longingly at me. "I just want you to know," he said, "that this has been the happiest week of my life. I never want it to end. I just want to stay here with you forever. You are the most fun person I know. I love you so much."

I knew what he meant. I wanted to stop time, freeze us there, in our moonlit dream. We both knew, though it was unspoken, what lay ahead. We walked down the path to our room arm in arm and went to bed. That night he had a psychotic episode. The next morning he remembered nothing.

Chapter 21

If there is a meaning in life at all, then there must be a meaning in suffering. Suffering is an ineradicable part of life, even as fate and death. Without suffering and death human life cannot be complete.

—Viktor E. Frankl, *Man's Search for Meaning*

It was the end of August and we were in East Hampton at Grey Gardens. I always had a big birthday party for Ben on the Saturday night closest to his birthday, which was the twenty-sixth. It was his favorite party of the year. In 2014 it was Ben's ninety-third birthday. Though he would insist "I don't want all that fuss," he was quick to peer over my shoulder to check on the seating arrangements.

Ben was agitated, confused, and weak that day, though he had slept most of the morning and afternoon. There were more than forty invited for a seated dinner. He was lying on the bed, watching me get dressed, his favorite thing to do, and held up his hand, our signal for me to come over and take it. He looked at me with a mixture of sadness, apology, and maybe a little embarrassment. "I don't think I'm going to make it, babe," he said. I kissed him and told him it would be okay if he didn't feel like it. Everyone would understand. If he felt up to it, he could come downstairs later.

Trying to put on a brave and cheerful face to greet our guests was extremely difficult. I managed to get through cocktails and announced dinner. As I led the way to the dining room, who should appear at the bottom of the steps but Ben, tan and gorgeous and dashing as usual in his Turnbull and Asser shirt with the white collar, white striped pants, a dark sweater, and the brightest smile you've ever seen. He was the host. He greeted everyone warmly, shook their hands, clapped them on the back, remembered their names—and if he didn't he called them "chief" or "gorgeous." He was the handsomest man in the room and the cockiest. He was Ben, my husband, the man. He had rallied yet again.

The party was a smash. Ben carried it off. He was clearly having a great time. The birthday cake arrived and he blew out the candles. I made a wish, wishing that he would keep living. I began the toasts, telling Ben how much I loved him. What followed was one fabulous encomium after the other. Ben lit up. According to the toasts, Ben was clearly the greatest editor, man, human who ever lived. The more people drank the more over the top the toasts became. Steve Kroft gave a fabulous toast and then was so wound up that he gave it again, cheered on by the rowdy guests.

Then Ben tried to respond. He couldn't and was clearly frustrated. He kept saying my name. It was becoming uncomfortable. I knew what he was trying to say, what he had said after all his birthday parties. I put my hand on his and said, "You can just say you love me if you want. You don't need to say anything else." He couldn't get the words out. "I think everyone needs another drink," I said loudly to the group and everyone seemed happy to let Ben off the hook. I got up and put my arms around his shoulders and whispered to him how much I loved him and how proud of him I was.

Suddenly, he was exhausted. He quietly got up and slipped out of the room. The party went on. *Oh, Ben, how I wanted you to be able to stay and have a good time and be the life of the party the way you always were. How I wanted you back.* I couldn't wait to get up to my bed and hold him in my arms. I went upstairs and crawled into the bed and engulfed him. He had been asleep, but he knew I was there.

"I tried to say I loved you but I couldn't," he said. "I'm sorry, babe."

"You were fantastic tonight," I whispered. "Everyone said so. You really pulled it off."

"It was a wonderful party," he said. "You always do it so well. . . ."

He dozed off. I cried myself to sleep.

The doctors had told me Ben was in perfect health. He could live another five years. Yet I knew in my gut that night, for the first time, that he was leaving me. I lay in bed with Ben and thought about praying. As with Quinn, the night before his heart surgery, I didn't know who to pray to. I didn't know what to ask for. Did I really want Ben to live this way, or get worse, for another five years? I didn't know what I wanted. I wasn't angry. I felt defeated. I had always managed to overcome everything bad that had happened to me. But this? I didn't want to drag Quinn down by letting him know how hopeless I felt. All I had to turn to was God. And God just wasn't there for me at that moment.

• • •

It was Thursday, September 11, 2014. Ben would be dead in a little over a month, but I couldn't have predicted that. We were moving forward with life as usual, our new normal. Ben was tired but in a good mood. He was always happy to see his doctor, Michael Newman, and we had a jovial conversation with him about Ben's overall health. Ben said he was slowing down but felt fine. Michael asked the nurse to take Ben for a blood test. When he left, Michael shut the door and sat down.

"I'm putting Ben in hospice care," he said.

"I'm sorry?" Clearly I hadn't heard him correctly.

"I'm putting him in hospice care."

"What does that mean?" I asked. "He's not dying. He's healthy as a horse. There's nothing medically wrong with him. He sleeps a lot and is confused, but the geriatric psychiatrist said he could live for five more years."

"I know," said Michael quietly. He was not just Ben's doctor. He was mine and Quinn's as well. He was also a close friend. We spoke shorthand. He was always honest with me, and beyond empathetic. He loved Ben too. We just looked at each other.

"How much time does he have?" I asked finally.

"Maybe four months but I doubt it," he said. "Probably two."

"But, Michael, how do you know? What are the signs?"

"I just know," he said. "I've been doing this a long time."

I was in such shock that I couldn't respond. I couldn't take it in. Here was my husband I loved so much, joking and laughing with Michael just a minute ago and now he would be gone in two months? I couldn't wrap my head around the idea. Michael picked up the phone and called the head of hospice and arranged for his favorite nurse, Vallerie Martin, to come to our house to meet Ben that week. I sat there like a zombie. The nurse brought Ben back into the room, all smiles. Michael explained that he was going to send a nurse over to the house once a week to see him, so he wouldn't have to be constantly coming downtown to the office. Ben didn't seem to think anything of it. Neither of us mentioned hospice. When we left, as we were waiting for the elevator, I put my arms around Ben and hugged him as hard as I could.

Our usual exchange took on an even greater meaning: "I love you, Ben."

"Me too, babe."

. . .

A few days later, I received a letter from Oak Hill Cemetery, which is at the top of our hill in Georgetown on R Street at Thirtieth. Ben and I had bought a plot there some years earlier. The cemetery is a "garden cemetery," one of the most beautiful in the country. At the time the only available plot was down the hill in a sort of gulch right on the road, which I found depressing. However, we bought it because we wanted to get grandfathered in. We could upgrade later.

The letter said Oak Hill was trying to create more space and had decided to sell eight plots for mausoleums along the small road that ran behind the entrance garden. Would I be interested? I would. The coincidence of the timing was astonishing. Although, as I understand the universe, I now know better than to call a gift like this a coincidence. Caroline Casey had taught me the term synchronicity, or meaningful coincidence. She always told me to watch for periods of increased synchronicity—these periods, she said, are when the magic happens.

I made an appointment to meet with the superintendent of the cemetery on that Thursday, September 18, in the afternoon. I had already agreed to do an interview at midday with Brian Lamb of C-SPAN. It was to be a wide-ranging conversation about On Faith, how the website was doing, and my life in general.

I had only told a few close friends that Ben was in hospice care—clearly still not really knowing what it meant. He wasn't sick. He was confused and slept a lot, but he still knew us all. He was still Ben.

Brian began the interview by asking questions in general, but at some point he asked me how Ben was doing. By that time our friends and many of his old colleagues knew that Ben had dementia, but that was the extent of it. I remember starting to talk about Ben and having an out-of-body experience. It wasn't me talking. There was this person sitting in a chair and I was floating above her listening to her tell Brian, very calmly, solemnly but not emotionally, that her husband was dying and had been put under hospice care. She clearly had no qualms about what she was saying. She was very matter-of-fact. She talked about how taking care of him was a spiritual experience. I nodded to myself. She was right. I hadn't thought of it that way. I hadn't thought of it any way except that taking care of him was what I was meant to do, what I was called to do, what I had to do, but mostly what I really wanted to do more than anything in the world. Taking care of Ben was sacred. She kept talking. I agreed with everything she said; she said it better than I could have. Where was she finding the words? It felt like a stream of consciousness, as if she had to tell this, had to get it out, had to let people know.

When the interview was over and Brian thanked her, I came back into myself. I had no feeling at all. I got up to leave. Several of the producers came up with tears in their eyes to tell me how moving the interview was, but I didn't remember what had been said. I managed to sleepwalk my way out of there and get home. I needed to see Ben, to reassure myself that he was still there.

Then I went to the cemetery and chose a plot that was in the front for a mausoleum. It didn't occur to me then, in the state I was in, that anyone, much less Ben, would ever be in it. It just gave me a sense of comfort knowing it was there.

* * *

Ben's hospice nurse, Vallerie, began visiting regularly. Ben still had no idea she was a hospice nurse. Or maybe he did. He had no idea I was planning his funeral. Or maybe he did. She and I discussed the fact that we had not talked about death. We decided that he didn't want to. He hadn't asked Michael Newman or Vallerie or me a single question about his health.

I was moving full steam ahead with funeral planning. It was a strange yet welcome distraction, a way to keep my hands busy and my mind occupied. Actually, nothing can stop me when I'm in that state. As Ben would say, my "motor was running." In some ways, I'd never been so calm and undistressed in my life. I had called the National Cathedral and spoken to Dean Gary Hall to set up an appointment with the staff. I had lined up the choirs, a tenor, a band, the food and a tent for the reception, the programs, the evergreens for the church. I hadn't cried. I had too much to do and not enough time, although I still hadn't accepted it yet. I was planning all this just in case. . . .

A week or so before Ben died, Vallerie was conducting a "routine" checkup on Ben. She was trying to get a sense of where he was. Suddenly he turned serious. He looked at Vallerie and me.

"When am I leaving?" he asked.

"What do you mean, Ben?" I responded. He seemed puzzled that I didn't understand.

"When do I have to go?" I looked at Vallerie. Was he saying what I thought he was saying?

"Go where, Ben?" I asked. He appeared frustrated and impatient.

"When am I going home?"

"You are home, Ben," I said, taking his hand. "You are home."

He closed his eyes and leaned his head back on the sofa. Vallerie motioned to me to leave the room with her. We walked into the kitchen.

"He's asking when he's going to die, isn't he?" I said, barely able to keep it together.

"Yes."

I knew that "going home" was the closest we were going to get to speaking about his death. His spirit was in me and mine in him. We didn't need to say anything to each other. He knew and I knew. We both knew.

. . .

That same night Bob Woodward and Elsa Walsh came to see Ben. Everyone wanted to say good-bye. Ben came alive—it was amazing how he would rally. I fixed him a drink as I did every night. We laughed and talked. He was really coherent. Ben and I sat together on the sofa, he held my hand tightly and swung it back and forth. He was so loving and affectionate and talked about what good care I was taking of him that it nearly made me cry. Elsa too.

Ben gave Bob the finger at one point, which really meant he was back. Bob was thrilled. After they left, I took him upstairs to help him shower and get him ready for bed. He was in a particularly feisty mood. I had a hard time with him in the shower and finally had to undress and get in with him as I sometimes did when he couldn't wash himself. When I got him out, I started to dry him off. At one point the towel brushed up against his private parts.

"Ouch!" he yelled.

"I'm so sorry," I said. "Did I hurt you?"

He glared at me. "If you hit my balls one more time, this party is over."

I burst out laughing. I looked up at him to see how upset he was, and he had a mischievous grin on his face. It was Ben. I stood up and put my arms around him, both of us still dripping wet, and held him for the longest time.

That night, after his shower, as I was walking him to his side of the bed, he stopped on my side and sat down. I had on a little silk night shift. He pulled me to him and began to run his hands underneath it, caressing my body, kissing me all over, telling me how beautiful I was, how desirable I was, how much he loved me. I knew he wanted to make love to me. I wanted him to as well. That part of our lives had never ended. But I knew he couldn't. He knew he couldn't too. We just held each other. I have never known such longing. I have never known such sorrow.

. . .

Because the house had been busy with family and friends throughout that week—everyone wanting to say good-bye—both Ben and I were exhausted, although he seemed to be holding his own. I finally decided to stop having people come by. He couldn't handle it anymore.

That weekend Quinn and I decided to take Ben to Porto Bello again. We didn't know how many weekends he had left, and the weather was going to be beautiful, sunny and crisp. We could have a fire, which Ben loved. We had a hard time getting him in the car, and he slept the whole way down. We had told Vallerie we were going, and she said she would alert the hospice people down there. I took my hospice kit with me. By the time we got to the country Ben couldn't get out of the car. When we finally got him into the house, he didn't want to sit by the fire. He wanted to go to bed, but we had to carry him up the stairs. I almost decided to put him back in the car and drive home, but it was already dark and I figured if he hadn't improved by the next day, we'd go back.

We got him in bed and he went right to sleep. The next day he couldn't get out of bed. He was practically catatonic. I called Vallerie. They couldn't get a hospice nurse over to us because they weren't on the same plan or something. It was all very confusing. Quinn had called his friend Stephen, whose wedding we had had at Porto Bello the weekend before. Stephen's father, John Ball, was the priest at the Episcopal Church in St. Mary's City across the river from us. He dealt with hospice all the time, but he couldn't get a nurse over either. Ben was really sinking, and I was in a panic. He wasn't making any sense, just talking gibberish. I spoke to John, who thought Ben might be dying. He called his friend the local doctor, who agreed with his diagnosis. I was practically hysterical. I didn't want him to die at Porto Bello. We had no hospice care. The police would come. We'd have to get his body to Washington. I didn't know what to do.

John showed up at the house and suggested he give Ben last rites. He and Quinn and I gathered around Ben in our bedroom and placed our hands on him as we prayed. I had never heard last rites before except in books and movies. I felt as if I were in a movie. It was unreal. The movie was going to be over soon and then we could go to sleep and in the morning everything would be okay. I wrapped myself around Ben, weeping. Quinn was holding me, stricken. It was all happening so fast. Ben seemed only vaguely aware of what was going on.

Father Ball began with this prayer: "Almighty God, we lift up your servant Ben, and we thank you for his life. . . . Help him to know you are right there with him holding his hand as you lead him gently home." He continued praying: "We remember, O Lord, the slenderness of the thread, which separates life from death and the suddenness with which it can be broken." He then said the Lord's Prayer and anointed Ben on the forehead with oil.

After the prayer of commendation, he ended with a blessing: "May the peace of God which passes all understanding keep your heart and mind in the knowledge and love of God and of his son, Jesus Christ, our Lord. The blessing of God, Father, Son, and Holy Spirit, be with you now and remain with you always. Amen."

Not since Quinn's wedding had I been so immersed in prayer. His words were not only not off-putting but welcome and deeply comforting. I felt Ben was safe, in good hands, cherished, and he would be taken care of. I believed for that moment that Ben was in God's hands.

Ben began breathing a bit more steadily and I persuaded John to leave, promising to call him if Ben died. I made Quinn go to bed and clung on to Ben for the rest of the night, counting his irregular breaths, my hand on his heart. I finally fell asleep. Sunday morning he was still alive. But he was definitely dying. John Ball got the doctor to come over to see if we could get back to Washington in a car or if we needed to get an ambulance or if we should let him die where we were. I was adamant that we take him back to Washington. The doctor felt we could get him back alive if we gently put him in the car with the seat all the way down and pillows around him, which we did. We made it home quickly and had him in our bed by midday. He was so happy to be there and so was I. I curled my body around him and never left him until he died two days later.

For those two days Ben was surrounded by family and friends. Quinn later told me that on the last day Ben was able to speak he saw that he could barely keep his eyes open. When Quinn asked his father if he was okay, Ben threw up his hands and said, "Yeah, of course. I'm fine. Don't worry." Later that day Quinn had gone back and lay down on the bed with him. Ben lifted his head, just barely, looked over his shoulder, and said to him: "I got a good feeling about you . . . I love you." Those were his last words to Quinn. What a send-off.

Leslie Marshall, Ben's former daughter-in-law, who lived across the street, was there the whole time. I don't know how I would have made it through without Leslie. She came every day to give

Ben a hug and keep up my spirits. Ben's daughter, Marina, and his stepdaughter, Ros Casey, were also with us every day. Other family members came in and out. He seemed to recognize everyone. Bob and Elsa came by again and came upstairs. "Ben," I said, "it's Bob and Elsa." "Bob Woodward," shouted Ben and practically sat up, stretching his arms out for a hug. "Yaaaaay!" They stayed only a short while, and he collapsed back into his pillow. Eden and Jerry Rafshoon came too, but Ben was beginning to drift off. Soon I asked everyone to leave. I wanted to be alone with him.

When the house was finally quiet, I turned to Ben, the light still on, still holding him tightly and I looked him in the eyes. "I love you, Ben," I said simply.

He looked at me with such adoration I will never get over it. I don't expect to see that look in anyone's eyes again. Most people may not be lucky enough to see it even once.

"Me too, babe," he said.

Those were the last words he spoke to me.

. . .

Ben drifted off to sleep. I didn't know that he wouldn't regain consciousness. I thought I would see him in the morning, talk to him, tell him again that I loved him. Have him tell me he loved me. That would never happen.

October 20 was our thirty-sixth wedding anniversary. I whispered to him that he couldn't die before that. He had to live out that day for me, for us. He didn't try to get up that night but his breathing had taken on a rasping quality. He would breathe in, with a breath full of sound, followed by a long silence that seemed like an eternity and then, when I thought he had drawn his last breath, he would breathe in again. I slept fitfully, on and off, too afraid to let myself go for fear he might die.

The next morning, Quinn was right there. He didn't leave Ben's side, sitting in a chair next to the bed and holding his other hand. Carmen brought in some balloons and flowers. All of us made a big fuss over Ben and our anniversary. He was not responding. I still had so many things I wanted to say to him. I lay in the bed next to him all day, reliving our wedding, reminding him of what a spectacular day it was, a beautiful sparkling October day and how I was so happy that I collapsed in his arms in tears when I was saying our marriage vows in front of Judge Bazelon.

I know he heard me. I began to caress his face and his head, tracing the outline of his profile over and over again, so as to memorize it, as if I were reading Braille. I thought if I kept touching him, I could keep him from leaving me.

I held his hand, only letting go to get up and use the bathroom. I would warn him not to die while I was gone. When I let go of his hand, he would clench and unclench his fingers until I got back. We went through the whole day like that. I smoothed his forehead, kissed him, and lay with my head on his chest, listening to him breathe laboriously, counting his heartbeats, praying for him to live, praying for him to die.

That night, our last together, our anniversary night, I turned out the lights and I reminisced to him about our honeymoon night. What happiness we had shared. What passion we had shared.

I needed that closeness again. He was wearing his favorite French gray-and-navy-striped long-sleeve T-shirt, so worn that it was raggedy around the neck and sleeves. I took it off. I had an overwhelming primitive urge to taste him—the same urge I had the night before Quinn's surgery when I thought he might die. This time I knew Ben was going to die. I began to kiss him all over and kept going until I was exhausted and he and I were both slick with my tears. Then I just lay on top of him and let him do the breathing for both of us until I fell asleep.

I didn't sleep long. Finally I rolled over and held his hand and listened to him, listened to him dying. One thing I know for sure. God was in the room with us that night.

. . .

The next morning I began to give Ben morphine. I had the kit and gave him a syringe full every half hour or so. Vallerie arrived in the late afternoon. His breathing had become really erratic. The pauses in between breaths made each one seem like the last. Even then, though, if I let go of his hand for a second, his fingers would start to wiggle. But then it happened; he took one last deep breath, let out a huge shudder, and seemed to sink back in his pillow. I kept waiting for the next gasp, but it never came. *Please, Ben, one more breath.* Nothing. His hand loosened in mine, even though I wouldn't let go.

Quinn put his head on his father's chest and began to sob. Ben's mouth was open. Vallerie came over and closed it. Then she called hospice. They called the funeral home. I lay there holding him, the family surrounding him.

What was I supposed to do now?

When Ben and I decided to get married we had less than a week to arrange our wedding. He wouldn't let me tell anyone. He didn't want to get scooped by the *Star*, our rival newspaper. I suddenly realized with all the family in the room and people downstairs in the house, the word would get out quickly that Ben had died. My journalistic instincts took over. It was 7:30 P.M. If I called now, we would make the first edition.

The *Washington Post* broke the story online and we made the first edition. Ben would have been so happy.

The funeral home came to get his body and took him away. I was beyond exhausted. I asked everyone to leave and took a shower, took my first Ambien in a year, and passed out. I had taken Ben's French T-shirt, rolled it up, and clutched it in my arms like a baby pillow. I would sleep with it every night from then on.

. . .

The following morning I woke up alone in my bed. Something was wrong. Something was missing. Then I remembered. Ben was gone. My sister, Donna, went to the funeral home with me. Somebody had to view the body. I didn't want to. I wanted to remember him alive, even the way he was at the end. Donna came back from the viewing shaking her head. "You don't want to see him," she said. "He doesn't look like Ben."

Of course he wouldn't when that much energy and life and light goes out of a person, and Ben had more than most. It couldn't be Ben. But where was he? What had happened to all that energy? It had to be somewhere. I wanted so badly to feel it, but I didn't. I wanted a visitation but I hadn't had one. I wanted a sign.

"Ben," I kept repeating to him under my breath, "let me know you are here with me."

That night I went to bed, I started to turn out my light. Just then the light on Ben's bedside table on the other side of the room went on. It stayed on for several minutes. At first I was stunned. "Oh, Ben, you are here. Thank you for letting me know. I love you so much. I miss you terribly already." His light flickered several times as though he were responding in kind. Then it went dark.

I threw myself on his pillow hoping by some miracle he would materialize. But it was just his pillow.

The next morning Carmen and I checked the lightbulb to make sure it hadn't burned out. It was fine. It still is.

. . .

The days before the funeral were a total blur. There would be three thousand mourners at the National Cathedral. It would be broadcast on C-SPAN. I was drowning in names, lists, programs, limousines, seating, music, tablecloths, flowers, menus, what to wear. Each thing I did had the mundane about it, yet I had a vision of the spectacular. It had to be. For Ben.

I spent hours going over the service, what music should be played and when, what readings, who the speakers, pallbearers, and ushers would be, in what order they would speak. Ben's and my song was "Evergreen." I would have the same Irish tenor who sang at Quinn and Pari's wedding sing it before the official service began. I wanted no flowers, only masses of different evergreens banked along and in front of the altar. I wanted one white rose to place on Ben's casket. He always gave me roses for our anniversary. I wanted a color guard with the American flag, "Taps," his favorite hymns, a choir. The dean of the cathedral, Gary Hall, was incredible, and the whole staff helped me plan the ceremony according to the protocol of the Episcopal Church.

My family had arrived from California and the house was full, thank God. The phones were ringing, the doorbells were chiming, notes and flowers and food were being delivered constantly. There was no time to grieve. The day of the funeral arrived. Oddly, I felt no emotion and was not at all nervous. Everything had been planned. I woke up, had some yogurt, and got dressed. It was strange but I had the feeling I was dressing for my own funeral. I put on each piece of clothing, each piece of jewelry (I wore Ben's family necklace, the same one I wore at our wedding) with ritualistic deliberation. I did my hair, put on my makeup, dabbed perfume (Sortilège) at my neck and on my wrists as though it would be the last time.

I slowly walked out of my room and down the stairs to the hallway where the whole family was waiting, everyone in black. Ben's children, grandchildren, stepchildren, their children, nieces and nephews—there must have been forty or fifty all together. There were limousines waiting for everyone. I gave people their car assignments. In ours, I told Quinn, would be him and me and Ben. I had forgotten. Ben would not be in our car. Ben was dead. Ben would be in his coffin in the long black hearse in front of us.

I got in the car and we drove to the National Cathedral. As we pulled up I saw a throng of people lined up to enter. We, the immediate family, were shown to the holding room. Vice President Joe Biden, whom I had known since he was first elected to the Senate, and his wife Dr. Jill Biden came into the room to give their condolences.

Finally it was time for the service to begin. I was still strangely unemotional. We filed out of the receiving room and took our places behind the casket in order to walk down the aisle. I stared straight ahead, not wanting to make eye contact with anyone for fear I would lose my control. I was determined not to cry. I carried a white rose to place on Ben's casket. I kissed the rose and placed it on the coffin. We took our seats in the front row, Quinn next to me, and the service began.

For me, the National Cathedral has always been a place of transcendence. I've always felt close to God or something higher than myself in that space. I often go there in the midafternoon when the sun pours in through the stained-glass windows and sit and meditate and pray. Even the spires of the cathedral seem to be lifting their arms to God, beseeching, praising.

It's a place where I feel I can go to ask for help. I feel something is there, something that gives me solace and comfort, something that reinforces what I now call my faith. I feel cherished there. I am never alone.

For the funeral service, some of the rituals were dictated by church rules and one of the hymns was requested by Ben. The rest of the service I planned. I wanted, above all, to honor him in a way that would be fitting to his personality. There was sadness, yes, but I wanted people to feel joy as well. It was an exquisite outpouring of love for Ben. Ben's daughter, Marina, and stepdaughter, Ros Casey, did readings, as well as Bo Jones and Jerry Rafshoon. Michael Newman said Kaddish. Tributes were given by Carl Bernstein, Tom Brokaw, Don Graham, David Ignatius, Walter Pincus, and Bob Woodward. Somehow I managed to keep it together, partly by listening so hard to everything each person said about a man that I knew they loved too.

The most difficult part of the service, the part I had been dreading had arrived. Quinn was going to eulogize his father. He had come to me the day before the funeral, in tears. "I can't do this, Mom," he said. "I'll never make it." He had written his eulogy but I had not seen it. He was confident about what he had to say.

"Yes, you can," I told him. "You can because Dad will be with you the whole time. He will be standing beside you with his arm around your shoulder and he will make sure you can do it."

He didn't seem convinced. I prayed he would have the courage. He did. He soared. Among his sentences that flew out into the cathedral that day were some that struck me as creating a full picture of the father he had just lost:

*A lot of people have been talking about my father as a legend,
and a lion, and a giant, and he was a huge, huge man. But for
me Dad was majestic because he was the simplest man I ever
met. . . . He taught me that if you do the little things well and
treat everyone with respect it can take you so much further than
you ever anticipated. . . . My father was also the happiest man
I ever met. I grew up with him telling me that my happiness
made him happy. He never complained—about anything. . . .
Everyone who ever met him wanted more of him. . . .*

*. . . My father had the deepest voice, the broadest chest, and
the loudest heart of any man I ever met. I used to put my head on
his chest as a kid, and his heart would be so loud I would have to
move my head over to the right side of his chest. Your heart is still
beating, I would tell him, and he would laugh.*

Quinn's voice broke from time to time, but he managed to control
his emotions just when it looked like he would fall apart. Near the
end Quinn said this:

*Losing him has been hard, but it has already made me stronger.
It is as if something inside me clicked. I used to be someone others
might need to take care of, but now I feel ready to take care of
others. My mom is no weakling, as you know, but I will take
care of her. Maybe the old man is hitting me with those piercing
eyes of his again. He doesn't need to say anything. I can't see him
anymore, I can't hear him—but I get the message: "Hey, buddy,
it's your turn. Get it right, kid."*

I dug my nails into my hands. I bit my lip. I clenched my teeth, I
sucked in my stomach. I tried to breathe as rapidly as I could. I thought

I might faint. I knew that if I let go at that moment I would never recover. I was overcome with wrenching grief. Then I heard a sobbing noise to my left. I turned and saw both Vice President Biden and Secretary of State John Kerry visibly moved. The vice president had his head buried in his handkerchief and was crying openly. (Later he would write Quinn a personal note telling him what a wonderful job he had done. "I gave my father's eulogy," he told Quinn. "Yours was better.")

Then I realized that everyone in the church was crying. Everyone but me. Strangely I felt buoyed by the tears. I prayed. *Please help me be strong.* I began to feel stronger. Somebody heard me.

. . .

The clouds, when we walked out of the cathedral, were dark and low and menacing, and gusts of wind suddenly whipped around us, tossing my hair up over my head as we got into the car. I suddenly realized that Ben was not with us. How could that be? It was always Ben and Quinn and me.

The immediate family drove to Oak Hill Cemetery in Georgetown where we would leave Ben's casket to be temporarily buried in a crypt in the chapel until I could build a family mausoleum for him and for us.

The chapel is a beautiful Gothic structure built in 1850 and designed by the famous architect James Renwick. Small—it probably seats fifty people—with lovely amber and gold stained-glass windows, it is set among trees surrounded by a garden and a number of tombstones, including those of Katharine Graham and her husband, Phil.

Once the family had gathered, Dean Gary Hall said a blessing over Ben. It was then that I completely fell apart. I went over to kiss the coffin and collapsed on top of it, sobbing so hard I couldn't move.

Slowly, the other members of the family left the chapel so I could be alone with him. How was I ever going to leave him there? How was I ever going to go on without him? How was I ever going to pull myself together for the reception? I had made it this far. I had to make it through the rest of the afternoon. I had to do it for Ben. Now more than ever, I wanted him to be proud of me.

It was always Ben who was there to console me. He would take my head and rest it on his huge barrel chest and put his strong arms around me and his big hands would caress my hair and he would say in his deep gravelly voice, "It's going to be okay, baby." Now there was nobody to do that.

Now I was alone. Ben was in this box I was lying on top of. Never to come out. He would not be at home to greet our guests with me as he always had been. I would greet them on my own. I had to. And I had to go, to leave. To leave him there alone.

. . .

The reception for nearly one thousand people was in a tent in the backyard. I went in the kitchen door and ran into the bathroom to check my face. My eyes were red and swollen, but at least there was no mascara streaming down my cheeks.

I made my way down the back steps to the tent and was engulfed by people the minute I arrived. From then on it was just a giant swirl of people and hugs and kisses and compliments on the service and somebody putting a drink in my hand and smiling and greeting and accepting condolences, murmuring thank-yous and listening to great Ben stories and turning to grab hands and hear more thank-yous. I was feeling dizzy from all the noise and the laughter and the faces. The one thing I remember thinking was that I had to concentrate on something to keep my mind off the fact that Ben had died.

Finally the last guests departed and I went up to the house with the family to relax. The food from the tent had been brought up to the house and put on the dining room table. I realized I was hungry and someone got me a plate and another glass of wine. I was sitting in the library on the sofa when Ben's grandson Marshall, weeping, joined me. After kissing Ben's coffin, he had stepped out of the chapel to compose himself. He found he was face-to-face with a majestic eight-point buck. Instinctively, he pulled out his cell phone and took a photo, which he showed me. It was Ben.

I was still sitting there when Donna came over and sat by my side. Suddenly, without any warning, a gigantic wail erupted from inside me. It was so full of anguish that it shocked even me. I didn't know it was going to happen. I didn't know where it had come from. Everyone in the room froze. It kept coming. I couldn't stop. I didn't want to stop. I had to let it out. If I didn't, my body would explode. All that pain that had been building up for years and especially in the last week just kept pouring out of me.

Donna held me. Nobody knew what to do. There was no relief possible. Those who were in the living room came rushing in to see what had happened. I could hear whispers and flurries and questions. There was nothing to be done. I was inconsolable.

Finally there was a moment when I slumped over with exhaustion. There was nothing left inside me. No emotion. Nothing.

The next thing I remember was waking up in the morning, reaching over for Ben, realizing he was not there and that that's the way it would be for the rest of my life. I got up, put on my black clothes, and went downstairs for breakfast.

Chapter 22

Since age two I've been waltzing up and down with the question of life's meaning. And I'm obliged to report that the answer changes from week to week. When I know the answer, I know it absolutely. As soon as I know that I know it, I know that I know nothing.

—Maya Angelou, quoted in *The Meaning of Life*

Nothing outside of my bubble of grief had any effect on me. I felt like the famous bubble boy. I could hear people talking to me. I could see them. I could respond, but they were all outside.

Somebody e-mailed me the poem "Funeral Blues," by W. H. Auden. These four lines were especially wrenching:

He was my North, my South, my East and West,
My working week and my Sunday rest,
My noon, my midnight, my talk, my song;
I thought that love would last forever: I was wrong.

How could I have been so wrong? How could I ever really not have taken the reality to heart that Ben would die? I guess I didn't believe it because he was so fully alive, so invincible. I was lost without him.

. . .

I never even thought about what color I was going to wear in the
weeks and months following Ben's death. It wasn't that I thought I
was supposed to wear black. It's just what I automatically pulled out
of the closet, day after day. Nobody remarked on it. I didn't know
how long the mourning period was "supposed" to be. I didn't think I
had to do one thing or another, according to some long-ago-written
prescription. Looking at the many lively colors in my closet—the
reds, pinks, blues, even the whites—I was repelled. It was unthinkable that I could wear anything but black. It would have been a sac-
rilege. I don't know why. I just felt it.

I had signed a contract to write this book some time before Ben's
death. It was after talking with Mark Tauber about a piece I wrote
on the importance of the labyrinth Ben and I had created at Porto
Bello that I walked every day when I was there. I had met Mark
through my work on On Faith and he suggested that I think about
writing a spiritual memoir, one that touched on the multiple religious and quasi-religious influences in my life. I viewed the idea
as a way to walk with and talk to myself about the different phases
I had passed through, to look back at what I thought and believed
along the way.

I didn't start writing in earnest until a few weeks after Ben died.
Suddenly I felt driven to pour it all out. I had never kept a diary or
journal. I never wanted to be a person so enamored with herself as
to think every thought, feeling, and act needed to be recorded. I also
didn't want to be an observer of my own life. I wanted to live in real
time. The book took on a whole new urgency, a palpable way to deal
with my grief. It became all-consuming. Even when I wasn't actually
writing, I was ruminating about what it all meant. Little did I know

how significant this book would become to me. The whole process saved me.

. . .

Ben's decline in those last few years had made it impossible for me to concentrate enough to write. I was focused only on him. Now that he had died, he was foremost in my thoughts all the time. I saw him in my mind's eye, felt him ever present, and at the same time I wanted to make more sense of the meaning of it all, what I'd found all those decades before and what I'd lost with his death. My mind immediately turned that thought around to the idea of what I might find while moving forward without him.

It was a painful time, but cathartic in ways. On the outside, I was going through the motions, seeing friends, going to small dinners, the movies, anything to take my mind away from the reality, if only for minutes at a time. Everyone, I found out quickly, has a different way of grieving. One friend of mine whose husband died suddenly in a car crash never spent one evening alone for the first year. Another, whose wife had been ill for a long time but died unexpectedly, hardly went out at all and is still in mourning five years later. Yet another, whose wife died after a four-year illness, was in a relationship with someone else within six months.

I will often hear people criticizing others for their way of dealing with grief and loss. I feel strongly that criticism is unwarranted, certainly not if no one is hurt by the mourner's words or behavior. If people turn to booze, dancing all night on tables, having affairs, going to a silent retreat at a monastery, disappearing from the social scene, I say do what you want to do because in the grieving process that is often what you're compelled to do, what you *have* to do. It's so hard to get away from the grief. It chases you into dark corners and holds you captive. But it can be assuaged, tamed in a way, made less wild, omnipresent, or inescapable.

I chose life. That meant being around the people I loved and who loved me and especially around those who loved Ben. Quinn was my rock, and we went to as many places with each other as we could. His divorce from Pari was final only weeks after Ben's death. They had been separated since the April before but we never told Ben.

I went out a lot and found that I was able to laugh. A group of us had dinner and organized a trip to the movies to see *Fifty Shades of Grey* and giggled all the way through. I refused to be morose in front of others. I also found myself trying to cheer them up. That made me feel better. I did most of my grieving privately. Nobody really wants to be around someone who is grieving. Grief permeates the atmosphere.

The focal point of my day was to visit the cemetery chapel where Ben's body was temporarily buried in a crypt in the floor until the mausoleum could be built. I always lit a candle in the chapel and would lie on the carpet on the aisle over his crypt, as close as I could get to him, and weep until I was ragged. I begged him—prayed to him actually—to help me through this. There really were times when I didn't think I could ever be happy again.

Occasionally, the force of my grief would shock me. Once during a visit, I tried to pull back the carpeting and lift the lid on the floor to get to him. I stopped myself even before I realized I didn't have the strength. When I had run out of tissues and was limp from emotional exhaustion, I would wend my way home, sated with grief until the next day when I would do it all over again. I was never so thankful to have that warm chapel as during the freezing weather when I would otherwise have been standing over an icy plot of newly dug earth shivering and keening out in the open.

. . .

The first Valentine's Day after Ben died may have been my lowest point to that date, especially since it was the first year we wouldn't be going to La Samanna. I couldn't sit still, I paced, I walked, I cried. Nothing worked to make me feel better.

For reasons I still do not understand, I decided to stop wearing black on that very day. It wasn't as if I had stopped loving Ben or stopped grieving any less. It wasn't as if I wanted to be with another man. The idea was unthinkable then. I simply felt a slight quickening in my heart, a longing for what we had had together, and I couldn't imagine that I wouldn't have those feelings again.

Around that time I met someone I found attractive, a man who had recently lost his wife. He couldn't have been more different from Ben. The last thing I wanted was an ersatz Ben. At that point I couldn't imagine anyone who could replace him.

On the other hand, I was beginning to feel sexual. Did I feel ashamed? No. Did I feel guilty? A little. On some level, even being drawn to someone else seemed like a betrayal. My overall feeling, though, was of being alive. I wanted what Ben and I had, and that included sex.

I never was intimate with this man, but he activated that essential part of me, which I thought had died with Ben. I could see that I might one day feel happy again. Besides, I really knew that's what Ben wanted for me. I knew because he had told me so.

By then I had begun to wear navy blue, the closest color to black, then went on to lighter blues and purples and lavenders. It wouldn't be until Easter Sunday services at the National Cathedral that I would break out the pink—shocking pink, no less. Looking back, I still think it was too soon for that about-face.

. . .

At the end of February I went back to the monastery in Berryville for another silent retreat. All the attendees were given little diaries or blank books. This time I wrote in mine. I was so sad I didn't really feel like going to meals or services and often fled to my room, took a shower, and read books on the significance of silence and various meditations.

I decided to walk down to the Cool Spring Natural Cemetery. There were more stones than before, marking the newly buried under mounds of earth. One caught my eye. The stone simply read: "Jody" 1941–2014. Under the stone was a faded and torn blue shirtwaist dress with tiny bouquets of dried flowers. I envied Jody and I wanted to trade places with her, but couldn't (and wouldn't) because of Quinn. I felt sorry for those she had left behind. I walked down to the river, sat on the bank, and meditated. I couldn't stop thinking about Ben and all the memories of being on the river in West Virginia, our times on the rocks, surrounded by the woods. Ben with his ax and his chain saw, clearing brush and cutting down dead trees, burning piles of autumn leaves, coming back to the cabin covered in soot, a wide grin on his face he was so happy to see me. I went up and sat by the chapel for vespers. The sound of the river in the distance was soothing. It was a warm day, in the sixties, and as I sat there I noticed tiny flowers budding near the steps, little white ones, and bluets even though there were no buds on the trees yet. The sun was going down. The cows in the nearby field were lowing. The old monks were chanting prayers about Jesus. A lovely peace settled over me.

That night I went to the chapel in the guesthouse and sprinkled my head with holy water and lay down in front of the altar with my arms spread out, totally surrendering to my grief. How could I go from such anguish to such peace and then spiral back down to such pain again so quickly in that short span of time? This undulating experience of profound, naked emotions was all a mystery to me. It was also piercing, overpowering, raw, uncontrollable, and exhausting. Patricia Campbell Carlson wrote, "Grief and gratitude are kindred souls, each pointing to the beauty of what is transient and given to us by grace." I couldn't agree more.

I wanted the retreat to go on and on, in part because I was totally alone with Ben, connected with him, nothing and no one else. I felt closer to him there than I had since he'd died.

When the retreat was over, we sat in a circle to share our experiences. I was determined not to fall apart. But when I was asked how it had been for me so soon after Ben's death, I broke down. I talked about "Jody" at the cemetery and how I wished I could trade places with her. I couldn't believe I was so open and forthcoming around these people I hardly knew, but it was good to be able to talk about it and make that confession. When I finished, there was a hushed silence, and when I left, everyone hugged me. I felt safe.

· · ·

In May I went with a friend to an overnight retreat in the Maryland countryside. It was to focus on the enneagram, which the Enneagram Institute describes as a "tool for understanding ourselves and others." As with my devouring Linda Goodman's *Sun Signs* at an earlier stage in my life, or looking for answers and meaning from so many different sources throughout my days, I saw the enneagram as another way to arrive at some insight into myself.

Earlier in the year I had been introduced to the enneagram by the noted Franciscan friar, writer, teacher, and philosopher Richard Rohr, founder of the Center for Action and Contemplation. After that first meeting, I had read one of his books, *Falling Upward*, about the second half of life, which I read intently since it dealt with loss and grief and moving forward. I had sat next to and interviewed Rohr at a PathNorth event in Washington and found him truly inspirational. After learning about the enneagram from him, I immediately took the test—or more appropriately, filled out a questionnaire, which turned out to be astonishing in its accuracy, as it seemed to fit me to a T.

The enneagram consists of nine personality types, each with a corresponding number. My basic personality type turned out to be Type Two, the Helper, which was the equivalent of saying that this descriptive word was the role that best fit me most of the time, the one that came closest to how I might describe myself. This was good news and bad news, I learned. My deadly sin is pride, which I guess is better than gluttony, but I'm sure some would beg to differ.

The model elaborated on the personality types: "At their best," Twos are "unselfish and altruistic, they have unconditional love for others." The danger for Twos is to give too much of themselves and then feel hurt or resentful when the giving is not reciprocated. They can be smothering and possessive. I recognized some of those traits in myself and was revolted by them. This is not an easy test to take— with some questions that are hard to answer honestly, and the results are often difficult to confront.

I had surely been a helper all my life and those traits served me well as I was dealing with the illnesses of first Quinn, then my mother and father, and then Ben. But until Ben started failing, he often balked at what he felt was my overattentiveness and tendency to want to run his life. In fact, it was a running joke in our family and among our friends. At every birthday party I had for Ben, there was always at least one teasing toast about how Ben was totally dominated by me. Sometimes, when I really wanted to annoy him, I'd tell him that it was well known in Washington that he was the most pussy-whipped (one of his favorite words) man in town, which would make him absolutely crazy. As you can imagine, Ben would rather go down fighting than allow himself to be pushed around by anyone, especially his wife.

What was particularly discouraging was the fact that this attitude was not lost on Quinn, and like father like son, he began to push back at me too. I did a lot of soul-searching around this issue and now see that they were both right. I just couldn't see it at the time. I was trying, especially in my therapy with Steven, to understand it. There was one funny moment when I was trying to boss Steven around and he, unaware—a very rare thing for him—kept backing his chair away from me until he was finally up against the wall. I pointed this out to him, accusing him of trying to escape me, and we both burst out laughing, but it was emblematic of a very big issue of mine—what he called "the too muchness of Sally."

I so wish I had had that insight while Ben was alive and well. I wish that he could have taken the test too. It would have been such a gift to both of us, because Ben's probable personality type was a nice fit with mine and also explained a lot about times when we had our struggles. Sadly, this had been about the time that Ben really began to need me the most, but instead of being able to back off from some of my pushiness, I had to double down on my caretaking, which threw me off and set me back on my road to progress. Of course, as Quinn began to lose his father, he became needier as well. After Ben died, I had to regroup with Steven, get my bearings. I had to get back to trying to find "my own True Self." I had to find the new Sally who could be "brought to deeper and deeper levels of understanding and insight, love and grace," as Rohr wrote in one of his introductions to the enneagram on his website that he titled "Knowing Ourselves." I so wanted to know myself more and desperately wanted to be that person of "understanding and insight, love and grace."

I saw myself (rightly or wrongly) as pretty much in the healthy range of the Twos except for one thing: gossip. I realized I would never be able to improve on that score. I was toast. Happily, my saving grace has been that I recently learned the word *gossip* comes from "gospel." Except for malicious gossip, it can be healthy, a way to connect with and be interested in other people.

Rohr quotes Carl Jung about his point "that so much unnecessary suffering comes into the world because people will not accept 'legitimate suffering' that comes from being human. . . . Ironically, this refusal of the necessary pain of being human brings to the person ten times more suffering in the long run."

That didn't seem to be my problem. I feel that I gave in to my grief and allowed myself to suffer in a way that got me through and would continue to get me through the worst times. From the beginning of the first year without Ben, I took to heart the idea that grieving was beneficial and the only way to work through it was to allow myself to experience it rather than deny my feelings.

I began having dreams again about Ben. He kept coming back and appearing in the dreams alive. Everyone was so excited. "Ben is back!" they would exult. "Yay!" I was devastated and totally at sea. In my dreams, I was the only one who realized he was dead. I kept trying to convince them that he wasn't here, that he had died, that he would not be coming back. In my dreams I even went so far as to go to the *Post*'s newsroom to plead with people to accept the truth. I couldn't go through his decline, death, and funeral again. I had the dream over and over. I still have it. I think that what I'm dreaming is my own need to convince myself that he is gone.

On my birthday, I spent an hour and a half with Steven discussing this. Acceptance was really the hardest part. I wasn't there yet. Oddly I never experienced anger or guilt during the first year without Ben—and haven't still. I was expecting to but it never happened. I really believed that I had taken the best care of Ben that I could have. How could I possibly be angry? He had lived to be ninety-three and had had, as he wrote in the title of his book, "a good life." Besides, there was so much suffering in the world; mine was nothing compared to what so many went through. I never once asked "Why me?" but rather "Why not me?"

. . .

We had always spent every August at Grey Gardens. The summer after Ben died was to be no different. I started making plans to spend the month on Long Island, but something held me back. A voice in my head kept telling me not to. This is where Ben and I had spent so many years on our vacation, full of rest and relaxation and friends and lots of love and laughter. I somehow knew going back there would not be a way for me to move forward and would be no relief from the grief. I decided to rent out Grey Gardens for the whole summer, rent a place in Corsica for part of July and August, and invite friends to come and stay so I wouldn't be alone. I chose Corsica because I wanted to be in France, but didn't want to go anywhere Ben and I had been together. It's a French island, off the coast of the south of France, famous as Napoleon's birthplace. The terrain and the people have a reputation of being slightly untamed in their beauty and natural setting. It was not a tourist mecca, another mark in its favor.

In the weeks before leaving for Corsica, I was in a frenzy of activities—continuing to work on the book, working on the website, remodeling a new studio apartment in New York, planning the trip, packing, and checking on the construction of the mausoleum. A large part of the frenzy was because I had decided to have a ceremony to commemorate the first anniversary of Ben's death. It became clear at some point that the mausoleum was going to be finished at about the same time as the anniversary. I had decided that, rather than have him moved unceremoniously, it would be nice to have some sort of occasion to consecrate the mausoleum and bring Ben properly to his final resting place.

At first I didn't know what to call this day or any kind of ceremony. The Christian faith doesn't really have a name for this sort of thing, but there is a Jewish ritual called *yahrzeit*. It's a German word. *Yahr* means "year" and *zeit* means "time." A year's time from the death of a loved one. The Jews unveil the tomb on the yahrzeit. October 21 would be the anniversary of Ben's death and this would be its unveiling.

Several days before I was to leave for Corsica, I got a letter from the Washington Home and Community Hospices, the group that had kept such an incredible watch over Ben in his last weeks and days. I had been receiving helpful mailings from the group, but this one was special. "Dear Friend," it read, "it has been nine months since the death of your loved one. . . . Many of our family members find the nine months' mark to be difficult in its own way." Included was a list of suggestions for coping with grief. How appropriate and how uncanny! Who would have thought nine months had passed and that this often was a troubled milestone? What was so particularly disconcerting and agitating about this mark in the calendar of death? But it seemed to explain much of what was going on with me. Three sentences in the letter particularly spoke to me. "Accept yourself— your pain, your emotions, your own way of healing, and your own schedule for doing so," the letter read. "To cry, to experience your pain and express it is a sign of strength and love and is necessary for healing." I needed to hear that almost as confirmation of how I was reacting to loss. It was also comforting to read another thought they shared: "Always remember that your grief will ease and that you will reestablish your life."

. . .

I decided to live those three weeks in Corsica with abandon. I invited a number of friends to visit and we had a magical time, sleeping late, eating croissants for breakfast, discovering new coves and small beaches for swimming, hiking to waterfalls, lunching in small villages, walking in ancient hill towns, and returning to the villa for naps. We would have cocktails either on the terrace overlooking the sea or on the rocks by the beach, our rosé the exact color of the sunset, then long lingering wine-filled dinners with typical Corsican dishes. I wore only bikinis, as did every woman we saw on the beach. (Of course I wouldn't have dreamed of doing that in this country.)

The local vineyard was a few kilometers away, and we were treated to a tour and wine tasting by the owner, a tall, swarthy, Corsican hunk. He was in jeans and a tight-fitting black T-shirt. His salt-and-pepper hair was tousled and he was slightly unshaven. He was also the mayor of the town. When I remarked to him during the tour that I loved the island, he replied suggestively, *"Oui, nous sommes très sauvages!"*—Yes, we are very wild!

I melted.

Needless to say, I took all my houseguests for the next few weeks to visit the vineyard, and everyone insisted I invite the mayor for dinner. The truth is I really wanted him for more than dinner. I was tempted, but I just wasn't ready. If I'd been alone, I might well have. Who knows? Anyway, I'm glad I didn't. I thought the first time after

Ben needed to be special. I needed to be with someone I really cared about. It would not have been unlike going to bed with someone for the very first time. I knew I would be ready at some point, and that more than anything I wanted someone to love and to make love to, to love me and make love to me. I knew for sure that I would have that again.

I had been hoping for relief in Corsica and I found it. For me, it turned out to be the best thing I could have done at the time. It was calming and reassuring and full of life. While I was there I happened on this prayer, which I promptly copied onto one of the pages of my calendar: "Raphael, lead us toward those we are waiting for, those who are waiting for us. Raphael, Angel of Happy Meetings, lead us by the hand toward those we are looking for. May all our movements, all their movements, be guided by your Light and transfigured by your Joy."

Saint Raphael, an archangel, was not well known to me, but I loved the idea of an angel of happy meetings. It turns out that Raphael is also the angel of marriage, healing, travel, and joy. I immediately adopted him as one of my guardian angels. I love that the words *light* and *joy* are together in this prayer. I had been hoping for relief from the dark and some letup of my sadness, and I found that too. A month after I returned from Corsica, I came across this in my astrology readings: "New moon eclipse, dark of the moon, themes of grief and loss, abandonment are arising, purify home and body to become clean. Channel for eclipsing of an old state of life followed by a rebooting of a newly wired system."

Chapter 23

The meaning of life is ours to create, again and again, for every individual and generation. Only by creating and re-creating the fabric of meaning can we live. . . . Meaning is what human beings create from what they see and hear and remember. . . . Meaning is what we weave with each other and with patterns passed down from the past, selecting, discarding, embroidering, twisting the threads together to draw every man and woman and child into a larger whole.

—Mary Catherine Bateson, quoted in
More Reflections on the Meaning of Life

What followed Ben's death was truly a year of mourning—deep and unpredictable and intense. It was a sad and surreal year, when I alternated between feeling totally numb and devoid of emotion and experiencing moods that fluctuated daily or even hourly, from highs to lows and lower lows. Certainly, friends and family were there for me and helped hold me up. Focusing on the quotidian was another big comfort. Those everyday moments somehow, in their very ordinariness, reinforced the idea I could actually take small steps that would eventually move me forward.

For a time I felt untethered, like George Clooney in the movie *Gravity*, as he floated off into space. I've gone from lamentations to *saudade,* a Portuguese word that has become one of my favorites and seems to have been created just for people who have experienced great losses. *Saudade,* a longing for someone you love who is absent, or as Wikipedia defines it: "a deep emotional state of nostalgic or profound melancholic longing for an absent something or someone that one loves."

My days have been filled with *saudade*. It's different from grief. It permeates your bones. The Greeks had a word for it too: *imeros,* or yearning.

As the grief dissipates, *saudade* remains. As there is a difference between grief and depression, there is a difference between yearning and depression. I've not felt depressed since Ben died. Sad, but not depressed. That sadness has morphed into *saudade*.

The day after Ben's funeral when I went to visit him at the chapel, he was already under the floor in the aisle under the rug. As I had placed a white rose on his casket at the cathedral, now I was having one delivered to the chapel every Monday. Even though the weather had suddenly turned cold, the chapel was heated. I went every day, sometimes for several hours. It was my place to cry, to find that blessed release. At first I tried sitting on the bench but it was too distanced from him. Then I began to lie on the carpet over his coffin and I felt I could almost feel his arms around me. I could whisper to him that I loved him and he could hear me. It was so peaceful there and so cozy that there were times I almost fell into a trance, times when Ben would come alive and I could feel his warmth as the sun shone through the yellow panes of the stained-glass windows. The few days I couldn't get there I was almost desperate from missing him. The more I went there, the more I realized how important it was for me that I would have the mausoleum to go to when it was finished.

What both helped and hurt me was being close to Ben during my visits to the cemetery. But at the same time, what made me feel inordinately better was my preoccupation during that year with working on creating the mausoleum. I met often, both at home and at the cemetery, with the architect, Stephen Muse, to start drawing up plans.

From the beginning, I knew exactly what I wanted. I wanted the design to represent the two sides of Ben. On the one hand, I felt we needed to somehow depict his love of country, his total Americanness, his belief in and adherence to the highest values and morals of his homeland, and his exuberance in celebrating it. I also wanted the building to show his love for the beauty of nature; his longing for the quiet for contemplation; his need for space for emptying his mind; his days in the woods chopping down dead trees, clearing brush, staring for hours at his bonfires as he burned the day's offerings.

The idea of a neoclassical building was pretty obvious. Surprising to some, Ben had been a Greek major at Harvard. He loved everything about ancient Greece, glorying in its architecture particularly. Despite having been brought up in Boston, Ben loved everything about Washington. This was his kind of town, and he was a creature of the city. He saw its architecture echoing that of the Greeks. He adored the glistening white marble monuments, almost temples, the classic columns and carved statues. He thought Washington was simple but majestic and viewed the city as grand.

What more fitting surroundings could we give him than a truly Greco-Washington tomb. Stephen and I settled on a small white granite building with three key parts to it: columns, a stained-glass window, and a wooden door behind iron gates. We easily decided on Doric columns as best representative of Ben's simplicity and unostentatiousness. For the window, Quinn suggested we copy an antique wall hanging Ben had bought at a flea market that had hung in his office for more than forty years. It depicted a furled flag in a bald eagle's mouth. Because the bald eagle is the official national emblem of the United States, it was also completely apropos.

I wanted the iron gates at the entrance to be in the shape of a tree, similar to the giant oak tree photographed by Ansel Adams, also the official national tree of the United States. The font on the mausoleum would be the font used by the old *Washington Post*. There is also a verse of one of his favorite poems about trees—and souls—etched on the floor.

There would be room for six caskets. Ben and Quinn and I could all be together. It gave me a feeling of such security. We could always have a home. The three of us are homebodies. As an army brat who never lived in one place for more than a year and a half, little is more important to me than having a permanent home. It was to Ben, too. When I say home, I'm not just speaking of a dwelling, but of a psychological home, an emotional home, a spiritual home. To me a home is where love is and love is where home is. Ben and I created a home for each other and for Quinn. I believed this would one day be a new home where we could be together. Wherever Ben was, that is where home would be. The main thing is I wanted to exalt Ben. Someone asked the artist Elaine de Kooning, widow of the great painter, Willem de Kooning, what it felt like to paint in her husband's shadow. She replied, "I don't paint in his shadow. I paint in his light." I had the good fortune to live in Ben's light.

. . .

Rituals had become a very important aspect of my spirituality. They offer access to a well of comfort and divine connection in my life.

This was not always the case. Before Quinn was born, rituals were not of interest to me. In fact, I was revolted by them. I scorned them when I was even younger. I found them shallow, mawkish, self-indulgent. Thinking about my feelings then, I can see that a lot of what bothered me about the idea of rituals was the fact that I was afraid of my own sentiments and emotions. In a way it was a bit like being an angry atheist. I think I was protesting too much, especially given that later in my life rituals would come to mean so much to me. Maybe, too, it was that I felt that so often rituals were meaningless, misused, even dishonest.

It was an interesting paradox for me, though I didn't get it as an adolescent and even as a young woman. I hated rituals because I thought they were superficial, and yet I was afraid of them because subconsciously they carried so much meaning. Sometimes you hate the thing you're actually drawn to the most or are repulsed by some of the negative things that remind you of yourself.

These words—*revolted, dishonest, hate*—were extreme words to use, but looking back, it's how I felt. Finally, another decade or so on, I realized I hadn't stopped to consider that rituals often made many people feel good, and I only gradually came to understand that my view of not liking them, and therefore not wanting to participate in them, was self-centered and selfish.

Over time rituals have become hugely important in my life. Ritual has become more and more a part of that deepening interest in religion and faith, a way to express my feelings and my beliefs, a way to connect to others and to the divine. They were cherished opportunities. They give me hope because they hold out the possibility that I can be elevated in some way.

I once did a column for the *Washington Post* about the idea of the "sacred table," which for me is really the heart of a home. Family and friends gathering together is a sacred time. When I wrote the book *The Party*, I dedicated it to my parents "who taught me that successful entertaining is really about generosity of spirit." My parents were from the South, where hospitality is a religion, making people feel warm and welcome, having them leave one's home feeling affirmed. I agree. There are few better ways to express your love, respect, affection, and friendship than to gather people around your table.

Henry David Thoreau once said that getting up early can be a sacrament. Not for me. Cocktail hour is my sacrament. Twilight is my favorite time of day. The French have a phrase for it—"*Entre le chien et le loup,*" between the dog and the wolf—referring to the time of day when the shepherd can't tell whether that shadow is his dog guarding the sheep or a wolf planning an attack. Bernard DeVoto, a historian and critic, wrote a wonderful little book, *The Hour: A Cocktail Manifesto*. In it he wrote, "This is the violet hour, the hour of hush and wonder, when the affections glow and valor is reborn."

Dinner, the table, companionship, sharing, laughter, bonding, connecting—what could be more fulfilling, what could be more fun? It always fascinates me how people think of Washington as a cold, hard cynical place. Certainly Washington is a town where power can be all-consuming, but for exactly that reason, people here tend to be closer than in most communities. Despite the omnipresent public rancor, the real Washington is where people go to the same churches or synagogues or mosques, where their children go to the same schools, where people go to one another's funerals, christenings, weddings, and graduations.

Rituals become even more important in a place where the stakes—the life and death stakes—are so high. Krista Tippett talks about ritual as a kind of container for trauma. Courtney Martin, an On Being columnist, wrote: "Rituals are so powerful because they provide structure for the full spectrum of our emotional lives: the births and the deaths, the union and the disintegration."

Gathering people around my table may be my favorite ritual. As Tim Shriver says, it was also the way that Jesus had communion with others. "Jesus was a real party boy," says Shriver. "Half the scenes, half the parables in the Bible are parties. There are weddings, feasts, celebrations, and they are all parties. . . . The prodigal son ends in a party, the wedding feast of Cain is a party, the parable of the poor man Lazarus is outside of a party. Everybody is having a party all the time and Jesus goes to parties and he's always drinking and eating with the bad people, the naughty people, the outsiders."

Having covered parties for the *Washington Post* and written a book on entertaining, I have often been asked what party in history would I most like to have attended. My immediate answer is the Last Supper. The last thing Jesus did before he died was to have a party with those he loved. They shared bread and wine. It was sacred, holy, a sacrament, a communion. He chose to celebrate his life around a table with his closest companions. I hope that is the last thing I do. I'd like to die the way my mother did, with a glass of champagne in her hand.

· · ·

I can rid myself of something by writing on a piece of paper what I want to let go of and throwing it in the fire, or floating it down a stream. I can say prayers and send them off in any direction. I can always light candles to help illuminate all that was being said and heard around a sacred table. Many of the rituals that I participate in—weddings, christenings, funerals, walking the labyrinth, Christmas and Easter, Yom Kippur, Rosh Hashanah, Shabbat, and Ramadan—all give new meaning to my life. When I see the effect that rituals I create have on people, it gives me a sense of meaning. Nothing gives me more pleasure than surrounding myself with friends, sitting at a table with candles and good food, wine and good conversation. I love the idea that I can bring happiness to others, that I can introduce a bit of the sacred, a slant of light, a measure of joy into someone else's life. I want my guests to leave my table feeling honored and affirmed. There is magic in that for me.

. . .

Ritual was one of the reasons that a yahrzeit appealed to me. A yahrzeit is part of a prescribed order, a tradition of a community, a ceremonial act in which we could honor Ben. One idea of the yahrzeit is that when the year of mourning is over, "mourners are expected to return to a normal life." The sixteenth-century code of Jewish law says, "One should not grieve too much for the dead and whoever grieves excessively is really grieving for someone else." I understand that, but I don't know what it means to grieve excessively. Nobody can define an individual's grief. Everyone is different and everyone grieves differently. I knew that at some point I would have to move on to a more normal life, but there were days when I found the idea of that completely unthinkable. There were other days when I thought I was going to make it.

I realized I would not be able to end the mourning period overnight, to divorce myself from the grief, but it also meant that I wouldn't be the "widow" anymore. Not that that's a title anyone would aspire to, but there is a sacred quality to it. People are more tender, gentle, and respectful of you. I needed that. It's almost as if you are wearing your grief in plain sight, no matter how hard you try to hide it, and people are acknowledging it.

When I decided to have a yahrzeit, to consecrate the mausoleum and to commit Ben's body, it seemed like a wonderful idea, a beautiful ritual. However, it seemed so unlikely, if not impossible, that only a year later I could somehow get on with my life, "move on," reenter the real world. It seemed unimaginable that somehow my grief would dissolve. "One should not grieve too much . . . ?" I don't understand that.

I have discovered that you can't go around grief and that the trajectory of grief is not a straight line. Walking the woods in the cemetery, as I have done many times since Ben died, sometimes with Quinn, mostly alone, I have come to see grief reflected in its topography. There are hills and vales, peaks and gulches, smooth paths and rocky ones, sunny spots and dark areas. Sometimes there is silence, sometimes noise. Almost always I am filled with a sense of peace. When I come to the cemetery to mourn, I feel Ben is with me and I will be able to carry on.

I trusted that the ritual of a ceremony would at least open the door to the possibility of a bit of closure, a measure of peace.

Chapter 24

For one human being to love another: that is perhaps the
most difficult of our tasks; the ultimate, the last test and
proof, the work for which all other work is but preparation.

—Rainer Maria Rilke, *Letters to a Young Poet*

For many reasons, I was looking forward to Ben's yahrzeit. The mausoleum was nearly finished. I had invited a hundred close friends and family. The ceremony was sure to be beautiful and meaningful for all of us. There would be a tent in front of the mausoleum, overlooking the woods. A harpist and flutist would play "Afternoon of a Faun" by Debussy. At the stroke of noon when the bells tolled twelve times, Ben's casket would be rolled from the chapel and moved into his new home. Quinn and I would follow him and say good-bye.

This would be my way of purifying, eclipsing an old state of life, rebooting. I felt more and more the need to get through this year of formal mourning, to come out the other side. I don't know exactly what I was expecting, but I did feel there would be a kind of before-and-after difference. I was depleted from this grieving. I had to find a new way to live. I guess I had a fantasy that, magically, at the end of that year, the burden, the heavy weight of sadness, would be lifted and I would find my way back (or forward) to a new normal. How naive. As I would discover, it would not be that easy.

The grief would sneak up randomly and ambush me. It was as if I were walking down a country road, stepped on an IED, and watched my body parts fly in all directions. Someone I know was in a terrible accident recently. He was distraught when he was told he would lose his legs. It was only when he began to have feeling in his limbs, then excruciating pain, that he begged the doctors to amputate. I hated not having much feeling after Ben died, but when the real pain set in, I wanted to die.

Washington, after Corsica, was as difficult as Corsica had been good. I was back home again. But Ben was not. I began to have frightening symptoms of a heart attack—severe chest pains, dizziness, shortness of breath. I had blood tests and EKGs, which showed nothing wrong. I was fine. Only I wasn't. It happened a second time. More tests, another EKG. This time I was diagnosed with "broken heart syndrome." It's a real thing. That's what I had.

· ; ·

Ben was not the only worry I had. I was heartbroken for Quinn as well. Quinn had been alone since he and Pari had divorced. And now he was grieving the loss of his father.

For years I had been seeing a tarot card reader, Patricia McLaine, who had recently retired. It wasn't until then that I went to a psychic tarot card reader to talk about Quinn. She told me I had a wonderful son whom I loved very much and he loved me. She said he would be very happy and successful all his life. She also said he would meet and fall in love with someone within the next year. She would be the child of parents from another country, and her work would have something to do with politics. Soon after the reading, Quinn met Fabiola Roman, and it was love at first sight. Her parents are from

Bolivia and she was born there. She is the executive assistant to the president and CEO of the National Center for Missing and Exploited Children. Happily, they're engaged. I'm crazy about her. She is beautiful inside and out and has brought such happiness to Quinn. I really believe Ben sent her to him.

Never count out Quinn Bradlee. He is his father's son and the joy of my life.

. . .

While I was planning Ben's yahrzeit, a friend called me and told me there was a piece in *Elle* magazine I had to read. It was written by a friend of hers, journalist Lisa Chase, whose husband, *New York Observer* editor Peter Kaplan, had died the year before. It was about Lisa Chase's experience contacting Peter through a medium, Lisa Kay. She had actually had a conversation with her husband through this woman.

She began her article, "Up until a year ago, I'd never visited a psychic, never had my palms or tarot cards read. I wasn't exactly a skeptic, but you have to trust the people who practice such things, you have to buy into their cosmologies, and I didn't, quite."

Four months after Peter died, Lisa Chase talked to two friends who had lost loved ones and both had consulted a medium. Lisa Chase called Lisa Kay. Normally Lisa Kay doesn't do readings on the first call, but she told Lisa Chase that Peter was there. "He's here," she said. "He wants to talk now." Lisa Chase began taking notes. The conversation that ensued included information that only she and Peter could possibly have known.

"In the immediate aftermath of the call," wrote Lisa Chase, "I was filled with euphoria and flooded with an intense wave of love for him."

Like a good journalist Lisa Chase began to interview professionals about mediums. She spoke to a physician's assistant and a Ph.D. She also spoke to psychotherapist Sameet M. Kumar, Ph.D. He asked her, "Are you trying to get me to tell you that I don't believe in this? Because I do. . . . I've heard hundreds of these stories over the years."

When I read her piece, it was too much for me. I got Lisa Chase's number and called her right away. She couldn't have been more sympathetic and supportive. She reiterated what she had said in the piece about having been a skeptic. I told her I was not. She highly recommended Lisa Kay and gave me her number. At first I was terrified to call, but then I couldn't stand it. About a week before Ben's yahrzeit I picked up the phone and dialed the number.

I told her about Ben. She was immediately responsive. She told me that I couldn't escape grief. "Our loved ones are around us but on a higher vibrational frequency."

She said my mother and father had died around the same time of year as Ben. (They both had died in the month of September.) "There's a grouping coming around. I'm getting the loss of others."

"I'm now connecting with Ben," she said. "He's talking to me. He told me not to do the reading now. You need the space to feel all of this."

"Are you writing a book?" she asked me. "He sees your book. He says 'I'm in it. My picture's in it. I'm so handsome.'"

"Who is Frank Rich?" she asked. "Ben says you were with him recently."

As it turns out I had been in New York the week before at an HBO screening of the film *The Diplomat* about my late friend Richard Holbrooke. At the after-party I was sitting with journalists Frank Rich and his wife, Alex Witchel, and I was telling them about Ben's mausoleum and the upcoming yahrzeit. I had known Frank and Alex a long time, but we weren't close friends and I hadn't seen them in years.

Lisa Kay said that Ben says he was around you that whole evening. She then told me that in talking to me through her he said, "You mentioned me. I like all of this publicity I'm getting. Thank you for honoring me."

"He wants you to know that he's very much connected to you. He's around you and he is supportive. He also says he will be with you the whole time during the yahrzeit, as will your mother. It's very beautiful what you are doing." She tells me he's laughing and says to feel free to make jokes.

When the call had begun and she had contacted Ben, I collapsed. I knew he was there. She was telling me things nobody could possibly know except him. She said she hadn't intended to tell me so much, but that she had no idea Ben would show up as strongly as he did. I wasn't surprised. That was Ben. She said she didn't want to do the real reading for at least another month. I told her I would call her then. It took me days to recover. I kept going back and reading the notes in total disbelief. I felt devastated by talking to him, knowing he was really there but also euphoric at the same time for the same reason. The difference was that I couldn't touch him.

I couldn't get up the courage to call her again right away. Every time I thought about it, which was often, I didn't think I could bear the experience of having him and not having him. It wasn't until six months after the yahrzeit that I called her back. She again connected with Ben immediately. "Ben wants you to have another relationship," she said. Ben had always told me he hoped I would marry again. He was, after all, twenty years my senior and he wanted me to be happy. I always teased him that if anything happened to me first, he would be snapped up in a matter of weeks. There would be babes lined up to bring him casseroles. He didn't deny this. Ben needed to be taken care of. He hadn't been without a woman in his life since he was nineteen.

He also said I taught him many things. (It's true. One thing I taught him was how to be softer.)

Lisa told me that Ben was saying that I had been in quite a state of emotion for a few weeks and was experiencing a terrible grief and that he has been around me a lot. Then she said, "He asks if you saw his slippers on the floor."

I had just come back from a three-day weekend in Las Vegas to celebrate the birthday of my friend lawyer David Boies at the Wynn Hotel. I had had a luxurious room. At the foot of my king-size bed was a pair of lady's white terry cloth hotel slippers. After dinner the first night I came back to the room having had a good time but feeling really sad and missing Ben. It was the first big thing I had gone to without him, and I was feeling very much alone. I got ready for bed and walked over to the other side of the room to adjust the temperature. I looked at the other side of the bed and on the floor was a large pair of men's brown terry cloth slippers. I fell apart. There was nobody there to wear the slippers, nobody to share the beautiful bed with me. I took the slippers and threw them in the closet. The next night, the same thing happened. I went to the other side of the room and there were the slippers that the hotel maid must have replaced.

I told Lisa about Las Vegas. Then she told me what Ben was saying to me: "I was there with you. You talked to me. I slept in the bed with you that night." He was. I did. He did.

Lisa told me that this is the worst year for grieving and also the year of acceptance, when I begin to understand that he is dead. She said I must not rush out of this state: "People have so little awareness of grief." Lisa also told me he remembered a romantic night at Harry Cipriani's in Venice. "I miss those days," he said. Then he said to me, "I am so proud of Quinn. I hope he knows it." He told Lisa that Quinn would fall in love with someone very soon and that she would be of a different nationality (a confirmation of my feeling that Ben sent Fabiola to Quinn). He told me not to worry about Quinn, that "he just learns on a different channel."

Ben also said to her that he's met some interesting people on the other side. He told her he had spoken to his former antagonist Richard Nixon.

"Who's Jack?" Lisa asked me. I told her it must be Jack Kennedy. "He says he's seen him many times—Bobby too—and had dinner with him." He also wanted me to say hi to Ethel Kennedy when I ran into her. "She's tough," he said. "She has a lot of moxie." (*Moxie* was one of Ben's favorite words.) He wanted me to say hello to Nick. Nick Pileggi is a close friend who was married to Nora Ephron. Nora had died in the summer of 2012 and Nick was grieving too.

"He wants me to tell you, 'You'll always be my bride, my girl.'" He said, "She's still a girl. She's always young at heart. So am I. Here." Lisa said he was pointing to his heart.

We ended this session with Lisa telling me again not to avoid grief. "Your book will be part of the healing process," she said. "Grieving goes up to three years. It's like a scar. Don't escape it. It's messy, up and down. It's not linear. Don't judge it. Writing will help you."

It has. It definitely has. So has time. I am obviously not a skeptic about this conversation. It's hard for me not to believe something or someone was there in those two or so hours when Lisa Kay was telling me things only Ben and I could have known. All I can say is that this conversation was enormously comforting, as were those Lisa Chase had. That can't be a bad thing.

That last conversation with Ben gave me so much comfort. He repeated that I should remember that I was not alone, he would always be with me. Yet one of the hardest things for me would be learning to say "I" instead of "we."

. . .

October 20 was our wedding anniversary, the day after which would be the yahrzeit. Somehow I needed to celebrate our anniversary together for the last time. I arranged for a cocktail party at the chapel, where Ben's casket had been taken out of the crypt and was in the center of the room. I had my whole family from California with me, a few very close friends, and Ben's grandchildren and Quinn. We went up to the cemetery at twilight with hors d'oeuvres, plenty of booze, candles, and music. We had an anniversary party right there, gathering chairs around to sit in a circle, to talk and laugh and tell stories. We all talked to Ben as if he were still alive, still with us. The music was joyful and I felt happy and relieved the year was over and that I had made it through without completely falling apart. I felt his presence keenly, his support and his love. He was there watching over me. I would occasionally get up and put my head on his casket and whisper to him. I knew that it would be the last time. The next day he would be locked inside a granite wall forever. This was the closest I would ever be to him again. I wanted to stay there forever, in the candlelight, drinking my rosé and toasting Ben. But the evening had to end. We walked down the hill solemnly to where dinner was waiting for us. Ben would not be at the head of the table.

I knew then that I could live with loss. I would be okay. Ben had given me that strength through his love. I had no regrets about our life together. That made the ending of that long year so much easier. The next day I would start the beginning of my new life.

· · ·

The day of the yahrzeit dawned. It was a sparkling day, the cloudless sky the color that blue was meant to be, the leaves turning, a sweet breeze blowing. I couldn't have prayed for anything more perfect. The guests were seated under an open tent on the lawn, facing both the chapel and the mausoleum. A harp was playing.

Unlike the funeral, I was very emotional and very nervous. Unfortunately, the numbness had worn off. I was feeling conflicted, still grieving, but I had a sense of relief and anticipation—relief that the year was over and anticipation of what life might bring.

I also had a sense of apprehension that I wouldn't be able to shake the grief. The reason I was scared was because I hadn't spoken at the funeral, and here I was to be the only speaker. Now it was all on me and I felt the pressure.

Quinn and I waited in the chapel with Ben's casket until the chapel's bell chimed. As the casket was being slowly rolled down the path to the mausoleum, Quinn and I walked behind. I was moved that when we passed the tent, everyone stood. We watched as the undertakers placed Ben's casket in the granite enclosure and then sealed him in forever. I kissed the wall where his name was engraved and ran my fingers over his birth and death dates, almost as a final realization that he was really gone.

Gary Hall, dean of the National Cathedral, committed Ben's body, gave a blessing, and consecrated the mausoleum. I then stepped to the lectern and looked out at our friends who were gathered. I felt totally embraced and strengthened. I began with a joke—which Ben would have loved—about the pretentiousness of the mausoleum:

*I know. It's completely over the top. Here's the conversation I've
been having with Ben about it in my head. "Jesus Christ, Sally!
What were you thinking? This is the most pretentious bloody (only
he didn't say bloody) thing I've ever seen. It's embarrassing. We'll
be laughed out of town. You can't be serious. Holy Moly (only he
didn't say Moly)."*

I continued on a more serious vein:

*I don't need to tell anyone here that Ben was larger than life, that
he was a giant of a man, that he filled a room. He was all of those
things and more. It makes it easier to understand my grief, then,
to know what a huge emptiness he left behind and how hard it
will be for me to ever find that kind of energy and charisma and
love of life again. But I take heart in the poem in our program, "A
Thousand Winds," to know that in many ways Ben did not die. I
take heart in the knowledge that he loved me with all of his heart.
How lucky I was to have had him. I take heart in knowing that
he is here with me today and always. He wants me to finish my
grieving so I can return to a normal life. I do understand that.*

I then read aloud the last stanza of one of Ben's favorite poems,
"When Great Trees Fall," by Maya Angelou, written after James
Baldwin died, which is etched on the floor of the mausoleum.

> And when great souls die,
> after a period peace blooms,
> slowly and always
> irregularly. Spaces fill

with a kind of
soothing electric vibration.
Our senses, restored, never
to be the same, whisper to us.
They existed. They existed.
We can be. Be and be
better. For they existed.

. . .

I did a lot of reading on grief over that year after Ben died. There were many memorable and affecting pieces that I read and thoughts that resonated with me, but one in particular struck me as incredibly close to the actuality of my own experience. It's from the introduction to Kevin Young's anthology *The Art of Losing: Poems of Grief and Healing:*

> To lose someone close to you is to enter an experience no amount of forethought or hindsight can free you from. You must live through grief. You cannot outsmart it, nor think through the fact of someone's being gone, and forever. You must survive the sorrow. . . . With luck, one emerges from grief not just with emptiness, but wisdom—though of a kind you'd gladly unlearn for your loved one to return.

Determining to reclaim the joy in life, I needed and was receptive to all the help I could get, from any direction. I sought inspiration and welcomed words of understanding and cheer and those that would help me stay on the path I'd chosen. I needed an anthem. It came unexpectedly at a cabaret in New York where I went one night with friends. I love cabarets. The songs were mostly out of the great American songbook, so old-fashioned and romantic. I was sipping my wine in the dimly lit room and wishing I had somebody that night to hold hands with and kiss in between love songs. The singer announced one of her old favorites. I had never heard it, but even the first strains sounded familiar. It's called "Here's to Life" and had been made famous as the signature song of jazz singer Shirley Horn. If ever there was a song meant for me to hear at just the right moment, this was it. It set me on the path I needed to follow and embrace for the last part of my life. I think it was a gift from Ben. *This one is for you, Sal,* he seemed to be saying. It was perfect.

HERE'S TO LIFE

No complaints and no regrets
I still believe in chasing dreams and placing bets
But I have learned that all you give is all you get
So give it all you've got.

I had my share, I drank my fill
And even though I'm satisfied I'm hungry still
To see what's down another road beyond a hill
And do it all again.

So here's to life
And every joy it brings
Here's to life
To dreamers and their dreams.

Funny how the time just flies
How love can go from warm hellos to sad goodbyes

And leave you with the memories you've memorized
To keep your winters warm.

For there is no yes in yesterday
And who knows what tomorrow brings or takes away
As long as I'm still in the game I want to play
For laughs, for life, for love.

So here's to life
And every joy it brings.
Here's to life
To dreamers and their dreams.
May all your storms be weathered
And all that's good get better
Here's to life, here's to love, and here's to you . . .

Epilogue

I get up. I walk. I fall down. Meanwhile, I keep dancing.

—Rabbi Hillel

Some years ago, soon after I had started On Faith, Ben and I attended a Washington Post Company board dinner hosted by Don Graham, the company's chairman. I was delighted to be seated next to Barry Diller, head of IAC/InterActiveCorp. Although he was not particularly religious, I had been told he was positive about the website. He asked me a number of questions about it and about me, then leaned toward me and asked quite simply: "Do you have faith?" I was frozen and couldn't answer. He repeated the question. Stricken, I simply looked at him. Nobody had ever asked me that. I realized that despite the website, which I had named myself, I had little idea what the word meant and little idea whether I had it. I certainly had no idea how to respond. Finally, I said to him, "Barry, do you think you could catch the waiter's eye? I'd love another glass of wine."

Surprisingly, I'm not sure I could do justice to trying to answer the question any better today. People often ask how I would define myself religiously, what I believe, what label fits me. I've tried on a lot of positions, beliefs, denominations, and faiths over the years. At one point I even wrote that dancing was my religion. Somewhat embarrassing now, but then it didn't seem far from the truth. In the end, none of these identifiers I've taken on felt like a perfect fit, and I've discarded most of them.

The labels "seeker" and "searcher" don't work for me. I think we're all seeking meaning in life so it doesn't tell anyone much. I used to like the idea of being a "somethingist." At one time, I adopted the label when I thought people were using it to acknowledge that they believed in something, but couldn't make a definitive statement about what that something (or Something) might be. I fell into that grouping in certain respects. Later I saw a definition of *somethingist* in the Urban Dictionary as "a person who defines their beliefs in a somewhat annoying manner," and I began to think that this label was a little too cute and way too simplistic.

Religious humanist or *secular humanist* doesn't really describe who I am either, and neither *atheist* nor *agnostic* works for me. *Agnostic* never has, in part because if an agnostic is a person who believes that nothing is known or can be known about the existence of God, then that covers most of us to begin with. An atheist is someone who denies the existence of God. From a very young age, I clung to the idea that I was a confirmed atheist. As I've written, though, I came to understand that even if I was uncertain about the existence of God, I was never someone who didn't believe. I believed in many things, certainly in magic and mystery and meaning. I was not a doubter about the importance of gratitude. I was not skeptical about the beauty of all living things. I was not doubtful about the power of love, grace, and passion. We cannot live without grace, and we should never live without passion—in love, in work, and in our beliefs.

I believe that life inherently has great meaning, potentially for everyone. I am not negative, not a pessimist, not a cynic. I am definitely not a nihilist. If I had to choose one word for where I am spiritually and philosophically at this moment in my life, it would be *transcendentalist*. "The Transcendentalist" according to Ralph Waldo Emerson, "adopts the whole connection of spiritual doctrine. He believes in miracle, in the perpetual openness of the human mind to new influx of light and power; he believes in inspiration, and in ecstasy." When I first read that quote, I felt I could not have described myself better in terms of spiritual doctrine. I believe that there are miracles.

Most dictionaries don't recognize the word *Christian* with a small *c*, but I like to think that I am also just that, a christian, by which I mean a good and compassionate person, ethical and moral, embedded in core values, someone who cares about others. These are qualities I admire in people and with which I was brought up. Not that I always measure up to them—I'm no angel—but I try, especially as I get older.

I also believe that being a christian (unlike a Christian) doesn't mean one has to believe Jesus is the son of God. My view is that a christian believes in something supremely good (which of course Jesus was), and I do believe that that good comes from a creator, although I don't know what form it takes. My human mind cannot imagine that first there was nothing and then there was the universe. We can't create the divine ourselves. We can only contribute to it in certain ways and we can certainly experience it. It's that beauty and that great and ultimate good I'm seeking.

The reality is that in the end I have my own religion. I made it up, helped along by a close reading of Thomas Moore's lovely book *A Religion of One's Own*. Nobody has the same religion. At one point, Moore writes, "The more traditions I study and borrow from, the deeper my spiritual life becomes." And so it is with me.

Emerson is often quoted as having said, "Every church has a membership of one." Even with three thousand people in a cathedral or mosque or synagogue, each one has his or her own faith, own beliefs, own relationship with whatever she or he calls God. It's simply how you worship, what you believe, how you breathe. Nobody can get inside another person's mind and heart. Nobody can decide for you how to reinforce your goodness, or tell you with whom you're going to find love, or what's going to assuage your pain. For everyone faith is different.

A moment of epiphany for me was when I realized I am not an atheist (and likely wasn't ever) and that believing in magic is as legitimate as any religion or faith. It was an awakening, an illumination. I still had a long way to go. It was the idea of not being afraid to get closer to wonder and magic. The risk and the daring were worth it. I had been afraid to discuss my occultism for fear people would think I was crazy, and then I was reluctant to discuss my blossoming faith for fear my friends would think I had gone over the edge. Some of them did and do.

Looking back at these stories and the memories they brought to the surface has helped me more clearly articulate why I felt I needed the armor of being an atheist. I wanted to examine what would happen if I took off the armor and revisited those years and allowed myself to be vulnerable and open to a new way of thinking. I needed to take away that layer of defense and expose myself to greater understanding of my real beliefs. What I discovered writing this book was that I don't feel heavy anymore. I no longer feel confined and contained (imprisoned even) by that atheist label. I could finally see how unsuitable it really was. I could begin to move beyond this shackling that I had created for myself. That moment was enlightening and lightening at the same time.

. . .

Magic is an old concept. It comes from the word *magus* or *magi*, its plural. Most of us (certainly Christians) know the story of the three wise men or magi who came to visit Jesus in the manger. Magi were priests, practitioners of magic, astrology, and alchemy, with a depth of esoteric knowledge.

I'm willing to look anywhere for answers, clues, understanding, meaning. Openness is the key to any ideas that contribute to a meaningful life and cause no harm. Wicca is a relatively new religion that is ritualistic and can encompass all beliefs, some, or none. The basic tenet is the code or what is called the Wiccan Rede: "An it harm none, do what you will." Sounds pretty reasonable to me.

When I use the word *magic*, I know what I mean, but I believe it's hard to define concretely. I've concluded that it can't be defined but rather has to be felt, seen in a way, experienced and comprehended. I believe magic *is* based on faith and hope. It's like prayer. It can be found among the effects of prayer. It's powerful and supernatural and otherworldly. It's transcendent, transformative, and transporting. It's a gift, making us feel good, and can be used for the greater good as well. It's spiritual and uplifting at the same time. Magic is in the eye of the beholder, and everyone's a potential beholder. Magic is available to everyone and can be found everywhere—in the stars and on Earth. Magic is miraculous and sacred. (Thomas Moore proclaims that "nothing is not sacred," with which I heartily agree.) Anyone is free to define magic and translate it for themselves. You can call it religion or spirituality or God, Yahweh, Buddha, Allah, Zeus, or the Tooth Fairy.

Writing the stories in this book and discovering moments of enlightenment and enchantment have been magical. I feel as if I'm going forward in the right direction, as if a sense of peace has floated down on me, a greater connectedness to myself, to others, maybe even to the universe. Leon Wieseltier, author and religion scholar, prefers the word *enchantment* to *magic*. He suggests that if illusion brings you an enchantment, which it does for me, "you are perfectly justified in holding it because an enchanted life is a deeper and richer life than an unenchanted or disenchanted life." Max Weber, the founder of sociology, famously wrote that secularization renders a disenchantment or demagification (*entzauberung* in German) of the world. Finally I had come to understand the power of magic and enchantment.

I had contemplated magic—a touchstone from my childhood— and atheism, which grew naturally out of my shock at seeing those photos from Dachau so many decades ago. Faith was another matter. From the minute I froze in the face of Barry Diller's question to me about whether I had faith, I started asking questions of myself and many others. What I might have said to Barry at the time was that my religion was the First Amendment. Ben and I always had faith in the *Washington Post*. It took me years to find more answers to his question—and of course I'm still finding them.

Although this quote has been misattributed to Kierkegaard, it represents my thinking about faith: "Faith is walking as far as you can in the light and then taking one step more."

From a more religious stance, Jesus said to Thomas, as written in John 20:29 of the King James version of the Bible, "because thou hast seen me, thou hast believed: blessed are they that have not seen, and yet have believed." In other words, not that you have to see it to believe it, but that you have to believe it to see it.

. . .

When Ben's decline began, On Faith was a thing to do. After his death, I was looking for a thing to be, including a better person. Long ago, someone who was writing a book about people's epitaphs called and asked me what I would like my epitaph to read. He said he'd call back in a few weeks for my response. I told him there was no need to call back, I knew at that moment what I'd like etched in stone: "Good Wife, Good Mother, Good Daughter, Good Friend." I wouldn't change a word.

· · ·

Music, in the best and worst of times, has been exhilarating and consoling. On a daily basis it has been spiritually nourishing. The French word *chantepleure* (another word I love) means to sing and cry at the same time. I did a lot of that during the days before and after Ben's death. In fact I wrote about crying or breaking into sobs so many times in this book that I had to go back and seriously excise them with a red pen. Nonetheless, I take heart from these words of Washington Irving, which speak to me and seem another way of defining *chantepleure:*

> *There is a sacredness in tears. They are not the mark of weakness, but of power. They speak more eloquently than ten thousand tongues. They are the messengers of overwhelming grief, of deep contrition, and of unspeakable love.*

· · ·

Psychiatrist George Vaillant directed what is known as the Grant Study, a study undertaken at Harvard as part of a larger Study of Adult Development at Harvard Medical School. A number of men from the classes of 1939 through 1944, including Ben and Jack Kennedy, were followed throughout their lives since college. After writing several books on the subject, Vaillant concluded recently that the study showed one thing: "Happiness equals love. Full stop."

Which brings me to love.

Most of us are looking for the divine in our lives, searching for meaning and magic. Most important, almost all of us are looking for love, in its many manifestations.

What did Ben's death mean to me? I got religion or some sense of spirituality from the idea of love, self-sacrifice, mystery, and magic. It happened to me in a much clearer way at that moment. It illuminated for me the story of my life.

Being in love with a man on his deathbed is not romantic in the traditional sense, but I was more in love with Ben then than at any other time. I was in love with him every minute of every day, until the day he died. And I was more in love with him the day he died than I had ever been before.

I have faith in the power of love. That's the significance of the stories in this book. Ultimately loving is the most important thing a person can do. Giving and receiving love is encapsulated in another of my favorite words, albeit a rarely used one, *redamancy*, which means "the act of loving in return." George Sand was right when she wrote, "There is only one happiness in life, to love and be loved."

. . .

One of the many things I have learned is that you can't seek happiness to find meaning. You have to seek meaning to find happiness. To find meaning is not simply transcending the self; it's transcending the moment.

Thoreau wrote, "You must live in the present, launch yourself on every wave, find your eternity in each moment. Fools stand on their island of opportunities and look toward another land. There is no other land; there is no other life but this."

Living in the present is important, but equally essential is cherishing the memories and anticipating the future. I'm passionate about living life to its fullest—my life at this present moment, my life with all the people I care about, and my life in the larger world, in all the adventures to come.

I find in the end that I can't and will never stop asking questions. There is no way to know the unknowable, of course. My nascent quest for meaning and my understanding that there is no universal answer mostly came to me when Quinn was born. The same with God and faith. Everyone has his or her own idea of what gives their life meaning. Yet there are so many more questions to be asked. The more I know, the more I see what I don't know and the more aware I am of the richness that lies ahead in reading, learning, seeing, listening. When I look back on a life of questions, there are no right ones or wrong ones. It's only what feels right to me. This is only my story. I can't tell anyone how to be happy or how to be in touch with the divine or how to find meaning in life. I never had a plan for living. I just knew I wanted to love and be loved. We each have to find our own path.

Emerson, when he met friends he hadn't seen for a long while, had the habit of asking, "What has become clear to you since last we met?" I find that an important question to ask oneself from time to time.

What has become clear to me is that there is one question I will never stop asking: What do I plan to do with the rest of my "one wild and precious life"?

Acknowledgments

About a week before Ben died, he and I were both exhausted. Everyone had wanted to come and say good-bye, and he just wasn't up to it anymore, even though he didn't know that's why they were there. I was emotionally drained. Then I got a call from Ev Small, who had worked at the *Post* and for Kay Graham for twenty-five years and had been deeply involved in helping Kay with her Pulitzer Prize–winning book, *Personal History*. She had a picture of Ben she wanted to drop by. Ben knew Ev quite well, but I hardly knew her at all. I started to say that we weren't having any more visitors but something made me tell her to come by. She did, and Ben remembered her and was delighted. We talked for a while and I was immediately drawn to her. It had been a couple of years since I had signed my book contract and I hadn't written a word. Taking care of Ben had depleted me. Suddenly I blurted out, "Would you be willing to help me with my book?" It surprised me as much as it did her. I hadn't even thought about the book in months. She said she really didn't think so, that she had been working for other people and was anxious to do something on her own. I forgot about it. A week or so after Ben's funeral, Ev called. She thought she could at least talk with me about shaping the book. We met the next Tuesday and again every Tuesday for a few hours for over two years. Talk about synchronicity! As the book neared completion, we were meeting longer and longer hours and more days until the final month when we were practically living together. By the end, both of us, under enormous time constraints, were stretched to the limit, sometimes working until midnight. We began having a glass of wine at seven thirty, then seven, then six thirty, then six. I knew it was time to finish the book when I started eyeing the clock desperately at four thirty.

There are no words to describe what Ev did for me in these past two and a half years. She was at once my grief counselor, my shrink, my confidante, my teacher, my adviser, my editor, my researcher, my inspiration, my supporter, my warden, and my partner in writing this book. Ev immediately immersed herself in the subject of religion—checking endless books out of the library to recommend— interviewed me, talked through my experiences, encouraged me to write some things, urged me not to write others. She has an unerring sense of tone and language. I would like to say for the record that anything anyone finds objectionable, outrageous, or over the top in this book is *not* Ev's fault. Just know she tried to take it out. She would raise an eyebrow, hit me up again and again, and even though I faced her down from time to time—"This is my story, this is my truth"—she still managed to get me to cut out the most egregious parts. Sometimes I would write something completely unacceptable just to give her a win. She is also a tech wizard. There were times when she would have three versions of the manuscript on her computer and she managed to keep it all straight and make sense of things when I was glassy-eyed. Without Ev there would be no book. So my thanks and my love to Ev for keeping me going through the darkest times, with humor and intelligence and understanding.

Lucy Shackelford, "researcher to the stars," came into my life when she was working on Ben's papers, which we donated to the Ransom Center at the University of Texas. Lucy then turned her attention to my unorganized files. I have never seen anything like it. Lucy can find things that nobody ever knew existed. She unearthed so many documents, letters, photographs, and articles by me and about me and my family that I was truly stunned. Toward the end of the writing, she joined Ev and me in our marathon editing session. As is Ev, she is a stickler for facts, figures, and timelines. Both of them are meticulous. Lucy is also a computer genius. Lucy was completely unflappable when things got tense during late-night sessions. She was always there with a smile and a calming word. I don't believe there would be a book without Lucy either.

Nobody was more supportive of me during Ben's illness and death and the years afterward than Leslie Marshall. Leslie is the mother of three fabulous children, Ben's grandchildren and my step-grandchildren, Jo, Bea, and Marshall, whom Ben loved very much. For two years before Ben's death she and her husband, Bill Weld, moved into the house across the street. There was hardly a day that Leslie did not come over to give Ben a hug and kiss, tell him she loved him, and sit with him while he watched the news. Ben absolutely adored Leslie. She also was my handholder-in-chief. That involved drinking a lot of rosé out on the porch in the summer evenings, or by the fire during the winters after I had put Ben to bed. Leslie was there to listen and to commiserate. She really held me together as Ben declined. She loved Ben too. When he was dying she was in the room with me, along with other family members for those three days. After Ben died she took care of me, going up to the cemetery with me to visit Ben in the chapel, holding me when I cried. Leslie is a brilliant editor and read my book over twice, giving me encouragement and advice when I most needed it. Leslie personifies the definition of best friend. Never once in all of our relationship has there been an unkind or thoughtless word between us. She makes me feel like a million bucks and I truly love her.

Bob Barnett is the attorney extraordinaire in Washington. Bob has worked with Ben and Quinn and me on our books and has been a close friend for years. He has more energy, enthusiasm, and optimism than anyone I have ever known. He's so dear that it's hard to realize that Bob Barnett is not anyone to mess with. If you want somebody on your side, Bob is the only one to have. He also has a fabulous wife, Rita Braver. The two of them have been inordinately kind to the three of us throughout our lives and especially during this last ordeal. I owe them enormous gratitude.

Maricarmen Barrón helped me take care of Ben in those difficult last two years when I was overwhelmed. Nobody could have been more kind, loving, and devoted than Carmen, always cheerfully willing to do what both he and I needed no matter what time of day or night. She alone could get Ben to do things nobody else could. He loved Carmen and listened to her, often when he rebelled against me for trying to tell him what to do. She was and still is always there for Ben and Quinn and me, despite her own grief at losing him. She is still here now for Quinn and me. I couldn't have gotten through it without her.

Our doctor Michael Newman is everything a doctor should be. He treats the whole person, not just the illness. Even if we got hangnails he would ask, "What's going on in your life?" Ben counted Michael as not only the greatest doctor in Washington but as one of his closest friends. Michael treated the three of us with incredible care and attention and predicted Ben's death when nobody saw it coming. He said Kaddish at Ben's funeral at my request. He has been like a father to Quinn since then and an enormous comfort to me as well.

It was through Michael Newman that Ben and I met Steven Wolin, his closest friend and the most distinguished psychiatrist in Washington. Steven is the best thing that ever happened to the three of us. We started seeing him when Ben's personality began to change. Quinn began seeing him because of issues around his learning disabilities. The three of us would often go together, or separately, or two on one. Ben loved him and trusted him, and allowed Steven to help him through what Ben knew was the beginning of the end with grace and compassion. When I started seeing him alone, he literally, and I don't say this lightly, changed my life. He helped me discover the quest for faith that I had always had but never recognized, and steered me in the direction of what was to be my passion, both personally and professionally. Steven saw me through the death of my mother, a major trauma in my life, the constant problems Quinn was having at the time, Ben's loss of cognitive ability, and my own feelings of despair and loss of confidence. He made me believe in myself when it seemed that my world was falling down around me. He was there for me after Ben died, intelligent, consoling, and showing the way for me. Without Steven I'm not sure I would have made it, and there would certainly be no book today. I thank him with all my heart.

There is no more decent person in this world than Don Graham. He worked closely with Ben first as a reporter under him and then later as his publisher. Mostly though, Don was a cherished friend. Don stood by Ben during the horrible Janet Cooke episode. He also insisted Ben stay on after Ben suggested it was time to retire. He even gave him an office next to his and appointed him vice president at large, a title that made them both laugh. It was Don who suggested out of the blue that I do a religion website, in the dark ages of the Internet, which sent me careening off on a whole new fulfilling direction in my life. It was Don who, when Ben had been diagnosed with dementia, wanted Ben to keep his office, had lunch with him on a regular basis, and made sure he had the support of everyone on the floor until Ben stopped going in a few months before he died. Don and his wife, Amanda Bennett, have been incredible in their support of me since, taking me to movies and dinner at the lowest moments. Thank you, Don and Amanda, for being extraordinary friends.

Bob Woodward and Elsa Walsh were there for Ben and me and Quinn every step of the way. Bob and Ben developed a father-son relationship during Watergate, which only got stronger as the years went by. Ben loved Bob like a son and was extremely proud of him. Elsa and I became the closest of friends as well. The four of us have spent a lot of time together, vacationing, having dinners, spending every Christmas together, weekends, and just hanging out. Bob and Ben trusted each other completely. They came to see us a lot when Ben was failing, and Ben always lit up when they arrived. Elsa went with me to the funeral home after Ben died to discuss logistics. Their lovely daughter, Diana, is a part of our family. They were the last friends to talk to Ben on his deathbed. Since then they have taken care of Quinn and me with concern and love. I only hope to be as good a friend to them as they have been to us, to me.

I needed one last look at my book before the final edits and that task went to Kevin Sullivan and Mary Jordan, "grande reporteurs" as Ben would call them, at the *Post*. Ben hired Mary when she was a mere child. Kevin was Ben's very last hire. I needed two seasoned, hard-nosed journalists who would tell me the cold hard truth. They did. Because of them I made quite a few important changes that I think make this a better book. (Ev was thrilled.) Kevin and Mary also became very close friends of ours and have traveled with us and hung out with us with their great kids, Kate and Tom, for years. Their laughter and optimism and Irish enthusiasm really carried the three of us through the roughest times, and they have been there for Quinn and me since Ben died.

My sister, Donna Robbins, though in California, was extremely close to Ben, and after his death she took Quinn and me in for Christmas, saving us from an unbearably sad holiday. Donna and her three children, Christopher, Schuyler, and Courtney, were with us that first Christmas without Ben and spent every summer in East Hampton with us during those magical years when we were all healthy and happy. Donna and I have been through all the ups and downs of life together, especially close because as army brats we never lived in any place long enough to put down roots. Donna's outgoing, energetic, and embracing personality have kept me sane through the years, and I love her very much. The same goes for my brilliant brother, Bill, a practicing Buddhist whose calm and peaceful demeanor always gives me solace.

Ben's daughter, Marina, has been a part of my life since Ben and I got together, and Marina and I have become very close. Marina was there in the room with us as were her children, Miles and Beth, who came to see Ben at the end. Marina has been lovingly supportive both to Quinn and me throughout this whole time.

Ben's stepdaughter, Ros Casey, stayed with me in the room with Ben until he died, creating a calm environment when chaos was looming. Ben adored Ros, and her presence was precious to him. She has been a dear friend to me as well over the years.

Greta Williams, and Anna and Joe Bradlee, Ben's other grandchildren, were among the lights of his life. He adored spending time with them and was so proud of them all. Greta produced his first great-grandchild shortly before he died.

Carol Leggett was Ben's secretary. Nobody could ever have been more constant, loyal, caring, kind, and devoted than Carol. She protected him from everything and everybody, sometimes including me, especially as he began to fail. Carol, who would have loved to retire, stayed on until Ben died, watching out for him, making him comfortable, taking him to lunch, making him feel appreciated and important. She baked him his favorite blueberry pies until the end. That may have been the last thing he ate. He thought he'd died and gone to heaven. He did.

Friendship is everything and I simply could not have survived without my friends, especially those who looked after Quinn. David and Eve Ignatius were there for us. David even moved his office from the editorial section of the *Post* up to the ninth floor to be with Ben in his last two years. David is one of Quinn's new godfathers and has taken his responsibility for Quinn's welfare to heart. Angus and Sissy Yates have really stepped up to the plate. Angus is another of Quinn's new godfathers and has taken Quinn to lunch more times than I can count to shore him up after the loss of his father. Lisa and Michael Kelley, who live in St. Mary's County, have been there for Quinn since Lisa first hired him to work for her as a busboy at the Brome Howard Inn when he was fourteen years old. Lisa has been like a surrogate mother to Quinn and is one of his new godmothers. Lisa has been a strong and loving presence in his life and mine, especially since Ben died. Kyle Gibson, Quinn's other new godmother, has been close to Quinn since she worked with him on his first book and began visiting him at college. Whenever Quinn became depressed he would call Kyle and she would drop everything to take him out to dinner and listen and give him advice.

Those who were so important to me during all of this time, Eden Rafshoon and Jerry Rafshoon, were close to us since the Carter administration. We spent many wonderful vacations with them, and they spent a lot of time with us during Ben's final two years when it was difficult for him to socialize. Eden has been a constant friend before, during, and after Ben's death. I am so grateful for their friendship.

Bo and Bebe Jones had children Quinn's age, Teddy and Lindsay, and we began vacationing together when the kids were little. Bo was the *Post*'s general counsel and later publisher and one of Ben's dearest friends. We spent, and still do spend, every Christmas Eve together and always had a fabulous time together as families. Bebe is an analyst, and her friendship and insights have been especially valuable to me during these past few years. They are and always will be cherished friends.

Paul Richard, the *Post* art critic and my wise counselor for over forty years, may well have saved the republic with his advice to me during Watergate. His wife, Deborah, and Dorothy Jackson did an exquisite job planning and organizing Ben's yahrzeit. Shelby and Mary Lee Coffey have been close friends, and Shelby, once the Style editor, has been a dear friend, supporter, and confidant for at least four decades. Michael and Affie Beschloss have been close friends and supporters. Toni and Jamie Goodale have been friends from college, and Toni was on the phone constantly from New York to give words of encouragement. Mary Hadar was a former Style editor and one of Ben's closest female friends. Mary always made Ben laugh and he loved seeing her, especially in his last days. Pari Bradlee was a constant support throughout, and came over most days (even after she and Quinn had separated) to give Ben a hug and say hi, as we didn't want to upset him with the news. She has been unbelievably concerned for both of us since Ben died.

I started going to Caroline Casey for astrological readings nearly forty years ago. Caroline is a true intellectual, and her readings have been and still are insightful and illuminating. She has guided me, over this time, toward my North Star. She is funny and compassionate and caring. I also credit her with literally saving Quinn's life with her reading of his chart before he had heart surgery. She has been dead right about me, about Ben, and especially about Quinn, convincing us that against all odds he would survive and thrive. Which he has. She has never, ever been wrong.

Stephen Muse designed the most beautiful mausoleum ever for Ben at Oak Hill Cemetery. It was a joy to work with Stephen as we had when we renovated our house, Porto Bello, in southern Maryland. Stephen was not just a brilliant architect, the best in Washington, but a kind and compassionate friend who gently got me through such a distressing time.

I would like to thank Tim Shriver, my "spiritual adviser," for his wise counsel and his advice during the writing of this book. Timmy and his wife, Linda Potter, have been friends for over thirty-five years, and Tim has been a constant supporter of my quest for meaning.

Leon Wieseltier also gave good advice, and his brilliant and erudite conversations helped me in my thinking through a lot of my positions. Mike McCurry was also helpful in talking with me about the religious and political atmosphere in Washington. Frank Foer, over a long lunch, came up with not only the theme of the book but the title: *Finding Magic*.

Without Mark Tauber, there would be no book. I first met Mark when he was publisher of HarperOne, and we immediately became fast friends. I had just started the *Washington Post* website blog On Faith. He read a piece I wrote on labyrinths for *O* magazine, and he suggested I write a spiritual memoir. I wasn't ready at the time, but he eventually wore me down. Mark believed in me. I signed a contract around the time that Ben began his decline into dementia, but I was incapable of writing anything then. It wasn't until after Ben died that I realized I had to write my story. Mark was a true mentor, with a deep intelligence and a great sense of humor. He knew exactly what it was that I should write and talked it out of me, always encouraging and enthusiastic. He was the most involved publisher I've ever worked with—and the best.

At HarperOne I would like to thank my editor Mickey Maudlin for his enthusiasm, Jan Baumer for her first edits and encouragement, Adrian Morgan for the beautiful cover, Anna Paustenbach for calmly delivering bad news about deadlines, Laurie McGee for copyediting, Trina Hunn for lawyering and her excitement, Jennifer Jensen for marketing and being on top of it, Noël Chrisman for a truly professional job as production editor, and finally Suzanne Wickham, publicity director, to whom I am now surgically attached. Suzanne was immediately on board, knowledgeable, and plugged in with a lot of great ideas and is fun to work with. She said she could be reached night and day, 24/7, and she wasn't kidding. To all of you, my thanks.

My support system at home has been invaluable. Jody Evans, my personal assistant, has been with us since before Ben began his downward spiral. Jody remains unruffled during even the greatest crises, always taking things in hand and making sure it goes well. She helped organize the events around the funeral with total calm and patience when it looked as if things were really going to fall apart. Jody was an early reader of the manuscript, and when I asked her if there was anything in it she found over the top, she laughed and said, "That's just you!" Jody also has enormous patience with the fact that my computer and my cell phone hate me and are always malfunctioning. It seems her main job is to keep me from smashing them in frustration.

Sally Thacher runs the finances. Poor Sally! She has the worst job in the world, which she carries out with good humor and affection, especially when she says we need more money. Sally has been handling this for years, and Ben and Quinn and I could not function without her running our lives.

Aaron and Jenny Meisinger run the farm at Porto Bello, and they are rocks. Aaron loved to work out in the woods with Ben and Quinn, and later, when Ben was no longer able, Aaron would stand around with Ben and Quinn while Ben burned brush, his favorite thing. They have been fabulous with Quinn, who loves to go there for solace and peace, especially now that his dad is gone.

Yolanda Arispe has been a quiet and constant support in the house, always volunteering to help out or stay late when we need her, especially during the time Ben was sick and afterward when Quinn needed her.

And speaking of Quinn, I never knew one could feel such love for another human being until he was born. It continues to amaze me that I could love him more each day. As they say, it's as if my heart were running around in someone else's body. He is my life. He has overcome more than most people, and his resilience in the face of illness and disabilities is extraordinary. Ben always said he admired Quinn more than anyone he knew, and he meant it. So do I. Quinn is funny and smart and kind and loving, and he never gives up. He often quotes his father when he's discouraged. "Nose down, ass up, push forward." That he has done all his life. When Ben died, Quinn promised in his eulogy at the funeral that he would always take care of me, and he has. Hardly a day goes by that he doesn't call or come see me just to make sure I am fine. He astounds me every day with his wisdom, his accomplishments, and his determination. Now he is engaged to the fabulous Fabiola, and with her beautiful daughter, Khloe, and their dog, Teddy Roosevelt, he will start his own family. I am so proud of him and who he has become.